POLITICAL THEORY AND

INTERNATIONAL RELATIONS

POLITICAL THEORY AND

INTERNATIONAL RELATIONS

Charles R. Beitz

PRINCETON UNIVERSITY PRESS

PRINCETON, NEW JERSEY

Contents

Preface   vii

Introduction   3

Part One.   International Relations as a State of
     Nature   11
     1. The Skepticism of the Realists   15
     2. The Hobbesian Situation   27
     3. International Relations as a State of Nature   35
     4. The Basis of International Morality   50
     5. From International Skepticism to the
     Morality of States   63

Part Two.   The Autonomy of States   67
     1. State Autonomy and Individual Liberty   71
     2. Nonintervention, Paternalism, and
     Neutrality   83
     3. Self-determination   92
     4. Eligibility, Boundaries, and Nationality   105
     5. Economic Dependence   116
     6. State Autonomy and Domestic Social Justice   121

Part Three.   International Distributive Justice   125
     1. Social Cooperation, Boundaries, and the
     Basis of Justice   129
     2. Entitlements to Natural Resources   136
     3. Interdependence and Global Distributive
     Justice   143
     4. Contrasts between International and
     Domestic Society   154
     5. The Rights of States   161
     6. Applications to the Nonideal World   169

Conclusion   177

Works Cited   185

Index   201

Preface

POLITICAL theorists have paid insufficient attention to a variety of philosophically interesting and practically important normative problems of international relations because they have accepted uncritically the conception of the world developed by Hobbes and taken over by many recent writers. By accepting the conception of international relations as a state of nature, they have committed themselves to the view that international relations is primarily concerned with "the rivalries of nation-states, and with the traditional *ultima ratio* of those rivalries—war."[1] As a result, other pressing questions of contemporary international relations have been neglected, and the current debate about new structures of world order has taken place without benefit of the insight and criticism that political philosophers should provide.

This book is an attempt to work out a more satisfactory international normative political theory through a critique and revision of orthodox views. To assert the possibility of international political theory, one must first reexamine the traditional image of international relations as a state of nature and purge it of its skeptical elements. The traditional alternative to this view, which I call the morality of states, must be reconstructed to correct for the persistent misunderstanding of the notion of state autonomy. The result is a third view of international morality, which might be described as cosmopolitan.

Many people helped me to develop these thoughts. It is a pleasure to record my thanks to these people here.

Thomas Scanlon and Dennis Thompson supervised the preparation of an earlier version of this book as a doctoral dissertation in the political philosophy program at Princeton and continued to help when I undertook extensive further revisions. It is impossible to imagine more supportive advisors or rigorous critics. They cheerfully read a seemingly endless

[1] Stanley Hoffmann, *The State of War*, p. viii.

series of drafts of the manuscript and provided warm
encouragement in the periods when my doubts and second
thoughts gained the upper hand. In a larger sense, I benefited from their efforts, with others, to create a flourishing
community of interest in political theory at Princeton, in
which writing a thesis could be, and was, a pleasure. For all of
this, and for their continuing friendship, I am most grateful.

Huntington Terrell stimulated my interest in international
ethics when I was an undergraduate at Colgate and has en-
couraged my work in this area ever since. He read the present
manuscript with exceptional care and pointed out many philosophical errors and infelicities of language that I would not
have noticed otherwise. I am indebted to him for this, and for
teaching me some Socratic virtues, as well: he combines a
skepticism of received ideas with a conviction that moral philosophy can meet the highest analytical standards without
sacrificing relevance to practical affairs.

Several other people commented on the manuscript in its
various incarnations. Paul E. Sigmund and Robert C. Tucker
offered criticisms at my final public oral examination for the
Ph.D. and were good enough to amplify their remarks later.
Written comments on a subsequent version from Brian Barry
and Robert O. Keohane helped me to improve the argument
in many ways. Portions of the manuscript were reviewed and
criticized by Jeffrey Hart, William Hirsch, David Hoekema, J.
Roland Pennock, and Sheldon S. Wolin. I benefited from
their criticisms and suggestions even when I was not persuaded by them, since I was at least forced to make my own
views clearer.

I was lucky to have the help of Eleanor Bennett in the
preparation of the final manuscript. She not only brought
order out of a chaos of revisions, but also contributed a good
measure of whatever literacy the manuscript now possesses. I
am also happy to thank Paula Smith for her careful and efficient work on the index.

For financial support at various stages of my work, I am
grateful to Princeton University, the Morris Abrams Award
in International Relations, and Swarthmore College. The discussion of international distributive justice is based on my

article, "Justice and International Relations" (*Philosophy and Public Affairs* 4, no. 4 [Summer 1975], pp. 360-89), portions of which are reproduced by permission of Princeton University Press, the holder of the copyright.

Finally, I owe debts of a different kind to my parents, Jean and Richard Beitz, whose sacrifices made possible much of my education; and to Sherry Swirsky, my best friend, whose encouragement of my work on this book has meant more to me than I can say.

Swarthmore College
October 1978

POLITICAL THEORY AND
INTERNATIONAL RELATIONS

Introduction

IN THE modern history of political theory, and in most contemporary discussions of problems of political philosophy
as well, international relations appears largely as a marginal
affair. The image of a global state of nature, in which nations
are conceived as largely self-sufficient, purposive units, has
been thought to capture the relative absence of moral norms
governing relations among states. At one extreme of the
tradition—represented by Machiavelli, Bodin, and Hobbes—
international theory has denied the existence of any controlling universal rules in relations between states, substituting
raison d'état as the highest norm. Even when the possibility of
international moral ties has been granted—for example, in
post-Grotian writings on international law—these ties have
been held to be substantially weaker than intranational moral
bonds precisely because of the absence of supranational political authorities. The only problem in international relations to
have gained significant theoretical attention is the justification
and prevention of war—the main form of social intercourse
in the global state of nature.[1]

However justifiable this neglect has been in the past, many
recent developments compel us to take another look at the
"recalcitrance of international politics to being theorized
about."[2] These developments include the increasing sensitiv-
ity of domestic societies to external economic, political, and
cultural events; the widening gap between rich and poor
countries; the growth of centers of economic power beyond
effective regulation by individual states; the appearance of
serious shortages of food and energy caused, at least in part,
by the pursuit of uncoordinated and uncontrolled growth
policies by national governments; and the increasingly urgent

[1] See, for example, the following remark in the introduction to a widely
read contemporary work of analytical political philosophy: "In relations between states the problem of establishing a peaceful order overshadows all
others." Brian Barry, *Political Argument*, p. xviii.

[2] Martin Wight, "Why Is There No International Theory?," p. 33.

demands of third world countries for more equitable terms of participation in global politics and economics. To put the point in language more familiar to discussions of this subject, the rise of "welfare questions" in international forums, and of "low politics" in diplomacy, parallels the increasing impact of international arrangements and transnational interactions on human well-being. It is not that "high politics"—that is, the threat and avoidance of war—has become unimportant, but rather that it represents only one of many problems for which solutions must now be sought at the international level.[3]

These changes in international relations have a threefold relevance to political theory. Since states can no longer be regarded as largely self-sufficient political orders, the image of a global state of nature no longer provides an obviously correct picture of the moral relations among states, persons of diverse nationality, and other actors in the international realm. The orthodox theoretical image of international relations and many practical principles thought to follow from it require critical examination and modification in the face of the new and not-so-new facts of world politics.

At the same time, the attempt to formulate a more satisfactory normative theory puts the facts in a new light and suggests empirical questions that have been answered insufficiently thus far. The answers to such questions might form part of the justification of international normative principles, or they might be required to determine how international principles apply. In either case, a normative theory appropriate to the contemporary world raises questions and suggests problems that deserve greater attention from students of international relations.

Third, and perhaps most important, one must consider the relation of political theory and international practice. Political theory arises from a perception of the possibility of choice in

---

[3] None of the arguments in this book actually turns on the claim that international interdependence is something new. Indeed, it seems more likely that the growth of the world economy did not follow, but rather accompanied, the rise of the modern state. Both were part of the same historical process. Thus, interdependence is at least as old as the modern state. See generally Immanuel Wallerstein, *The Modern World-System*.

political affairs. This possibility is presupposed by criticism of the established order as well as by engagement in efforts to change it. When choices are to be made regarding the ends and means of political action, or the structures and rules of institutions and practices, it is natural to ask by what principles such choices should be guided. An important function of the political theorist is to formulate and examine alternative principles and to illuminate the reasons why some are more persuasive than others. Now the developments that have undermined the orthodox theoretical image of international relations have also weakened the practical consensus that the rules and settled expectations of the present world system are legitimate. An international debate is underway concerning the future structure of world order, but political theorists have failed to provide the kinds of guidance one normally expects from theory in times of political change. Recognizing this, it would be irresponsible not to try to work out the implications for our moral ideas of a more accurate perception of the international realm than that which informs the modern tradition of political theory. For only in this way can we more rationally understand our moral identities and assess the modes of political practice in which we engage.

WHILE a more satisfactory international normative theory is necessary, the would-be international theorist may expect to encounter a variety of obstacles that do not embarrass the political theorist of domestic society. Chief among these is a widespread if unreflective conviction that normative international theory is not possible, since for various reasons (discussed in part one, below) it is thought to be inappropriate to make moral judgments about international affairs. Another obstacle is that it is not clear what the program of international theory ought to be. The main problems of the political theory of the nation-state grow out of the interplay of a rich tradition of philosophical argument and the recurrence of a set of relatively well defined issues in popular political debate. International relations, in contrast, has neither so rich a theoretical tradition nor so well defined or recurrent a set of political issues. Third, our intuitions about moral problems in international affairs are less firm than our moral intuitions about domestic problems. Whatever one's view about the relation of intuitions and moral theory, it seems clear that the relative paucity of familiar and reliable intuitions about international problems will make it more difficult to formulate and justify normative principles for international practice. Finally, as I shall suggest, many international normative issues cannot be settled definitely without more satisfactory empirical information than is currently available. While empirical considerations are, if anything, more important in international than in domestic political theory, the social science of international relations is less advanced than the science of domestic society.

This book is intended to help lay the groundwork for a more satisfactory normative political theory of international relations. It is important to stress that I do not claim to provide a systematic theory analogous to those found in the familiar treatises on the political theory of the nation-state. In view of the difficulties noted above, this seems too ambitious a goal at present. Instead, I want to show that the obstacles to international theory are not insuperable and that there are international normative problems of sufficient practical importance and philosophical interest to warrant further theoretical effort. In addition, I hope to call into question some received views about international morality and suggest the plausibility of a more cosmopolitan and less state-centered perspective. But I do not regard my normative conclusions as final in any sense, and I have tried to indicate the directions in which criticism of my views seems most promising and further thought seems most needed.

Although my discussion is necessarily preliminary, I hope that it will have several kinds of value in its own right. The most important of these is that it can bring some conceptual clarity to an area in which confusion is endemic. If readers are not persuaded by my criticisms of prevailing views or by the alternative positions I outline, my discussion should at least illustrate the respects in which such views require more careful formulation and defense than they have heretofore received. Even when I make no attempt to resolve outstanding controversies, my analyses of the normative concepts involved in them should make clear what the controversies are about and what would be needed to resolve them. Further, while not pretending to offer a history of international theory, I have surveyed the tradition of international theory and indicated the ways in which elements of it are relevant to my main concerns.[4] The tradition is not, in general, very edifying, but nonetheless one finds suggestive formulations and illuminating arguments scattered about within it. Finally, I have given special attention to the relation of the empirical science of international relations and the normative issues of international theory. When possible, I have assessed relevant empirical considerations and shown how these require or incline us to accept some normative positions and to reject others. When necessary, I have tried to formulate unresolved empirical and theoretical problems in such a way as to show how further work on them would influence their resolution.

THIS book has three parts. Each part addresses distinct issues, but the discussion is progressive and suggests the outlines of a more systematic theory. Thus, I argue (in part one) that international political theory is possible, by showing that several arguments for skepticism about international ethics are

[4] By "the tradition of international theory" I mean the writings of the classical international jurists (like Grotius, Pufendorf, and Wolff); occasional remarks on international relations that appear in treatises primarily devoted to the political theory of the state (like Hobbes's *Leviathan*); and works that consider the causes of war and advance plans for world peace (like Kant's *Perpetual Peace*). Perhaps surprisingly, there is no single work that gives a comprehensive and scholarly analysis of the growth of international thought. The most helpful discussions are: Wight, "Why Is There No International Theory?"; Arnold Wolfers, "Political Theory and International Relations," pp. ix-xxvii; F. H. Hinsley, *Power and the Pursuit of Peace*; and Walter Schiffer, *The Legal Community of Mankind*. A detailed historical survey of the development of the idea of the law of nations, from Thomas Aquinas to the twentieth century, is available in E.B.F. Midgley, *The Natural Law Tradition and the Theory of International Relations*. See also F. Parkinson, *The Philosophy of International Relations*, which contains a helpful bibliography; A.C.F. Beales, *The History of Peace*; and F. Melian Stawell, *The Growth of International Thought*.

incorrect, and furthermore, that the international realm is coming more and more to resemble domestic society in many of the features usually thought relevant to the justification of (domestic) political principles. To support this claim, I examine the traditional image of international relations as a Hobbesian state of nature and argue that it is misleading on both empirical and moral theoretical grounds.

If international skepticism of the sort criticized in part one represents the dominant view about international morality, then views stemming from the modern natural law tradition (which I call the morality of states) might be said to represent the most widely held alternative. Like international skepticism, the morality of states makes use of the analogy of states and persons, but it draws the normative conclusion that states, like persons, have some sort of right of autonomy that insulates them from external moral criticism and political interference. This idea lies behind such principles of international practice as nonintervention and self-determination, and some now familiar moral objections to political and economic imperialism. I argue in part two that the analogy of states and persons is highly misleading here, and that the appropriate analogue of individual autonomy in the international realm is not national autonomy but conformity of a society's political and economic institutions with appropriate principles of justice.

Finally, I return to the analogy of international society and domestic society to discuss whether the two realms are sufficiently similar that arguments for distributive justice within the state carry over into international relations. Current debate about a new international economic order clearly presupposes *some* principle of international distributive justice; I argue that a suitable principle can be justified by analogy with the justification given by John Rawls in *A Theory of Justice* for an intrastate distributive principle. Although it is clear that states continue to have great significance for the world's political and moral order, I argue that the importance which for various reasons we must accord to states does not undermine the case for global redistribution. The argument is of the first importance for the current debate about reforming the international economic system, for its implication is that the existing global distribution of income and wealth is highly unjust. It is important, as well, for a more refined international political theory, because it suggests that the differences between the international and domestic realms, although significant in some respects, supply no reasons why such devices of domestic political theory as the idea of an original contract should not be extended to international relations.

I have said that this book is a first attempt to provide a political theory of international relations that is more systematic and more consonant with the empirical situation than traditional views. In the conclusion, I characterize such a theory as cosmopolitan (in Kant's sense) and distinguish it from international skepticism and the morality of states.

A consequence of the preliminary character of my remarks is that many questions must be left unanswered. Some of these questions are very important, for both empirical research and practical politics. If there is a defense for leaving such crucial matters open, it is that one cannot confront them responsibly without a prior grasp of the more elementary but also more basic concerns of this book.

I HAVE restricted myself to a few cursory remarks about the application of my views to problems of war and peace. Since these are often taken to be the central problems of international relations, their lack of emphasis in this book deserves some explanation. There are three main points. First, some issues related to war and peace—particularly those having to do with the concepts of violence and nonviolence, war crimes and the rules of war, and collective guilt and responsibility—have received considerable philosophical discussion in the past several years, often of very high quality.[5] They have not

---

[5] Two recent books are especially noteworthy: Michael Walzer, *Just and Unjust Wars*; and W. B. Gallie, *Philosophers of Peace and War*. Also, see the essays contained in three most helpful collections: Richard Wasserstrom, ed., *War and Morality*; Marshall Cohen, Thomas Nagel, and Thomas Scanlon, eds., *War and Moral Responsibility*; and Virginia Held, Sidney Morgenbesser, and Thomas Nagel, eds., *Philosophy, Morality and International Affairs*. On nonvio-

suffered from the general neglect of international relations by moral and political philosophers.

A second point is that some problems about the morality of war, like traditional questions of *jus ad bellum*, cannot be resolved without a more general theory of international right. For example, claims of justice in war often turn on claims that particular rights (e.g., to land) have been infringed or that rules of international conduct (e.g., those defining a balance of power) have been broken. Such claims furnish a justification for resort to war partly because they rest on principles that distribute rights to international actors and define a structure of international life that actors have duties to promote or uphold. But to explain why some such principles rather than others are morally best, one needs an international political theory. If this is true, then much of what I say in this book will be relevant to the problem of *jus ad bellum*, even though I have not usually drawn the connections explicitly.

Finally, I repeat a point with which I began. Contemporary international relations consists of far more than the maneuvers of states "in the state and posture of gladiators; having their weapons pointing, and their eyes fixed on one another . . . ; and continual spies upon their neighbors."[6] This additional activity raises distinctive moral problems to which solutions are increasingly essential, but which are likely to be overlooked because they fall outside the traditional conception of world politics. I certainly do not mean to suggest that the problems of war and peace are either unimportant or without philosophical interest; but, by setting these issues aside, I hope to show that other problems are at least as important, in some respects more basic, and of considerable philosophical interest in their own right.

---

lence and pacifism, see especially H.J.N. Horsburgh, *Non-violence and Aggression*.

[6] Thomas Hobbes, *Leviathan* [1651], ch. 13, p. 115.

PART ONE

International Relations as
A State of Nature

Morality, then, as the channel to individual self-fulfillment—yes. Morality as the foundation of civic virtue, and accordingly as a condition precedent to successful democracy—yes. Morality in governmental method, as a matter of conscience and preference on the part of our people—yes. But morality as a general criterion for the determination of the behavior of states and above all as a criterion for measuring and comparing the behavior of different states—no. Here other criteria, sadder, more limited, more practical, must be allowed to prevail.[1]

[1] George F. Kennan, *Realities of American Foreign Policy*, p. 49.

THE state, like other institutions that can affect people's well-being and their rights, must satisfy certain moral requirements if we are to consider it legitimate. It is by these standards that we evaluate the state's claims on us and orient our efforts at political change. The normative component of political theory is the search for such standards and for the reasoning that forms their justification.

We do not often take the same attitude toward the complex structure of institutions and practices that lies beyond the state. This is in accord with the modern tradition of political theory, but it is worth asking if there are reasons of principle for following tradition in this respect. In this part, I consider whether it makes sense to look for general principles of international political theory that can supply reasons for and against particular choices in the same way that the principles of domestic political theory guide choices about alternative policies within the state. Is normative international political theory possible?

Any attempt to lay the groundwork for normative international political theory must face the fact that there is a substantial body of thought, often referred to as "political realism," that denies this possibility. Skepticism about international morality derives from a variety of sources, such as cultural relativism, apprehension about the effects of "moralism" on foreign policy, the view that rulers have an overriding obligation to follow the national interest, and the idea that there can be no moral principles of universal application in a world order of sovereign states. In the first section of this part, I argue that none of these arguments supports international moral skepticism, either because such arguments involve elementary confusions or fallacious assumptions, or because they are incomplete.

A more sophisticated argument for international skepticism is that certain structural features of an anarchical world order make international morality impossible. This argument (reconstructed in detail in section 2) characterizes international relations as a Hobbesian state of nature, that is, as an order of independent agents, each pursuing its own interests, without any common power capable of enforcing rules of cooperation. The image of international relations as a state of nature has been influential both in the modern tradition of political theory and in contemporary thought about international affairs. Moreover, it yields a plausible argument for international skepticism and so deserves close attention.

The Hobbesian argument for international skepticism combines two premises, which I examine separately in sections 3 and 4. The first is the empirical claim that the international state of nature is a state of war, in which no state has an overriding interest in following moral rules that restrain the pursuit of more immediate interests. The second is the theoretical claim that moral principles must be justified by showing that following them promotes the long-range interests of each agent to whom they apply. I shall argue that each premise is wrong: the first because it involves an inaccurate perception of the structure and dynamics of contemporary international politics, and the second because it provides an incorrect account of the basis of moral principles and of the moral character of the state. Both premises are embodied in the image of international relations as a Hobbesian state of nature, and in both respects this image is misleading.

If my argument against the Hobbesian conception of international relations is correct, a main reason for skepticism about the possibility of international political theory will have been removed. In fact, I shall argue, one cannot maintain that moral judgments about international affairs are meaningless without embracing a more far-reaching skepticism about all morality—something, I assume, that few would be willing to do. However, a successful defense of the possibility of international political theory does not say much about the content of its principles. In section 5, I characterize the traditional alternative to Hobbesian skepticism (represented in the writings of various modern natural law theorists) as the morality of states and distinguish some of its basic substantive features, which are criticized in greater detail later in this book.

1. The Skepticism of the Realists

F OR many years, it has been impossible to make moral arguments about international relations to its American students without encountering the claim that moral judgments
have no place in discussions of international affairs or foreign
policy. This claim is one of the foundations of the so-called
realist approach to international studies and foreign policy.
On the surface, it is a most implausible view, especially in a
culture conscious of itself as an attempt to realize a certain
moral ideal in its domestic political life. All the more remark-
able is the fact that the realists' skepticism about the possibility
of international moral norms has attained the status of a professional orthodoxy in both academic and policy circles, accepted by people with strong moral commitments about other
matters of public policy. Although the realists have often used
arguments with deep roots in modern political theory, I believe that their skepticism can be shown to rest on fallacious
reasoning and incorrect empirical assumptions.

To support this view, I shall argue that one cannot consistently maintain that there are moral restrictions on individual
action but no such restrictions on the actions of states. I begin
by considering the distinction (implied by this argument) between (generalized) moral skepticism and what I shall call
international skepticism and show in more detail exactly what
is involved in the assumption that moral skepticism is incorrect. It should be emphasized that this is indeed an assumption; I make no attempt to provide a general argument
against moral skepticism.

One might be skeptical about the possibility of international
morality because one is skeptical, in general, about the possibility of all kinds of morality. Perhaps one thinks that all or
most people are incapable of being motivated by moral considerations, or that moral judgments are so subjective as to be
useless in resolving conflicting claims and in fulfilling the
other social functions usually assigned to morality. Whatever
its rationale, moral skepticism, and its derivative, skepticism
about political ethics, represent a refusal to accept moral ar-

guments as sources of reasons for action. Moral skepticism might take a variety of forms, including a denial that moral judgments can be true or false, a denial that moral judgments have meaning, or a denial that the truth of moral judgments provides a reason for acting on them.

Generalized moral and political skepticism might be countered to some extent by examining the arguments that support them. Probably these arguments would turn out to contain important confusions or deep inconsistencies. But one could not thereby demonstrate the possibility of social or political ethics; other arguments for skepticism could be advanced, and at some point in the attempt to counter them one would need to rely on substantive ethical or metaethical views to demonstrate the weaknesses of the skeptical arguments. This, however, would be to assume that skepticism is wrong, rather than to argue it. Generalized moral and political skepticism can only be shown to be wrong by exhibiting an acceptable theory of ethics and of its foundation, because one of the functions of such a theory is to explain the possibility of just those features of ethics that the skeptic claims not to understand. At a minimum, such a theory must distinguish morality from egoism and explain how it can be rational to act on reasons that are (or might be) inconsistent with considerations of prudence or self-interest. Indeed, the idea that considerations of advantage are distinct from those of morality, and that it might be rational to allow the latter to override the former, seems to be at the core of our intuitions about morality.[2]

In what follows I shall have to assume without discussion that some such theory can be provided. The leading controversies in metaethics are likely to linger for a long while, and progress in normative areas ought not to await a resolution of these other problems even though they are in some sense logically prior. Obviously, one would like to offer a sufficiently complete theory to meet objections on both fronts. But this seems beyond reach at present. Instead, I shall pro-

[2] For a further discussion, see Thomas Nagel, *The Possibility of Altruism*, pp. 125-42.

ceed on the assumption that we share some basic ideas about the nature and requirements of morality (which I refer to as moral intuitions) and see whether international skepticism is consistent with them.

One important source of international skepticism is cultural relativism. International lawyers and cultural anthropologists have documented wide disparities in the views of rationality and of the good prevalent in the world's cultures. These differences are reflected in the structures of various legal systems and in the attitudes customarily taken by different cultures toward social rules, collective ideals, and the value of individual autonomy.[3] In some cultures, for example, autonomy is readily sacrificed to the requirements of collective goals. In general, given any consistent ranking of social goods or any plausible view of how such rankings might be morally justified, it is possible (and often likely) that a culture or society can be found in which there is dominant a divergent ranking of goods or view of moral justification. If this is the case, a skeptic might say, then there are no rational grounds for holding one social morality superior to another when their requirements conflict. Any doctrine that purports to be an international morality and that extends beyond the least common denominator of the various social moralities will be insecure in its foundations. But, typically, the least-common-denominator approach will leave most international conflicts unresolved because these have at their root conflicts over which principles are to apply to given situations or which goods should be sacrificed when several goods conflict. Since principles adequate to resolve such conflicts are fundamentally insecure, the skeptic claims, no normative international political theory is possible.[4]

[3] For example, see F.S.C. Northrup, *The Meeting of East and West*, esp. ch. 10; and Adda B. Bozeman, *The Future of Law in a Multicultural World*, pp. ix-xvii, 14-33.

[4] This construction might account for Kennan's non sequitur: "[L]et us not assume that our moral values . . . necessarily have viability for people everywhere. In particular, let us not assume that the *purposes* of states, as distinguished from their methods, are fit subjects for measurement in moral terms." *Realities of American Foreign Policy*, p. 47; emphasis in original.

This argument can be met on two levels, depending on the kind of intercultural disagreement to which it appeals. If the skeptical appeal is to disagreements over, say, the rankings of various social goods or their definitions, it may be that there is no challenge to the possibility of valid international principles but merely to the contents of particular ones. A consideration of views held in other cultures might persuade us that our assumptions ought to be altered in some ways to conform with conditions of which we had previously been insufficiently aware. This may be true of disagreements about the relative importance of individual autonomy and economic welfare. We are accustomed to defending individual rights in contexts of relative affluence, but considerations of economic development or of nonindustrial social structures might move us to recognize a dimension of relativity in these defenses. I do not mean to take a position on this issue at this point; I only mean to note one way in which cultural variations might be accommodated within an international political theory. In this case we would recognize a condition on the justification of principles of right that had previously gone unnoticed. Here, considerations of cultural diversity enter our thinking as data that may require revisions of particular principles; they do not undermine the possibility of normative theory itself.

But skeptics might say that what is at issue is something deeper; since different cultures might have radically different conceptions of what morality is, we have no right to be confident that our conception is correct. This carries the argument to a second level, but now it is difficult to say what the argument means. Perhaps it means that members of some other culture typically count as decisive certain kinds of reasons for action that we regard as utterly irrelevant from the point of view of our own morality. If so, we may ultimately have to say that the other culture's conception simply is not morality, or, at least, that claims founded on that conception do not count against our moral principles, even those that apply globally. It might seem that this attitude involves some sort of intellectual imperialism because it imposes a conception on cultures to which the conception is quite alien. But surely this is not correct. At some point, having learned what we can from the views of others, we must be prepared to acknowledge that some conception of morality is the most reasonable one available under the circumstances, and go forward to see what principles result. Notice that this does not say that everyone must be able to acknowledge the reasonableness of the same assumptions; actual agreement of everyone concerned is too stringent a requirement to place on the justification of moral principles (just as it is on epistemological ones). Notice also that the problem of relativism is not limited to international ethics; intrasocietal conflicts might involve similar disagreements over fundamental ethical assumptions. In either case, it is enough, in establishing standards for conduct, that we be able to regard them as the most rational choices available for anyone appropriately situated and that we be prepared to defend this view with arguments addressed to anyone who disagrees. In this way we reach decisions that are as likely to be morally right as any that are in our power to reach. We can do no more than this in matters of moral choice.[5]

One need not embrace cultural relativism to maintain that moral judgments are inappropriate in international relations. Indeed, political realism more often starts from different premises. Some realists begin with the assertion that it is unrealistic to expect nations to behave morally in an anarchic world. For example, Hans Morgenthau, a leading realist, objects that "writers have put forward moral precepts which statesmen and diplomats ought to take to heart in order to make relations between nations more peaceful and less anarchical . . . ; but they have rarely asked themselves whether and to what extent such precepts, however desirable in themselves, actually determine the actions of men."[6] While conceding the existence of some weak ethical restraints on international behavior, Morgenthau argues that international morality is largely a thing of the past and that competing national interests are now the main motives in world politics. This, he claims, is as it should be: "[T]he state has no right to let its moral disapprobation . . . get in the way of success-

---

[5] There is a helpful discussion of some general issues of ethical relativism in Richard B. Brandt, *Ethical Theory*, pp. 271-84.

[6] Hans J. Morgenthau, "The Twilight of International Morality," p. 79.

ful political action, itself inspired by the moral principle of national survival."[7]

How shall we understand this claim? One version is that we will fail to understand international behavior if we expect states to conform to moral standards appropriate to individuals. If we seek something like scientific knowledge of world politics—say, a body of lawlike generalizations with at least limited predictive power—we are unlikely to make much progress by deriving our hypotheses from moral rules appropriate to individual behavior.[8] This seems fairly obvious, but perhaps Morgenthau's emphasis on it can be understood in the perspective of the "idealist" legal approaches to the study of international relations that he sought to discredit.[9] In any event, this version of the claim does not imply that we ought not to make moral judgments about international behavior when thinking normatively rather than descriptively.

Another version of the claim, which is encountered more often, is this: we are likely to make mistaken foreign policy choices if we take an excessively "moralistic" attitude toward them.[10] This might mean either of two things. Perhaps it means that a steadfast commitment to a moral principle that is inappropriate to some situation is likely to move us to make

[7] Hans J. Morgenthau, *Politics Among Nations*, p. 10. There is an ambiguity here regarding the moral status of the national interest as an evaluative standard. One might call this view a form of moral skepticism, or one might say that it demonstrates that there is a moral warrant for following the national interest. I argue below that the former is the more appropriate interpretation. It should be noted, however, that some realist writers—probably including Aron and Morgenthau—have clearly thought that they were arguing the latter view instead. On this ambiguity, see Hedley Bull, "Society and Anarchy in International Relations," pp. 37-38.

[8] On the other hand, we may be equally misled by the research hypotheses that follow from a variety of realist assumptions. There is a useful criticism of realism as a research orientation, rather than as a skeptical doctrine about international norms, in Robert O. Keohane and Joseph S. Nye, Jr., *Power and Interdependence*, ch. 2.

[9] As Charles Frankel suggests in *Morality and U.S. Foreign Policy*, pp. 12-18. See also Kenneth W. Thompson, *Political Realism and the Crisis of World Politics*, pp. 32-38.

[10] Hans J. Morgenthau, *In Defense of the National Interest*, pp. 37-38. Compare Dean Acheson, "Ethics in International Relations Today," p. 16.

Y

immoral or imprudent decisions about it. Or it might mean
that an idealistic or overzealous commitment even to an appropriate principle might cause us to overlook some salient
facts and make bad decisions as a result. Each of these recommends reasonable circumspection in making moral judgments about international relations. But neither implies that
it is wrong to make such judgments at all. What is being said is
that the moral reasoning regarding some decision is flawed:
either an inappropriate moral principle is being applied, or
an appropriate principle is being incorrectly applied. It does
not follow that it is wrong even to attempt to apply moral
principles to international affairs, yet this conclusion must be
proved to show that international skepticism is true. An argument is still needed to explain why it is wrong to make
moral judgments about international behavior whereas it is
not wrong to make them about domestic political behavior or
about interpersonal behavior.

It is often thought that such an argument can be provided
by appealing to the concept of the national interest. Thus, for
example, Morgenthau seems to claim (in a passage already
cited) that a state's pursuit of its own interests justifies disregard for moral standards that would otherwise constrain its
actions.[11]

Machiavelli argues in this way. He writes, for instance, "[I]t
must be understood that a prince, and especially a new
prince, cannot observe all those things which are considered
good in men, being often obliged, in order to maintain the
state, to act against faith, against charity, against humanity,
and against religion."[12] Machiavelli does not simply represent
the prince as amoral and self-aggrandizing. His claim is that
violation by the prince of the moral rules usually thought
appropriate for individuals is warranted when necessary "to
maintain the state." The prince should "not deviate from
what is good, if possible, but be able to do evil if constrained."[13]

[11] Morgenthau, *Politics Among Nations*, p. 10; see also his *In Defense of the National Interest*, pp. 33-39.
[12] Niccolò Machiavelli, *The Prince* [1532], XVIII, p. 65.
[13] Ibid; see also *Discourses* [1531], I, ix, p. 139, and II, vi, pp. 298-99.

Now Machiavelli is not saying that rulers have license to behave as they please, nor is he claiming that their official actions are exempt from critical assessment. The issue is one of
standards: what principles should be invoked to justify or
criticize a prince's official actions? Machiavelli holds that
princes are justified in breaking the moral rules that apply
to ordinary citizens when they do so for reasons of state.
Another statement of his view might be that rulers are subject
to moral rules, but that the rules to which they are subject are
not always, and perhaps not usually, the same as the rules to
which ordinary citizens are bound. The private virtues—
liberality, kindness, charity—are vices in the public realm because their observance is inconsistent with the promotion of
the well-being of the state. The rule "preserve the state" is the
first principle of the prince's morality, and it is of sufficient
importance to override the requirements of other, possibly
conflicting, rules which one might regard as constitutive of
private morality.[14]

Is Machiavelli's position really a form of international skepticism? The view that a prince is justified in acting to promote
the national interest amounts to the claim that an argument
can be given that in so acting the prince is doing the (morally)
right thing. But if this is true, one might say, then Machiavelli's view and its contemporary variants are not forms of international skepticism. They do not deny that moral judgments
are appropriate in international relations; instead, they maintain that moral evaluations of a state's actions must be cast in
terms of the relation between the state's actions and its own
interests. The distinction between international skepticism
and the Machiavellian view turns out to be like the distinction
between general moral skepticism and ethical egoism. One
pair of views denies the possibility of morality altogether,

---

[14] Machiavelli, *Discourses*, III, xli, pp. 527-28. There is, of course, an extensive secondary literature devoted to the explication of Machiavelli's position.
No doubt many would take issue with my reading of his view, but I cannot
enter the debate here. On Machiavelli's notion of *virtù* and its relation to the
national interest, see Sheldon S. Wolin, *Politics and Vision*, pp. 224-28 and
230-31.

while the other pair advances a substantive moral principle. However, in both cases, the distinction is without a difference. What is distinctively *moral* about a system of rules is the possibility that the rules might require people to act in ways that do not promote their individual self-interest. The ethical egoist denies this by asserting that the first principle of his "morality" is that one should always act to advance one's own interests. To call such a view a kind of morality is at least paradoxical, since, in accepting the view, one commits oneself to abandoning the defining feature of morality. Thus, it seems better to say, as does Frankena, that "prudentialism or living wholly by the principle of enlightened self-love just is not a kind of *morality*."[15] Similarly, to say that the first principle of international morality is that states should promote their own interests denies the possibility that moral considerations might require a state to act otherwise. And this position is closer to international skepticism than to anything that could plausibly be called international morality.

If Machiavelli's view is, after all, a version of international skepticism, it does not follow that it is incorrect. Perhaps there *is* nothing that could plausibly be called international morality. At this point, we can only observe that the position as outlined provides no reason for drawing this conclusion. Why should we say that right conduct for officials of a state consists in action that promotes the state's interests? It is not obvious that the pursuit of self-interest by persons necessarily leads to morally right action, and it is no more obvious in the parallel case for officials of states. The argument involves a non sequitur. At a minimum, what is needed to vindicate the national interest view is an argument to show that following the national interest always does produce morally right action in international relations.

There is a tendency to resolve this problem by bringing in considerations regarding the responsibilities of political leaders to their constituents. Leaders should follow the national interest, it might be said, because that is their obligation as

[15] W. K. Frankena, *Ethics*, p. 19; emphasis in original.

holders of the people's trust. To do otherwise would be irresponsible.[16] Leaving aside the fantasy of describing some
leaders as trustees, the difficulty with this approach is that it
involves an assumption that the people have a right to have
done for them anything that can be described as in the national interest. But this is just as much in need of proof as
international skepticism itself. In domestic affairs, few would
disagree that what people have a right to have done for them
is limited by what they have a right to do for themselves. For
example, if people have no right to enslave ten percent of
their number, their leaders have no right to do so for them.
Why should the international actions of national leaders be
any different? It seems that what leaders may rightfully do for
their people, internationally or domestically, is limited by
what the people may rightfully do for themselves. But if this
is true, then the responsibility of leaders to their constituents
is not necessarily to follow the national interest wherever it
leads, without regard to the moral considerations that would
constrain groups of individuals in their mutual interactions.
The appeal to the responsibilities of leaders does not show
that it is always right for leaders to pursue the national interest.

Faced with the charge that the national interest as an ultimate standard is indifferent to larger moral values (e.g., the
global interest or the welfare of the disadvantaged elsewhere), realists often expand the definition of the national interest to include these larger values. For example, Morgenthau claims at some points that the national interest of a
power must be constrained by its own morality.[17] Apparently
he means that the calculations that enter into the identifica-

[16] See, for example, Arthur Schlesinger, Jr., "The Necessary Amorality of
Foreign Affairs," pp. 72-73.

[17] Morgenthau, *In Defense of the National Interest*, pp. 36-37; see also his letter to the editor of *International Affairs*. There is a similar claim in Thompson,
Political Realism, p. 167. In the context of policy questions, Morgenthau is
more straightforward. For example, in a discussion of U.S. policy toward In-
dochina, he writes that intervention is justified whenever it advances decision
makers' best judgments of the national interest, notwithstanding the customary prohibition of interventionary diplomacy in international law and morality. "To Intervene or Not to Intervene," p. 430.

tion of the national interest should include the relevant moral considerations. This maneuver seems to allow him to maintain the skeptical thesis (i.e., that the rule "follow the national interest" is the first principle of international conduct) while avoiding the non sequitur noted above. But it is hard to believe that any serious skeptic would be satisfied with such a revised national interest view. What the skeptic wants to maintain is that the definition and pursuit of the national interest is not subject to any moral conditions. In other words, it would be inappropriate to criticize leaders on moral grounds for their choices of foreign policy goals and means. Now suppose that Morgenthau's revised view were accepted, but that a leader mistakenly failed to include in his calculations identifying the national interest the relevant moral considerations. Then, apparently, the leader's conception of the national interest could be criticized on moral grounds, a possibility that the skeptic wants to avoid. Morgenthau's claim that the national interest of a power must be constrained by its own morality seems to be an ad hoc concession to a position inconsistent with his own skepticism. A consistent skepticism about international ethics must maintain that there are no moral restrictions on a state's definition of its own interests, that is, that a state is always morally justified in acting to promote its perceived interests. The problem is to explain how this position can be maintained without endorsing a general skepticism about all morality.

In response to this challenge, the international skeptic might claim that certain peculiar features of the international order make moral judgments inappropriate. National sovereignty is often claimed to be such a feature. On this view, states are not subject to international moral requirements because they represent separate and discrete political orders with no common authority among them. Jean Bodin is sometimes interpreted as arguing in this way. He writes, for example, "[T]here are none on earth, after God, greater than sovereign princes, whom God establishes as His lieutenants to command the rest of mankind."[18] The sovereign power is

---

[18] Jean Bodin, *Six Books of the Commonwealth* [1576], I, x, p. 40.

exercised "simply and absolutely" and "cannot be subject to the commands of another, for it is he who makes law for the subject."[19] Such a sovereign is bound by obligations to other sovereigns only if the obligations result from voluntary agreements made or endorsed by the sovereigns themselves.[20]

Bodin tempers his view with the claim that even princes ought to follow natural reason and justice.[21] He distinguishes between "true kings" and "despots" according to whether they follow the "laws of nature."[22] While the discussion in which this distinction is drawn concerns what we might call internal sovereignty—roughly, a prince's legal authority over his own subjects—one might infer that a sovereign ruler's conduct with respect to other sovereignties might be appraised on the same standard. This would give moral judgment a foothold in international relations, but such appraisals, in Bodin's view, would lack one feature that seems essential to full-fledged moral judgment. This feature emerges when a comparison is made between international and internal sovereignty. While it is possible for sovereign rulers to break the natural law, this would not justify subjects opposing their rulers because there is no superior authority to which appeal can be made to decide the issue.[23] Analogously in the international case, one might argue (although Bodin is silent on this matter) that no prince can justify opposition to the policies of another prince on the grounds that the latter has violated natural law, because there is no common authority capable of resolving the moral conflict. Notice that this is not to say that no prince can ever justify opposition to the policies of others; it merely makes *moral* (i.e., natural law) justifications inappropriate.

My interest here is in the suggestion that the absence of a common judge provides a reason for skepticism about international morality. It is clear that on some (particularly positivist) views of jurisprudence, the absence of a common

---

[19] Ibid., viii, pp. 27-28.   [20] Ibid., p. 29.
[21] Ibid., pp. 33-34.   [22] Ibid., II, iii, p. 59.
[23] Ibid., v, p. 67.

judge shows that there is no positive law.[24] But, even if we grant the positivists' claim that there is no genuine international *law*, it is difficult to see why the fact of competing national sovereignties should entail there being no sense at all in *moral* evaluation of international action. We do not make such stringent demands on domestic affairs; there are many areas of interpersonal and social relations that are not subject to legal regulation but about which we feel that moral evaluation would be meaningful. Furthermore, in principle, it does not seem that the idea of a common judge plays a role in morality analogous to its role in law. Even if we do assume that there is a correct answer to every moral question, we do not assume that there is a special office or authority responsible for providing the answer.[25]

This is not enough to establish the possibility of international morality, however, for someone might say that it is not simply sovereignty, but certain special features of an order of sovereign states, that makes international morality impossible. A similar recourse is available to proponents of the view that the perceived national interest is the supreme value in international politics. In comparing international relations to the state of nature, Hobbes produced such an argument. Because it is the strongest argument available for skepticism about international normative principles, I shall consider it at length in the following sections.

2. The Hobbesian Situation

THE most powerful argument that has been given for international skepticism pictures international relations as a state of nature. For example, Raymond Aron writes: "Since states have not renounced taking the law into their own hands and remaining sole judges of what their honor requires, the

---

[24] For this argument applied to international law, see John Austin, *The Province of Jurisprudence Determined* [1832], lecture 6, pp. 193-94, 200-1.

[25] Compare Henry Sidgwick, *The Elements of Politics* [1891], XV, sec. 1, pp. 238-41.

survival of political units depends, in the final analysis, on the balance of forces, and it is the duty of statesmen to be concerned, *first of all*, with the nation whose destiny is entrusted to them. The necessity of national egoism derives logically from what philosophers called the *state of nature* which rules among states."[26] The necessity (or "duty") to follow the national interest is dictated by a rational appreciation of the fact that other states will do the same, using force when necessary, in a manner unrestrained by a consideration of the interests of other actors or of the international community.

The idea that international relations is a state of nature is common in modern political theory, particularly in the writings of modern natural law theorists.[27] It makes a difference, as we shall see, which version of this idea one adopts as the basis for understanding the role of morality in international affairs. Since most contemporary writers (like Aron)[28] follow Hobbes's account, we shall begin there.

According to Hobbes, the state of nature is defined by the absence of a political authority sufficiently powerful to assure people security and the means to live a felicitous life. Hobbes holds that there can be no effective moral principles in the state of nature. I use "effective" to describe principles with which agents have an obligation to conform their actions; effective principles oblige, in Hobbes's phrase, *"in foro externo"* and are not merely principles that should regulate a preferred world but do not apply directly to the actual world. Principles of the latter sort oblige *"in foro interno"* and require us only to "desire, and endeavor" that the world were such that conformity with them would have a rational justification.[29]

In Hobbes's view, one has reason to do something (like adhere to moral norms) if doing the thing is likely to promote

[26] Raymond Aron, *Peace and War*, p. 580; emphasis in original.

[27] See the references in Otto von Gierke, *Natural Law and the Theory of Society*, vol. 2, p. 288, note 1.

[28] Aron, *Peace and War*, p. 72.

[29] Thomas Hobbes, *Leviathan* [1651], ch. 15, p. 145; compare Hobbes, *Philosophical Rudiments concerning Government and Society* [*De Cive*] [1651], III, sec. 33, pp. 49-50.

one's interests, in particular, one's overriding interests in avoiding death and securing a felicitous life. Morality is a system of rules that promote each person's overriding interests, and hence to which each person has reason to adhere, only when everyone (or almost everyone) complies with them. In other words, a condition of the rationality of acting on moral rules is that one have adequate assurance of the compliance of others.[30] Hobbes thinks that adequate assurance of reciprocal compliance with moral rules can only be provided by a government with power to reward compliance and punish noncompliance. Where there is no such assurance—as in the state of nature, where there is no government—there is no reason to comply. Instead, there is a very good reason not to comply, namely, one's own survival, which would be threatened if, for example, one abstained from harming others while they did not observe the same restraint.

Hobbes gives two accounts of why the state of nature is sufficiently dangerous to render compliance with moral restrictions unreasonable. In the earlier works (*Human Nature* and *De Cive*) he relies heavily on the psychological assumption that people will be moved by the love of glory to contend with others for preeminence.[31] In *Leviathan*, he develops another account which relies less on substantive psychological assumptions and more on uncertainty. Here the claim is that some (perhaps only a few) people in the state of nature will be seekers after glory, but that prudent persons aware of this fact would become "diffident," distrustful, and competitive, always ready to protect themselves by all means available.[32] On both accounts the outcome is the state of war, "a tract of time, wherein the will to contend by battle is sufficiently known."[33] In such an unstable situation it would be irrational to restrict one's behavior according to moral rules, "for that were to expose himself to prey, which no man is bound to."[34] Thus,

[30] Hobbes, *Leviathan*, ch. 11, p. 85, and ch. 14, pp. 116-17.

[31] Hobbes, *Human Nature* [1650], ch. 9, pp. 40-41; *De Cive*, ch. 1, pp. 6-7.

[32] Hobbes, *Leviathan*, ch. 13, p. 111. This account also appears in the earlier works, although with less emphasis. See *De Cive*, Preface, pp. xiv-xv, and ch. 1, p. 6.

[33] Hobbes, *Leviathan*, ch. 13, p. 113.   [34] Ibid., ch. 14, p. 118.

Hobbes concludes, in the state of nature "nothing can be unjust. The notions of right and wrong, justice and injustice have there no place."[35]

Some commentators have thought this conclusion too hasty. For, they point out, Hobbes allows that covenants may be made in the state of nature, and that some such covenants give rise to binding obligations to perform even when performance cannot be shown to be in the interest of the agent. In particular, Hobbes says that covenants are binding on a person not only "where there is a power to make him perform," but also "where one of the parties has performed already."[36] Since Hobbes's definition of justice is the performance of covenants, it seems that he is committed to the view that justice *does* have a place in the state of nature, at least in cases involving covenants "where one of the parties has performed already." This position receives additional textual support from Hobbes's discussion of the ransomed soldier, in which he claims that such a soldier, having been released on promise of subsequent payment of a ransom, thereby incurs an obligation to make good on the promise even though there may be no common power to enforce it.[37]

These passages have led some to think that Hobbes does not hold what might be called a prudential theory of obligation, for he seems to say that there are cases in which one has an obligation to perform as one has agreed even though supporting reasons of self-interest are absent.[38] This is a difficult position to maintain since it is in direct conflict with other portions of Hobbes's text. For example, he claims, without qualification, that "covenants without the sword, are but words, and of no strength to secure a man at all."[39] Furthermore, Hobbes's own justification of the claim about covenants where one of the parties has performed already rests on clearly prudential arguments.[40] While I cannot argue this issue at length, I believe that these textual considerations, taken together with Hobbes's psychological egoism, support the view that his

[35] Ibid., ch. 13, p. 115.   [36] Ibid., ch. 15, p. 133.
[37] Ibid., ch. 14, pp. 126-27.
[38] See, for example, Brian Barry, "Warrender and his Critics."
[39] Hobbes, *Leviathan*, ch. 17, p. 153.   [40] Ibid., ch. 15, pp. 133-34.

theory of obligation is purely prudential; people have no obligation to perform actions when performance cannot be shown to advance their (long-range) self-interests.[41]

To say that persons situated in the state of nature have no obligation to follow moral principles is not to say that there are no such principles. Indeed, Hobbes proposes nineteen "laws of nature" as the constitutive principles of "the true moral philosophy."[42] These principles are such that it is in the interests of each person that everyone abide by them. Hobbes argues that life in a society effectively regulated by the laws of nature would be infinitely preferable to life in the state of nature, since, in the state of nature, where no one has an obligation to restrict his actions according to moral principles, "the life of man" is "solitary, poor, nasty, brutish, and short."[43] The problem posed by Hobbes's theory is how to create conditions in which the laws of nature would be effective, that is, would oblige "*in foro externo*." Hobbes thinks that a common power is needed to assure each person that everyone else will follow the laws of nature. The dilemma is that creating a common power seems to require cooperation in the state of nature, but cooperation, on Hobbes's account, would be irrational there. (Who could rationally justify taking the first step?) There appears to be no exit from the state of nature despite the fact that any rational person in that state could recognize the desirability of establishing a common power and bringing the state of nature to a close. Thus, while there are moral principles or laws of nature in the state of nature, they do not bind to action in the absence of a common power.

International skeptics have seized on this feature of Hobbes's theory to support the view that there are no effective moral obligations in international relations. This conclusion follows from the analogy that Hobbes himself draws between international relations and the state of nature: "But though there had never been any time, wherein particular men were in a condition of war one against another; yet in all times, kings, and persons of sovereign authority, because of

[41] For helpful discussions, see David P. Gauthier, *The Logic of Leviathan*, pp. 57-62; and J.W.N. Watkins, *Hobbes's System of Ideas*, pp. 55-64.

[42] Hobbes, *Leviathan*, ch. 15, p. 146.   [43] Ibid., ch. 13, p. 113.

their independency, are in continual jealousies, and in the
state and posture of gladiators; having their weapons pointing, and their eyes fixed on one another; that is, their forts,
garrisons, and guns upon the frontiers of their kingdoms;
and continual spies upon their neighbors; which is a posture
of war."[44] In such a situation, each state is at liberty to seek its
own interest unrestrained by any higher moral requirements:
"[I]n states, and commonwealths not dependent on one
another, every commonwealth, not every man, has an absolute liberty, to do what it shall judge, that is to say, what that
man, or assembly that representeth it, shall judge most con-
ducing to their benefit."[45] Supposing that moral rules cannot
require a man (or a nation) to do that which he (or it) has no
reason to do, the argument holds that it is irrational to adhere
to moral rules in the absence of a reliable expectation that
others will do the same.

    This seems to be the strongest argument that the skeptic
can advance, because it is based on the plausible intuition that
conformity to moral rules must be reasonable from the point
of view of the agent in order to represent a binding requirement. When the agents are persons, the force of this intuition
can be questioned on the ground that other things than self-
interest can come into the definition of rationality. A successful counterargument of this kind results in the view that some
sacrifices of self-interest might be rational when necessary to
achieve other goods. But this kind of counterargument is not
as obviously available when the agents are states, since it can
be argued that, as a matter of fact, there is far less assurance
that states would sacrifice their perceived interests to achieve
other goals.[46] Thus, even if Hobbesian skepticism about indi-

    [44] Ibid., p. 115. See also *De Cive*, Preface, p. xv; and *De Corpore Politico*
[1650], II, ch. 10, p. 228.

    [45] Hobbes, *Leviathan*, ch. 21, p. 201. Compare ch. 30, p. 342: "[E]very
sovereign hath the same right, in procuring the safety of his people, that any
particular man can have, in procuring the safety of his own body. And the
same law, that dictateth to men that have no civil government, what they
ought to do, and what to avoid in regard of one another, dictateth the same to
commonwealths."

    [46] Compare Edward Hallett Carr, *The Twenty Years' Crisis, 1919-1939*, pp.
166-69.

vidual ethics in the absence of government is rejected, it might still move us to deny the possibility of effective regulative principles for the conduct of nations.[47]

It is important to be clear about the conclusion to which the skeptic is committed by this argument. The conclusion follows from applying Hobbes's theory of obligation to international relations. Accordingly, we might reformulate the conclusion as the claim that the officials of states have no obligation to conform their official actions in international affairs to moral principles. Such principles are not effective when there are no reliable expectations of reciprocal compliance. However, this is not to say that it would not be desirable for all states (or their officials) to conform their actions to certain principles, or that some such principles, analogous to Hobbes's law of nature, cannot be formulated. It is only to say, to repeat Hobbes's phrase, that whatever international principles exist apply *"in foro interno"* but not *"in foro externo."*

As I have said, the moral problem posed by Hobbes's theory is how to create conditions in which the laws of nature would be effective. Characterizing international relations as a state of nature poses a similar moral problem. If international relations is a state of nature, it follows that no state has an obligation to comply with regulative principles analogous to the laws of nature. But it also follows that widespread compliance with such principles would be desirable from the point of view of each state.[48] Carrying through the analogy with the

---

[47] This seems to have been Rousseau's view. See "L'état de guerre" [1896; written 1753-1755?], pp. 297-99. Perhaps this explains the hesitation about questions of international political theory expressed in *The Social Contract*. See *Du contrat social* [1762], III, xvi, p. 98, note 2, and IV, ix, p. 134.

[48] Apparently Hobbes recognized that this would follow from his own characterization of international relations as a state of nature, but he did not argue for an international Leviathan. Perhaps the reason is his view that, since states in a posture of war "uphold thereby, the industry of their subjects; there does not follow from it, that misery, which accompanies the liberty of particular men." (*Leviathan*, ch. 13, p. 115.) To say the least, it is not obvious that this claim is empirically accurate. Furthermore, even if it is correct, it would not follow that international agreement on regulative principles for nations is not desirable, but only that such agreement is less urgent than the analogous agreement to institute civil government.

state of nature therefore raises two further questions: what is the content of the principles it would be desirable for every state to accept? How can conditions be brought about such that it would be in the interests of each state to comply with these principles?

That such questions arise as a consequence of the characterization of international relations as a state of nature may suggest that the skeptics are inconsistent in invoking this characterization to support their view. For the first question presupposes that it would be desirable that conditions be created in which states would have reason to comply with certain normative principles, and the second question at least suggests that it is possible to create such conditions. From this one might argue that states have an obligation to do what they can to establish the requisite conditions, at least when they can do so without unacceptable risk. If this is true, then international skepticism is false, since it would not be the case that states are not subject to any moral requirements.

Hobbes does not posit an *effective* obligation to escape the interpersonal state of nature because the actions necessary to escape from it are inconsistent with the actions required for self-preservation within it. To defend international skepticism against the difficulty noted above, one would have to argue that international relations, like the state of nature, involves conditions such that the actions needed to establish an effective international morality are inconsistent with the actions required for the preservation of states. In that case it would follow that states are not subject to any binding moral requirements. And, while it would still be the case that conformity with appropriate international normative principles would be desirable, it would be academic to inquire about their content since there would be no way of rendering them effective.

3. International Relations as a State of Nature

THE application of Hobbes's conception of the state of nature to international relations serves two different functions in the argument for international skepticism. First, it
provides an analytical model that explains war as the result of
structural properties of international relations.[49] It produces
the conclusion that conflict among international actors will
issue in a state of war ("a tract of time, wherein the will to contend by battle is sufficiently known") in the absence of a
superior power capable of enforcing regulative rules. Second,
the state of nature provides a model of the concept of moral
justification that explains how normative principles for international relations should be justified. This explanation holds
that since the basis of a state's compliance with moral rules is
its rational self-interest, the justification of such rules must
appeal to those interests states hold in common.

These two uses of the idea of an international state of nature are distinct because one leads to predictions about state
behavior whereas the other leads to prescriptions. While the
two uses are related in the sense that the predictions that result from the first use are taken as premises for the second,
they should be separated for purposes of evaluation and criticism. In the first case, we need to ask whether the Hobbesian
description of international relations is empirically acceptable: do the facts warrant application of this predictive model
to international behavior? Our question in the second case is
different: does Hobbes's state of nature give a correct account
of the justification of moral principles for the international
realm?

Let us look first at the predictive use of Hobbes's international state of nature. The description of international rela-

---

[49] In this sense, Hobbes uses the state of nature to give what Kenneth Waltz
has called a "third image" account of the causes of war—that is, an account
based on the image of international anarchy. See *Man, the State, and War*, pp.
159-86, in which Waltz concentrates on the third-image explanations given
by Spinoza and Rousseau.

tions as a state of nature leads to the conclusion that a state of war will obtain among international actors in the absence of a superior power capable of enforcing regulative rules against any possible violator. As I have suggested, this conclusion is required as one premise in the argument for international skepticism, for, on a Hobbesian view, the reason that no actor has an obligation to follow rules of cooperation is the lack of assurance that other actors will do the same. Indeed, each actor has a reason not to follow such rules, since, in a state of war, an actor might rationally expect to be taken advantage of by other actors in the system if it were unilaterally to follow cooperative rules. Even if we accept Hobbes's conception of morality, for international skepticism to be a convincing position it must be the case that international relations is analogous to the state of nature in the respects relevant to the prediction that a state of nature regularly issues in a state of war.

For this analogy to be acceptable, at least four propositions must be true:

1. The actors in international relations are states.
2. States have relatively equal power (the weakest can defeat the strongest).
3. States are independent of each other in the sense that they can order their internal (i.e., nonsecurity) affairs independently of the internal policies of other actors.
4. There are no reliable expectations of reciprocal compliance by the actors with rules of cooperation in the absence of a superior power capable of enforcing these rules.

If these conditions are not met by international relations, then the analogy between international relations and the state of nature does not hold, and the prediction that international relations is a state of war does not necessarily follow.

I shall argue that contemporary international relations does not meet any of these conditions. Let us begin with the first. It establishes the analogy between the state of nature and international relations by identifying states as the actors in international relations just as individuals are the actors in

the interpersonal state of nature. This may seem so obvious as
not to deserve mention, but it is very important for the skeptic's argument that this condition actually obtain. The radical
individualism of Hobbes's state of nature helps to make plausible the prediction of a resulting state of war because it denies
the existence of any other actors (secondary associations,
functional groups, economic institutions, or extended fami-
lies, to name a few examples) that might mediate interpersonal conflict, coordinate individuals' actions, insulate individuals from the competition of others, share risks, or encourage the formation of less competitive attitudes. The view
that states are the only actors in international relations denies
the possibility of analogous international conflict-minimizing
coalitions, alliances, and secondary associations. Since it is obviously true that such coalitions have existed at various times
in the history of international relations, one might say flatly
that international relations does not resemble the state of nature in this important respect.[50]

There are other types of coalitions besides State

The difficulty with this claim is that Hobbes himself allows
for the possibility of coalitions and alliances in the interpersonal state of nature.[51] However, he argues that these would
not be stable. They would, if anything, increase the chances of
violence among coalitions, and the shared interests that
would lead to their formation would not be long lasting.[52]

One might make similar claims to defend the analogy of
international relations and the state of nature, but it is not obvious that the claims would be empirically correct. Some alliances appear to confirm Hobbes's hypothesis that forming
alliances increases the chances of war, despite the fact that alliances are often viewed as mechanisms for stabilizing a balance of power and making credible the threat to retaliate on
attack.[53] On the other hand, several types of coalitions have
produced opposite results. For example, regional political
and economic organizations appear to have played significant

[50] Oran Young, "The Actors in World Politics."
[51] Hobbes, *Leviathan*, ch. 17, pp. 154-55.   [52] Ibid.
[53] See, for example, J. David Singer and Melvin Small, "Alliance Aggregation and the Onset of War, 1815-1914."

roles in the nonviolent resolution of international conflicts. They have also made it easier for national leaders to perceive their common interests in peace and stability.[54] The same seems true, although in a more limited range of circumstances, of global international organizations like the United Nations.[55] To Hobbes's view that coalitions (and, by extension, universal organizations short of world government) are unlikely to be long lasting, it can only be replied that the important question is how long any particular conflict-minimizing coalition is likely to endure. Clearly, one should not expect such coalitions to persist forever, but it is historically demonstrable that some coalitions have enjoyed life spans sufficiently long to defeat the claim that they have made no significant contribution to peace and cooperation.

The view that states are the only actors in international relations also denies the possibility that transnational associations of persons might have common interests that would motivate them to exert pressures for cooperation on their respective national governments. The view does so by obscuring the fact that states, unlike persons, are aggregations of units (persons and secondary associations) that are capable of independent political action. These units might be grouped according to other criteria than citizenship, for example, according to interests that transcend national boundaries. When such interests exist, one would expect that transnational interest groups or their functional equivalents might exert pressures on their respective governments to favor policies that advance the groups' shared interests.

Since the second world war, the number, variety, membership, and importance of transnational groups have all increased, in some cases dramatically.[56] Early academic attention to transnational interests focused on groups of specialists

[54] Joseph S. Nye, Jr., *Peace in Parts*, chs. 4-5.

[55] Ernst B. Haas, Robert L. Butterworth, and Joseph S. Nye, Jr., *Conflict Management by International Organizations*, esp. pp. 56-61.

[56] The most useful survey of the growth of transnationalism is provided by the essays in Robert O. Keohane and Joseph S. Nye, Jr., eds., *Transnational Relations and World Politics*.

(economists, labor leaders) and on functionally specific transnational organizations (the World Meteorological Organization, European Coal and Steel Community) and hypothesized
that successful collaboration with respect to some functions
would promote by a process of social learning collaboration
with respect to other functions. The resulting progressive
enlargement of areas of transnational collaboration was expected to undermine international political conflict by making clear to domestic constituencies and decision makers the
extent of transnationally shared interests.[57] Subsequent experience has failed to corroborate the early functionalists' hypothesis for all cases of functional collaboration, but there are
particular cases in which the hypothesized social-learning
process has taken root.[58]

Although the central hypothesis of the theory of functional
integration has been discredited, the insight that transnational interest groups might alter the outcomes of international politics by exerting pressures on national government
policy making has not. In fact, the effectiveness of such
groups in promoting their interests at the national level has
been illustrated in several quite different areas. Two important examples of politically effective transnational groups are
multinational corporations and informal, transnational
groups of middle-level government bureaucrats. In each case,
although to very different extents, it is clear that transnationally shared interests have sometimes led to substantial pressures on government foreign policy decisions.[59] As the difficulties of integration theory suggest, it should not be
inferred that the effect of rapidly increasing transnational po-

[57] The most influential early statement of this view is David Mitrany, *A
Working Peace System*. There is a revised formulation in Ernst B. Haas, *Beyond
the Nation-State*, part 1. For a review of the more recent literature, see Michael
Haas, "International Integration."

[58] See James Patrick Sewell, *Functionalism and World Politics*, parts 1 and 3;
and Ernst B. Haas, "The Study of Regional Integration."

[59] See, on multinational corporations, Joseph S. Nye, Jr., "Multinational
Corporations in World Politics," pp. 155-59, and the references cited there;
and, on interbureaucracy contacts, Robert O. Keohane and Joseph S. Nye,
Jr., "Transgovernmental Relations and International Organizations."

litical activity is necessarily to minimize the chances of international conflict or to promote international cooperation,
because a variety of other factors is involved.[60] In particular,
transnational political activity is unlikely to promote international cooperation in the absence of perceptions by national
decision makers of significant shared interests that would justify such cooperation.[61] The theoretical importance of the
rise of transnational politics lies elsewhere. It lies in the fact
that nation-states can no longer be regarded as the only, or as
the ultimate, actors in international relations, since their
actions may be influenced significantly by pressures from
groups that represent transnational interests. Depending on
the strength and extent of these interests, this new element of
complexity in international relations renders problematic the
Hobbesian explanation of why international relations should
be regarded as a state of war.

The second condition is that the units that make up the
state of nature must be of relatively equal power in the sense
that the weakest can defeat the strongest.[62] The assumption
of equal power is most obviously necessary for Hobbes's claim
that the state of nature is a state of war because it eliminates
the possibility of dictatorship (or empire) arising in the state
of nature as a result of the preponderant power of any one
actor or coalition. This assumption might seem unnecessarily
strong, since the possibility of dictatorship within the state of
nature might be ruled out with the weaker assumption that
no actor is strong enough to dominate the rest. However,
there is another reason for assuming equal power, and in this
case nondominance will not do. The further reason is to rule
out as irrationally risky, actions by any actor designed to promote the development of conditions in which moral behavior
(i.e., behavior according to the laws of nature) would have a
rational justification. In other words, Hobbes defines the state

[60] Donald P. Warwick, "Transnational Participation and International
Peace," pp. 321-24.

[61] As John Gerard Ruggie suggests. "Collective Goods and Future International Collaboration," p. 878.

[62] Hobbes, *Leviathan*, ch. 13, p. 110.

of nature so that both conformity to the laws of nature and action to escape the state of nature are equally irrational. The stronger assumption of equal power secures both conclusions, whereas, on the weaker assumption of nondominance, it could be argued that the relatively stronger actors may have obligations to work for changes in those background conditions that make moral behavior irrational for all. This would be because some such actions might be undertaken without undue risk to the relatively stronger actors.

Now our question is whether it is appropriate to make the relatively stronger assumption of equal power about contemporary international relations. It seems clear that this condition is not met; there are vast disparities in relative levels of national power.[63] David Gauthier has argued that the development and proliferation of nuclear weapons render these inequalities less severe and make international relations more like a Hobbesian state of nature than it had been previously.[64] But this is too simple. While the possession of nuclear weapons may increase the relative power of some states not usually considered major powers, it is not true that all or most states are developing or will develop operational nuclear arsenals. The likely result of proliferation is not a world of nuclear powers but a world divided between an expanded number of nuclear powers and a large number of states that continue to lack nuclear weapons. Gauthier suggests that it is not equal nuclear capacity but equal vulnerability to nuclear attack that secures the analogy of nuclear politics and the state of nature.[65] But this shift does not help, since states are highly unequal in this sense as well, as a result of their varying levels of retaliatory capabilities (and hence of deterrent strengths) and of nuclear defenses.[66] Also, as long as the

[63] It has been suggested that this is one reason Hobbes thought that the inconveniences of the international state of nature would not lead to an international Leviathan. States of unequal power and vulnerability can "secure their ends by treaties and alliances, rather than by a resignation of their sovereignty." Howard Warrender, *The Political Philosophy of Hobbes*, p. 119.

[64] Gauthier, *The Logic of Leviathan*, pp. 207-8.   [65] Ibid., p. 207.

[66] There is a detailed discussion of these issues in Albert Legault and George Lindsey, *The Dynamics of the Nuclear Balance*, esp. chs. 3-5.

deterrence system works, conventional-force imbalances—
which are often substantial—will continue to differentiate
strong states from weak ones. If this is true, then the most
that can be claimed about relative levels of national power is
that no state can dominate all the others. As we have seen, this
alone may be enough to show that compliance with moral
rules is irrational for any state, but it is not enough to show
that some states (the strong ones) do not have obligations to
try to change the rules of the international game so as to render compliance with moral rules more rational. As we shall
see, even the relatively weaker assumption is thrown into
question by some further characteristics of power in contemporary international relations.

The third condition is that the units be able to order their
internal (i.e., nonsecurity) affairs independently of the internal policies of the other units. (As economists would say, the
units must have independent utility functions once corrected
for security considerations.)[67] If the units in the state of nature were interdependent in the way suggested, then the pursuit of self-interest by any one unit might require cooperation
with other units in the system. The relations among parties in
the state of nature would then resemble a game of mixed interests rather than a zero-sum game. Thus, if the units were
interdependent, Hobbes's assumption that the pursuit of
self-interest by the parties in the state of nature will usually
lead to violent conflict would be undermined.

Again, it seems unlikely that this condition applies to international relations. It is increasingly true that the security and
prosperity of any one state depends to a greater or lesser extent on that of some or all other states. In terms of security,
this is reflected in the recognition that the great powers have a
shared interest in avoiding a nuclear confrontation, and this
justifies a measure of trust and predictability in their relations

[67] Hobbes, *Leviathan*, ch. 13, pp. 112-13. Actually, Hobbes's assumption
may be stronger than this. When men quarrel for reasons of honor and glory,
one might say that their utility functions are inversely related and hence
(negatively) interdependent. But the argument only requires the condition of
independence given above.

with one another.[68] The interdependence of state interests has recently been illustrated in the broad area of economic and welfare concerns as well. Here it has been argued that the success of states in meeting domestic economic goals (e.g., full employment, control of inflation, balanced economic growth) requires substantially higher levels of cooperation among governments than has been the case in the past.[69]

Such interdependencies explain the rise of international institutions and practices that organize interstate rivalries in ways that require cooperation if the practices are to be maintained and conflicts resolved by nonviolent means. In the economic area, these include the organizational and consultative practices of the International Monetary Fund and its rules governing adjustment of currency exchange rates, and the related rules of trade formulated in the General Agreement on Tariffs and Trade. Taken together, these institutions can be seen as the constitutional structure of international finance and trade; their role is fundamental in promoting or retarding the growth of trade, the flow of investment, and the international transmission of inflation and unemployment.[70]

There is no doubt that such practices and institutions (or "regimes," as they are sometimes called)[71] have come to occupy a far more important place in international relations than previously as a result of the increasing volume and significance of transnational transactions. They are noticeable primarily in economic relations, but they are also significant in other areas (for example, regulation of the oceans and of the atmosphere, control of resource use, coordination of

[68] This conclusion emerges most clearly from the debate over the application of game theoretic models of conflict and cooperation to nuclear strategy. See, for example, Anatol Rapoport, *Strategy and Conscience*, part 2. There is a thorough review of this literature in John R. Raser, "International Deterrence."

[69] Edward L. Morse, "The Transformation of Foreign Policies." For a helpful discussion of the recent debate about the extent and kinds of interdependence, see Richard Rosecrance, "Interdependence: Myth or Reality."

[70] Richard N. Cooper, "Prolegomena to the Choice of an International Monetary System."

[71] By Keohane and Nye, for example. *Power and Interdependence*, p. 19.

health policies).[72] As a result, the character of power in international relations has been transformed.[73]

Power might be defined, very roughly, as an actor's capacity to cause other actors to act (or not to act) in ways in which they would not have acted (or would have acted) otherwise. The use or threat of violence is a paradigmatic instrument of power because there are very few situations in which we can imagine violence or its threat not causing others to act. But there is nothing about power that limits its instruments to the instruments of violence. Threats of something other than violence, as well as positive inducements, might count as forms of power in appropriate circumstances. The instruments of power available to an actor are partly determined by the kinds of relationships in which the actor stands with respect to the other actors it wishes to influence. In particular, common membership in institutions or common participation in practices often constitutes nonviolent forms of power. Thus, for example, members of organizations like the United Nations can bargain their votes for desired actions by other global actors. Or, traders in some commodity (say, oil) can withhold the commodity from the market to cause others to change their behavior in prescribed ways.

It is difficult to say how the rise of these new forms of international power will affect prospects for recourse to older forms. One might expect the international role of violence or its threat to vary inversely with the density of international institutions and practices that serve important interests. Common institutions and practices of the kind described require stable environmental conditions for their operation and a measure of consensual support, at least from their more significant members. It is likely (though not necessary) that all or most participants would share an interest in minimizing the

[72] The literature is large; see, for example, Richard N. Cooper, "Economic Interdependence and Foreign Policy in the Seventies"; Edward L. Morse, "Transnational Economic Processes"; and Alex Inkeles, "The Emerging Social Structure of the World."

[73] Seyom Brown, *New Forces in World Politics*, pp. 112-17 and 186-90; and Stanley Hoffmann, "Notes on the Elusiveness of Modern Power."

chances that continued functioning of their institutions and practices will be undermined by outbreaks of violence.[74]

On the other hand, while agreeing that new forms of power have arisen as a result of the development of new actors and relationships in international politics, one might think that this is, in fact, a reason to expect the use or threat of violence to become more rather than less common.[75] Perhaps the rise of new forms of power simply reflects the fact that states demand more from international relations now than in the past. A common example is that now, unlike, say, the eighteenth century, states are widely committed to maintaining high levels of domestic employment. Success in this commitment often depends on other international actors following particular kinds of policies. Since more is at stake in international relations now than previously, one might conclude, states have more reasons rather than fewer for using violence or its threat to protect and advance their interests.

This position, while not entirely incorrect, seems to overstate the case. First, as I have pointed out, the international mechanisms that states rely on to pursue various domestic (especially economic) goals often require stable environmental conditions and broad consensual support. Both of these might be upset if a state resorted to violence to pursue its goals. Violence, in other words, might be self-defeating in such circumstances. Furthermore, the view assumes that various forms of power in international relations are interchangeable; for example, if one cannot obtain an objective with a nonviolent form of power (say, one's influence in the decision-making structure of international finance institutions), one can still obtain it with superior military power. But it is not clear that forms of international power are so interchangeable, especially in view of the increasing diversity of

[74] This appears to be Kant's view in the First Supplement to *Perpetual Peace* [1795], p. 114.
[75] This view derives from Rousseau. *Discours sur l'inégalité* [1755], pp. 203-6. See also Stanley Hoffmann, "Rousseau on War and Peace," *The State of War*, pp. 62-63. But see Hoffmann's more recent remarks in "Notes on the Elusiveness of Modern Power," pp. 191-95 and 205-6.

objectives that states and other actors seek in international relations. The use of military power may not only be self-defeating, but its costs may be too great, or it may simply be irrelevant to the objective being pursued.[76]

The fourth condition is that there be no reliable expectations of reciprocal compliance in the absence of an authority capable of enforcing moral rules.[77] Hobbes is guilty here of formulating an overly restrictive condition. It has been pointed out that the reliability of the expectations involved is more properly understood as a function of the degree to which there is a settled habit of obedience to moral rules in the society.[78] A common power might effectively raise the level of obedience or it might not; what matters to the state-of-nature argument is that the appropriate expectations are lacking. But this does not fundamentally damage the Hobbesian position. One need only redefine the state of nature as a situation in which there are neither settled habits of obedience to moral rules nor well-established moral conventions.

This modification of Hobbes's position should be applied in the comparison with international relations as well. However, even some (like Kurt Baier) who have proposed the modification have failed to apply it to the international case. According to Baier's reconstruction of Hobbes's argument, "the doctrine of the sovereignty of nations and the absence of an effective international law and police force are a guarantee that nations live in a state of nature, without commonly accepted rules that are somehow enforced."[79] But this empirical claim hardly stands up against evidence of actual international behavior. Although there is no international police force, the international community possesses a variety of devices for promoting compliance with established norms. These range from such mild sanctions as community disapproval and censure by international organizations to coordinated national policies of economic embargoes of offending

---

[76] For a further discussion, see Keohane and Nye, *Power and Interdependence*, pp. 11-19, 27-29.

[77] Hobbes, *Leviathan*, ch. 14, pp. 114-16.

[78] See, for example, Kurt Baier, *The Moral Point of View*, pp. 238-39.

[79] Ibid., p. 312.

states. As international organizations grow in size and scope, exclusion from participation in the production and distribution of collective goods (for example, information and technology) is likely to become increasingly effective as an additional sanction.[80]

Regardless of the presence or absence of such machinery for enforcement, a wide variety of areas of international relations are characterized by high degrees of voluntary compliance with customary norms and institutionalized rules established by agreement. These areas are primarily associated with specific functions in which many states take an interest, but from which no state benefits without the cooperation of the other states involved. Governments participate in a wide range of specialized agencies (the Postal Union, the World Health Organization, the U.N. Conference on Trade and Development, etc.) and in many sectional associations like military alliances (NATO, the Warsaw Pact) and regional trade and development organizations (the European Economic Community).[81] In addition, there are rules and practices that are expressed in other than organizational forms—for example, customary international law, the conventions of diplomatic practice, and the rules of war.[82] The sphere of economic organizations and practices presents even clearer evidence of the existence of a highly articulated system of international institutions.

Evidence of areas of cooperation in which expectations of reciprocal compliance are reasonable could be multiplied, but enough has been said already to defeat the claim that the absence of a global coercive authority shows that international relations is, in the relevant sense, analogous to a Hobbesian state of nature. It is worth pausing to ask why, in the face of such fairly obvious empirical considerations, people might

---

[80] See Roger Fisher, "Bringing Law to Bear on Governments"; Wolfgang Friedmann, *The Changing Structure of International Law*, pp. 89-95; Michael Barkun, *Law Without Sanctions*, esp. ch. 2.

[81] See Lynn H. Miller, *Organizing Mankind: An Analysis of Contemporary International Organization*, esp. chs. 3-5.

[82] A convenient discussion of these matters is in J. L. Brierly, *The Law of Nations*, esp. chs. 2-3.

continue to think that the analogy holds. Perhaps, H.L.A. Hart suggests, this is the result of accepting a more funda- mental analogy between the forms and conditions of inter- action among individual persons and among communities organized as states. States, unlike persons, are not of such rel- atively equal strength as to make possible, or perhaps even desirable, machinery for coercive enforcement on the model of domestic society. There is no assurance that an offending state can be effectively coerced by a coalition of other states, while the use of sanctions even by a preponderant coalition might involve costs far in excess of the benefits to be derived from general compliance with appropriate rules.[83] It might be added that states can coordinate relatively complex ac- tivities with less reliance than individuals on centrally ad- ministered coercive threats because of their more diversified administrative and information-gathering capabilities. As a result, in a world not hierarchically ordered on the model of domestic societies, one can talk of a "horizontal" ordering which nevertheless involves substantial expectations of recip- rocal compliance with rules of cooperation.[84]

This picture of international relations might seem to leave little room for war, and this might seem rather unrealistic in view of the massive violence that has marked the last hundred years. But I have not meant to argue that war is a thing of the past, nor that it is no longer in some sense the ultimate prob- lem of international politics. The point is that the concerns of international relations have broadened considerably, with the result that competition among international actors may often take a variety of nonviolent forms, each requiring at least tacit agreement on certain rules of the game that express impor- tant common interests of the actors involved. The actors in international politics, their forms of interaction and competi- tion, their power, and the goals the system can promote have all changed. While international relations can still be charac-

[83] H.L.A. Hart, *The Concept of Law*, p. 214.

[84] For a further discussion, see Richard A. Falk, "International Jurisdic- tion: Horizontal and Vertical Conceptions of Legal Order"; and Gidon Gottlieb, "The Nature of International Law: Toward a Second Concept of Law," esp. pp. 331-39.

terized as "a tract of time, wherein the will to contend by battle is sufficiently known," it has become more complex than
this as well. But this new complexity, which has both analytical
and normative importance, is likely to be obscured if one ac-
cepts the model of international relations as a state of nature
in which the only major problem is war.

If these empirical criticisms are correct, then, even if one
holds that states are obligated to observe moral rules only
when it is in their interests to do so, it seems that there are
some rules of cooperation that are binding on states. This is
because states have common interests, and there are reasonable grounds for expecting reciprocal compliance with some
rules that advance these interests even in the absence of a
higher coercive authority. Of course, a substantially more
sophisticated analysis would be required to identify these
rules.[85] Furthermore, when established practices are flawed
(in some sense yet to be specified), or when certain kinds of
actions or policies are not governed by established practices, it
is still not the case that no state has an obligation to improve
the system. Since states are of unequal power, it may be that
some states (those that are relatively powerful) can take re-
medial actions without incurring substantial risks. Thus, the
analogy of international relations and the state of nature fails,
and as a result neither of the conclusions of the Hobbesian
argument for skepticism carries over to international relations.

A final caveat should be added, if only because the point is
so often obscured. My claim that it is wrong to conceptualize
international relations as a Hobbesian state of nature does not
imply that the international realm should be understood for
all purposes on the analogy of domestic society. I have suggested, and will argue further in part three, that the two
realms are similar in several respects relevant to the justification of principles of social justice. But there are important differences as well. The institutions and practices of international relations perform fewer tasks than their domestic

[85] One appropriate framework for such an analysis is provided by
collective-goods theory. This project is begun in Ruggie, "Collective Goods
and Future International Collaboration."

counterparts, are generally less efficient, and are less capable of coordinating the performance of tasks in diverse areas. More important, from our point of view, international relations includes fewer effective procedures for peaceful political change, and those procedures that do exist are more prone to problems of noncompliance. Rather than assimilate international relations to the state of nature or to domestic society, it would be better to understand it as occupying a middle ground. As in domestic society, there are, in international relations, both shared and opposed interests, providing a basis for both cooperation and competition. But effective institutions for exploiting the bases of cooperation are insufficiently developed, and their further growth faces great obstacles. These considerations do not argue for the meaninglessness of talk about international ethics, but they do present distinctive problems for any plausible international normative theory. In part three, I shall explore in more detail how these problems might be faced.

4. The Basis of International Morality

THE second, prescriptive, use of the state of nature explains the justification of regulative principles for political or international life. It does so by showing that a principle or set of principles would be the most rational choice available for persons situated in a state of nature.

Hobbes argues that the first law of nature—that is, the first principle to which rational persons situated in the state of nature would agree—is "that every man, ought to endeavour peace, as far as he has hope of obtaining it"; this law is qualified by what Hobbes calls "the right of nature," namely, that when a man cannot obtain peace, "he may seek, and use, all helps, and advantages of war."[86] The justification of these prescriptions, as I have argued, is based on rational self-interest. The analytical use of the state of nature shows that

[86] Hobbes, *Leviathan*, ch. 14, p. 117.

compliance with the laws of nature in the absence of an effective agreement by others to do the same would not be in the
interests of any person. The prescriptive use of the state of
nature provides the grounds for inferring that this is a reason
not to comply with the laws of nature unless the compliance
of everyone else can be assured. "[I]f other men will not lay
down their right" of nature, "then there is no reason for any
one, to divest himself of his: for that were to expose himself to
prey."[87]

It is clear that the description of the state of nature, and of
the persons located in it, should express the point of view
from which regulative principles should be chosen. Hobbes
thinks that this point of view is adequately captured by the
idea of self-interest: principles for domestic or international
politics must be justified, respectively, by considerations of
individual or national self-interest. This view is expressed by
his description of a state of nature in which the parties do
what is in their own interests, and by his conception of a law
of nature as a rule "by which a man is forbidden to do that,
which is destructive of his life, or taketh away the means of
preserving the same."[88] Our problem in assessing the prescriptive use of the international version of the state of nature
is not, as it was with the analytical use considered above, to
determine whether there are common interests among states
that can support rules of cooperation, and whether the circumstances of international relations ever allow states to follow those rules without unacceptable risk. Instead, we must
ask whether the Hobbesian account, applied to international
relations, provides an acceptable theory of the justification of
international moral principles. There are two questions. First,
should the justification of principles for international relations appeal ultimately to considerations about states (e.g.,
whether general acceptance of a principle would promote
each *state's* interests)? Second, should the justification of such
principles appeal only to *interests*?

The argument that states should pursue their own interests
in the absence of reliable expectations of reciprocal compli-

[87] Ibid. [88] Ibid., pp. 116-17.

ance with common rules depends on the analogy drawn between persons in the interpersonal state of nature and states in international relations. But this analogy is imperfect. In the interpersonal case, the idea that persons can pursue their interests unrestrained by moral rules might seem plausible because we assume that each has a right of self-preservation. Hobbes's claim that the laws of nature are not effective in the state of nature follows from the empirical claim that compliance with laws of nature in such a situation could require a person to act against his or her legitimate interest in self-preservation. But this reasoning does not obviously apply in the international case. By analogy with the interpersonal case, the argument for following the national interest when it conflicts with moral rules would be that there is a *national* right of self-preservation which states cannot be required to give up. The difficulty is that it is not clear what such a right involves or how it can be justified. States are more than aggregations of persons; at a minimum, they are characterized by territorial boundaries and a structure of political and economic institutions. How much of this—to say nothing of such other elements of statehood as cultural tradition, social structure, and so on—is covered by the presumed right of national self-preservation?

The plausibility of the claim that there is a basic right of national self-preservation seems to diminish as the idea of statehood is expanded. For example, it might seem relatively unobjectionable to say that the national interest justifies some action or policy when this is necessary to preserve the lives of the state's inhabitants against an external threat. In this case, the analogy with the interpersonal state of nature seems most acceptable, because it can be argued that the state's right of self-preservation is based directly on its individual members' rights of self-preservation. The presumed right is less acceptable when it is not lives but a state's territorial integrity that is at stake, since there is not necessarily any threat to individual lives. Persons often survive changes in national boundaries. If we expand the idea of statehood still farther—say, another state threatens a particular government but does not threaten lives or territory—the analogy loses even more of its persua-

siveness. I am not arguing that persons would not have
legitimate claims against other states and persons in these
cases, but rather that these claims could not be based on individual rights of self-preservation. In each case, the grounds
on which pursuit of the national interest could be justified are
the effects of the external threat on other rights of persons.
These are not captured by the analogy with the state of
nature.

This point is obscured because the skeptical position carries
over the analogy of states and persons from the analytical and
descriptive use of the international state of nature to the prescriptive use. I have argued that this analogy is misleading
even in the analytic use. But even if this is incorrect, it would
not follow that the analogy may be employed appropriately in
justifying prescriptions for international behavior. It is easy to
see how one might be led to carry the analogy too far. When
the state of nature is used for analytical purposes and the actors are persons, there is no difficulty in using the same construct to justify principles of conduct, since these are in any
event to be based on a consideration of the moral properties
of persons. But when the state of nature is applied to international relations, one must recognize that analytical and prescriptive interests may require different interpretations of the
state of nature. If we wish to *understand* the behavior of states,
perhaps it would be helpful to view them as rational actors
which respond to international circumstances on the basis of a
calculation of their rational self-interest. (The analysis in section 3 suggests some doubts about the realism of rational-
actor models of international politics, but that is beside the
point at the moment.) But if we wish to *prescribe* principles to
guide the behavior of states, we are involved in a quite different sort of question. For then our justification of normative
principles must appeal ultimately to those kinds of considerations that are appropriate in a prescriptive context, namely,
the rights and interests of persons. If the idea of the national
interest plays any role in justifying prescriptions for state behavior, it can only be because the national interest derives its
normative importance from these deeper and more ultimate
concerns.

Those who wish to apply Hobbes's argument to international relations should say that the parties to the international state of nature, when it is used as a device for showing which rules of conduct are rational, are to be conceived as persons rather than as states. This state of nature is international in the sense that the parties to it are of diverse citizenship. But they are still persons, and their choice of rules for the behavior of states (on such a revised Hobbesian view) is guided by their desire to preserve themselves as persons rather than simply to preserve their states as states. The effect of redefining the international state of nature in this way is to limit the choice of international rules in accordance with the considerations advanced above. The parties would still agree to a principle that used the national interest as a guide to behavior in the absence of reliable expectations of reciprocal compliance with moral rules. But now they would limit the national interest to what is required to preserve their lives. On the other hand, where there *are* reliable expectations of reciprocal compliance, there is no need to appeal to the national interest to justify principles of international conduct at all. For in that case individual rights of self-preservation are assured by the existence of stable expectations. The important question in identifying justifiable rules of international conduct would then be the effects of mutual compliance with the various alternative rules on the other rights of persons.[89]

The national interest is often invoked to justify disregard of moral principles that would otherwise constrain choices among alternative foreign policies. Thus, for example, Morgenthau writes that "the state has no right to let its moral disapprobation . . . get in the way of successful political action, itself inspired by the moral principle of national survival."[90] It

---

[89] To say that the (prescriptive) international state of nature is made up of persons rather than states (or their representatives) is not to eliminate states from the purview of international theory. My claim here is that principles must be *justified* by considerations of individual rather than "national" rights. But there is no theoretical difficulty in holding that such principles still *apply* primarily to states.

[90] Morgenthau, *Politics Among Nations*, p. 10.

is tempting to interpret Morgenthau as claiming that "the moral principle of national survival" should receive greater weight in deliberations concerning foreign policy than those other principles on which officials might base their "moral disapprobation." If my remarks above are correct, however, this interpretation is unhelpful because it fails to remove an important ambiguity from Morgenthau's formulation and hence fails to explain why his view is plausible at all. The ambiguity concerns the scope of "national survival." When this means "the survival of the state's citizens," the view seems prima facie acceptable, but this is because we generally assume that persons (not states) have rights of self-preservation. When "national survival" extends further (for example, to the preservation of forms of cultural life or to the defense of economic interests) the view's prima facie acceptability dissipates precisely because the survival of persons is no longer at issue. In such cases the invocation of the national interest does not necessarily justify disregard of other moral standards. What is required is a balancing of the rights and interests presumably protected by acting to further the national interest and those involved in acting on the competing principle that gives rise to moral disapprobation. While it cannot be maintained a priori that the individual rights presumably protected by the national interest would never win out in such cases, the opposite cannot be maintained either. Yet this is exactly what an uncritical acceptance of Morgenthau's view invites. Thus, to clarify the issues involved in debates regarding foreign policy choices, it would seem preferable to dispense with the idea of the national interest altogether and instead appeal directly to the rights and interests of all persons affected by the choice. Similarly, nothing is gained, and considerable clarity is lost, by attempting to justify principles of international conduct with reference to their effects on the interests of states. It is the rights and interests of persons that are of fundamental importance from the moral point of view, and it is to these considerations that the justification of principles for international relations should appeal.

The other objection to the Hobbesian state of nature as a

device for justifying rules of international conduct goes deeper and requires further changes in the definition of the state of nature. This criticism is generally relevant to the view of ethics according to which moral rules oblige only when they can be shown to be in the interests of everyone to whom they apply. The view does not allow moral criticism of established practices (although it allows criticism on other, e.g., prudential, grounds) nor does it admit principles whose general observance might seem morally required but would not benefit every party. But both of these seem, intuitively, to be part of the idea of morality.

The issue raised by this objection, of course, is fundamental to ethics: how can anyone have a reason to do particular actions or subscribe to general practices that cannot be shown to work to his advantage when a more advantageous alternative is available? In other words, how is ethics possible? The question is made complex because it requires a joint solution to the problems of moral justification—in what sense is compliance with moral rules rational?—and of moral motivation—how can these rules move us to act? These questions deserve discussion in their own right, but this would carry us far from the subject of international norms. Rather than pursue the question in any depth here, I shall assume that we share some general intuitions about the nature of ethics and try to show that the Hobbesian view falls far short of them. Then I shall return to the problem of expectations of reciprocal compliance and ask how it is relevant to the justification of principles for international relations.[91]

The view that ethics is based on enlightened self-interest is inadequate. It fails to account for certain principles that intuitively seem to impose requirements on our actions regardless of considerations of actual or possible resulting benefit to ourselves. Elementary examples of such principles are the rule not to cause unnecessary suffering or to help save a life if that can be done at acceptable cost and risk. Although, in

[91] The most elegant and subtle recent discussion of the issues raised here is Nagel, *The Possibility of Altruism*; on Hobbes, see Thomas Nagel, "Hobbes's Concept of Obligation."

general, we are likely to think that others would behave similarly if they were in our shoes and were called upon to comply with these rules, it does not seem that this is the reason we would give for acting on them. Indeed, we would say that there may be at least some moral obligations that impose requirements on action regardless of the presence or absence of expectations of reciprocal compliance, and, a fortiori, of conventions and enforceable rules that institutionalize these expectations and enhance their reliability. If the notion of natural moral requirements has a clear reference, it is to these sorts of obligations which do not gain their binding quality from the expectations, conventions, and institutions of particular communities.

One might agree with all of this, but claim that some other principles are based on self-interest—in particular, principles of justice that require compliance with political institutions or actions aimed at their reform. The argument would be that only self-interest provides a sufficiently strong motive for the sorts of actions required by justice, since natural moral requirements (for example, those discussed above which are, perhaps, based on such moral sentiments as altruism) are too few and too weak to support a very extensive system of social cooperation.[92] However, the Hobbesian view is inadequate here too. For it seems impossible to justify on the basis of self-interest compliance with the general rules governing participation in institutions. Consider, for example, the principle of political obligation. In one formulation, this principle holds that those who have submitted to the rules imposed by an institution, thus restricting their liberty, "have a right to a similar submission from those who have benefited by their submission."[93] Any defense of this principle based on self-interest sooner or later runs into the free-rider problem—why should someone submit to a restriction when he can benefit equally from nonsubmission? It requires truly heroic empirical assumptions to defeat such objections without giving

[92] A view of this kind is expressed in Philippa Foot, "Moral Beliefs," pp. 99-104.
[93] H.L.A. Hart, "Are There Any Natural Rights?," p. 185.

up the claim that political obligation must be based on considerations of self-interest. But a Hobbesian view of ethics leaves no alternative.[94]

The Hobbesian position and that expressed by these intuitive reflections represent two points of view from which we might make choices about how to act. To assert that ethics is possible is to say that there are occasions when we have reason to override the demands of self-interest by taking a moral point of view toward human affairs. Speaking very roughly, the moral point of view requires us to regard the world from the perspective of one person among many rather than from that of a particular self with particular interests, and to choose courses of action, policies, rules, and institutions on grounds that would be acceptable to any agent who was impartial among the competing interests involved. Of course, this is not to say that interests are irrelevant to moral choice. The question is how interests come into the justification of such choices. From the point of view of self-interest, one chooses that action or policy that best serves one's own interests, all things considered. From the moral point of view, on the other hand, one views one's interests as one set of interests among many and weighs the entire range of interests according to some impartial scheme. Both points of view are normative in the sense that they may impose requirements on action—for example, by requiring us to subordinate some immediate desire to some other consideration: either long-range self-interest (on Hobbes's view) or the interests of everyone. But only the moral perspective allows us to explain the basis of such natural moral requirements (and perhaps some institutional ones as well) as may move us to act even when there is no assurance of reciprocal compliance, and hence no self-interested justification, available.

This conclusion may seem stronger than it is. While I have argued that the moral point of view is not irrelevant to political theory, I have not said anything about the content of the moral norms that should constitute its substance. Thus, while

[94] See the illuminating discussion of the relation of rational self-interest and ethics in David P. Gauthier, "Morality and Advantage," esp. pp. 468-75.

it follows that the putative absence of reliable expectations in international relations does not show the impossibility of international political theory, very little is obvious about the strength or extent of the theoretical principles appropriate to such an environment. In other words, there is a gap between the structure of moral choice and the content of the rules, policies, and so on that should be chosen to govern various realms of action. How the gap is filled depends on the morally relevant features of the realm in question.

This explains how it is possible, as I observed above, to reject Hobbes's general conception of the state of nature (and with it his moral skepticism) and yet persist in the conclusion that the only effective principle of international morality is that of self-preservation. The empirical situation might be such that, when it is appraised from the moral point of view, the most that can be said is that agents should each pursue his own interests. While I have argued that such an empirical situation does not exist in some important areas of contemporary international relations, it could exist, and if it did, the moral conclusions that would follow would be, so to speak, extensionally equivalent to those reached on Hobbes's view. There is an important difference, however; while these conclusions rest, for Hobbes, on considerations of enlightened self-interest, on the other view they are founded on a consideration of all affected interests, balanced by an (as yet vague) impartial process. Thus, my claim that international political theory is possible does not imply that its principles are the same as (or analogous to) those that characterize the political theory of the state. Surely one factor that one would consider in choosing international principles from the moral point of view is the relatively lower reliability of expectations of reciprocal compliance in international relations. If it turns out that this factor is morally relevant in particular contexts of justification, then it would certainly affect the strength and extent of the resulting principles.

The position I have sketched as an alternative to Hobbes's is a reconstruction of that taken by many writers of the natural law tradition. The most familiar of these is Locke. Like Hobbes, he specifically compares the relations of states to the relations of persons in the state of nature.[95] Unlike Hobbes, Locke argues that even the state of nature "has a Law of Nature to govern it, which obliges every one: And Reason, which is that Law, teaches all Mankind, who will but consult it, that being equal and independent, no one ought to harm another in his Life, Health, Liberty, or Possessions."[96] However, Locke paid little attention to the specific requirements of the law of nature as applied to international relations.[97]

Although less familiar to us than Locke, Samuel Pufendorf is far more instructive on the application of natural law to nations. His major work on the subject, *Of the Law of Nature and Nations (De jure naturae et gentium)*, is especially interesting because it explicitly takes up Hobbes's arguments and attempts to defend the natural law tradition against them while producing similar conclusions regarding the weakness of moral rules in international affairs.[98] Against Hobbes, Pufendorf claims that justice and injustice were "defined by natural law and binding upon the consciences of men . . . before there were civil sovereignties."[99] Furthermore, these principles are effective even in the absence of a superior power on earth who explicitly proclaims and enforces the law; it is enough if they can be regarded as commands of God "arrived at and

[95] John Locke, *Two Treatises of Government* [1689], II, sec. 9, pp. 290-91, sec. 14, pp. 294-95, and sec. 145, p. 383.

[96] Ibid., II, sec. 6, p. 289. Compare Gierke, *Natural Law and the Theory of Society*, vol. 1, p. 97.

[97] Only one chapter—chapter 16, "Of Conquest"—of the Second Treatise is devoted specifically to this subject. However, it has been argued that a concern for international problems animates much of the remainder of Locke's theory as well. See Richard Cox, *Locke on War and Peace*. This interpretation is highly speculative, and there is little direct textual evidence in its support.

[98] Anglo-American scholars have paid too little attention to Pufendorf as a political and especially as an international theorist. There is a useful, largely historical, discussion of his views in Leonard Krieger, *The Politics of Discretion*. A brief, and I think accurate, account of his view of the law of nations can be found in Walter Schiffer, *The Legal Community of Mankind*, pp. 49-63. The best work is in German. See the bibliography in Horst Denzer, *Moralphilosophie und Naturrecht bei Samuel Pufendorf*, pp. 375-85.

[99] Samuel Pufendorf, *De jure naturae et gentium, libri octo* [1688], VIII, i, p. 1,138 (the order of the phrases has been reversed). See also II, ii, pp. 158-59.

understood in any way whatsoever, whether by the inner dictate of the mind, from the condition of our nature, or the character of the business to be undertaken."[100]

Pufendorf has a próblem with principles for nations because he wants to derive essentially Hobbesian results from a moralized (one might say Lockean) image of the state of nature. Like Hobbes, he argues that principles for nations can be derived from principles for individuals in the state of nature by regarding nations as "moral persons." Then principles for nations would be just the principles for individuals writ large.[101] Yet he also holds that the result of reinterpreting the principles in this way is a group of principles weaker in several respects than their analogues for individuals. For example, he seems to hold that pacts and treaties are binding on nations only when they serve mutual interests, whereas promises among individuals bind regardless of such considerations.[102] Also, while he holds that individuals always have a reason to combine into states to escape the state of nature, he does not believe that nations have an analogous reason to form some sort of supranational federation or world government.[103]

The explanation for these apparent inconsistencies is that Pufendorf does not view international relations as precisely analogous to the state of nature for individuals.[104] The interpersonal and international states of nature are similar insofar as both are characterized by rough equality of strength of the units and lack of a common enforcer of laws.[105] In both cases reason determines the regulative principles. But other circumstances differ, and the contents of the principles vary accordingly. There seem to be two main respects in which the analogy fails to hold. First, Pufendorf claims that states are

[100] Ibid., II, iii, p. 219. Pufendorf is responding to Hobbes's claim in *De Cive* (III, sec. 33, pp. 49-50) that "laws of nature . . . are not in propriety of speech laws" outside of civil society.

[101] Pufendorf, *De jure naturae*, II, iii, p. 226; VII, ii, p. 983.

[102] Ibid., VIII, ix, p. 1,338; VIII, x, p. 1,342-43.

[103] Ibid., II, iii, p. 163; VII, i, p. 949-63.

[104] Ibid., VIII, vi, p. 1,292.

[105] Ibid., II, ii, p. 163; III, ii, p. 330; VIII, iv, p. 1,253.

less likely than persons to be moved by other-regarding considerations when these come into conflict with self-interest.[106] If this is generally true, then it can be argued that those forms of obligation that depend on the availability of other-regarding motivations (such as keeping promises) are correspondingly weaker. A further, and more fundamental, difference is that the safety and liberty of individuals is far less secure in the interpersonal state of nature than in a state of nature made up of independent nations. The "state or commonwealth" is "the most perfect form of society, and is that wherein is contained the greatest safety for mankind."[107] Because the "safety" of individuals is adequately assured by the organization of commonwealths, the international state of nature "lacks those inconveniences which are attendant upon a pure state of nature."[108]

Some aspects of Pufendorf's view of the international state of nature are subject to the same empirical criticisms that I have made against Hobbes's. In particular, Pufendorf seems to accept the view that states are the only actors in international relations, that they are largely noninterdependent, and that they entertain few reliable expectations of reciprocal compliance with rules and common practices. I shall not rehearse my criticisms of these views again here. The importance of Pufendorf's system is that it gives a more acceptable account than Hobbes's of why principles for nations may sometimes fail to be analogous to those for individuals in civil society. This possibility, which seems to be a common intuition about international ethics and is clearly captured in the relative weakness of customary international law, need not force us to the extreme conclusion that morality and the normative political theory that derives from it have no place in international relations. Indeed, it is impossible to maintain this view as a matter of principle short of adopting a thoroughgoing skepticism about all morality. It is more reason-

[106] Ibid., II, ii, p. 176; VII, i, p. 962. Pufendorf gives no account of why this is the case. Rousseau held a similar view. See above, note 47.

[107] Pufendorf, *De jure naturae*, VII, i, p. 949.

[108] Ibid., II, ii, p. 163. Compare Hobbes, *Leviathan*, ch. 13, p. 115.

able to explain the peculiar features of international principles as the result of empirical differences between the
domestic and international environments, viewed from a
common perspective of moral justification. If this is true, then
we can reformulate the relationship between principles for
individuals in the state of nature and for nations in international relations. Rather than derive the former and reinter-
pret them, putting nations for persons, to obtain international principles, we might choose another procedure. We
might, instead, regard the choice of international principles
as a problem of political theory in its own right, which is to be
solved independently of the choice of principles for persons
outside of civil society. Principles for persons in the state of
nature would then come into the discussion of international
theory in the form of arguments by analogy. While they have
no special status in the international context, they provide
guidance in formulating international principles just in case
the analogy between international relations and the state of
nature is in the relevant respects appropriate. But the justification of international principles is independent of this comparison; it is to be sought in a return to the machinery of
justification—which I have vaguely called the moral point of
view—that is the common foundation of principles in both
realms.

5. From International Skepticism to the Morality of States

THE most sophisticated argument available to the skeptic
flows from the characterization of international relations
as a Hobbesian state of nature. This position combines an
empirical analysis of international relations, according to
which no state has an interest in following cooperative rules,
and a theory of moral justification that holds that all moral
restrictions on action must promote the long-range interests
of the agent. If moral rules must advance the interests of

everyone to whom they apply, and if it is not in any state's interest to follow moral rules, then, the argument concludes, there is no international morality.

The first part of this position results from an analytical application of the state-of-nature analogy, and the second part from a prescriptive application of it. I have argued that both applications of the idea of the state of nature to international relations are inappropriate. First, when the international state of nature is viewed as an analytical device, it produces the empirically false conclusion that there can be no reliable expectations of reciprocal compliance with cooperative institutions and policies in the absence of an overarching world authority. Such an analysis tends to obscure the fact that the interactions that comprise international relations take a variety of nonviolent forms, many of which require cooperative maintenance of common rules. Even if it were true that morality is based on self-interest (that is, even if Hobbes were right about moral theory), international skepticism would be wrong for empirical reasons, for states have interests in following these rules, and there are circumstances in which it is rational for them to expect each other to do so.

However, I have argued that Hobbes is wrong about moral theory, and this leads to further reasons for rejecting international skepticism. When the state of nature is viewed as a moral construct, and interpreted as it is by Hobbes, it supplies an unacceptable account of the justification of moral principles, and a fortiori of moral principles for international relations. The Hobbesian view invites a justification of international principles in terms of the interests of states; but, even if Hobbes's metaethics were accepted, it is the interests of *persons* that are fundamental, and "national interests" are relevant to the justification of international principles only to the extent that they are derived from the interests of persons. More basically, moral requirements on action can have justifications other than the rational self-interest of the agent. For example, participation in common practices and institutions can be morally obligatory even when compliance with the appropriate rules in any particular case does not advance the agent's own interests. Further considerations (e.g., fairness, equality) should be taken into account in the design of such practices and institutions. Moreover, there may be circumstances not involving participation in standing practices and institutions in which action can be morally required even when it does not advance the agent's interests. This class is important because it includes actions that would promote the development of morally acceptable institutions.

These conclusions remove a main source of skepticism about the meaningfulness of moral judgments concerning international relations by undermining the most powerful argument available to the international skeptic. Unless one is willing to embrace a general skepticism toward all morality, the analysis of international relations as a state of nature does not yield the conclusion that moral judgments do not provide reasons for action when they concern the international realm.

To say that international skepticism is incorrect, then, is to say that international political theory is possible. But it does not say much more, and, in particular, it does not say anything about the substance of the normative principles that should govern action in the international realm. I have illustrated this by considering Pufendorf's critique of Hobbes: while Pufendorf rejects Hobbes's skepticism about the possibility of international morality, he proposes international principles that are very weak. There would be little difference, in practice, between following Pufendorf's principles and Hobbesian prudence.

If the Hobbesian view of international relations is the dominant one in the Anglo-American tradition, then the view represented by Pufendorf is the most widely favored alternative. We might call this view the morality of states, because it is based on a conception of the world as a community of largely *Pufendorf* self-sufficient states which interact only in marginal ways. States, not persons, are the subjects of international morality, and the most fundamental rules that regulate their behavior are supposed to preserve a peaceful order of sovereign states.

Two basic features of the morality of states are especially striking. One is the principle of state autonomy: like persons in domestic society, states in international society are to be treated as autonomous sources of ends, morally immune from external interference, and morally free to arrange their internal affairs as their governments see fit. The other is the absence of any principle of international distributive justice: in the morality of states, each state is assumed to have a right to the wealth of its territory, and there are no moral rules regarding the structure and conduct of economic relations between states. Taking these two points together, the morality of states might be understood as the international analogue of nineteenth-century liberalism. It joins a belief in the liberty of individual agents with an indifference to the distributive outcomes of their economic interaction.

In the rest of this book, I criticize these two elements of the morality of states. I shall argue that each is incorrect; and, while I cannot now provide a comprehensive theoretical alternative to the morality of states, I shall suggest several important respects in which the received view should be revised.

PART TWO

The Autonomy of States

[T]he recognition of sovereignty is the only way we have of establishing an arena within which freedom can be fought for and (sometimes) won. It is this arena and the activities that go on within it that we want to protect, and we protect them, much as we protect individual integrity, by marking out boundaries that cannot be crossed, rights that cannot be violated. As with individuals, so with sovereign states: there are things that we cannot do to them, even for their own ostensible good.[1]

[1] Michael Walzer, *Just and Unjust Wars*, p. 89. Walzer's position, as developed in this book, is not as absolutely noninterventionist as the quotation suggests.

PERCEPTIONS of international relations have been more thoroughly influenced by the analogy of states and persons than by any other device. The conception of international relations as a state of nature could be viewed as an application of this analogy. Another application is the idea that states, like persons, have a right to be respected as autonomous entities. This idea, which dates from the writings of Wolff, Pufendorf, and Vattel, is a main element of the morality of states and is appealed to in a variety of controversies in international politics. Most often, these controversies involve the principles of nonintervention and self-determination, or the claim that foreign investment and multinational corporate activity in poor countries are objectionable because they constitute external interference in what is properly a country's internal affairs.

While the idea of state autonomy is widely held to be a fundamental constitutive element of international relations, I shall argue that it brings a spurious order to complex and conflicting moral considerations. This idea is neither fundamental, nor adequate as a justification of either the supposedly derivative principles of nonintervention and self-determination or the moral objections to imperialism and economic dependence. Intervention, colonialism, imperialism, and dependence are not morally objectionable because they offend a right of autonomy, but rather because they are unjust. In various ways which I shall try to make explicit, such policies offend principles of justice that ought to characterize the relations of states and the relations of persons within states. This is not to say that there are never cases in which a right of state autonomy ought to be respected, but rather that such a right, when it exists, is a derivative of more basic principles of justice. Furthermore, there are many cases in which there is no obvious reason why a state's autonomy should be respected—the clearest are those involving colonialism, in which observance of a principle of autonomy would, in effect, protect imperial powers against demands for colonial self-determination.

I argue these points by examining the moral reasoning for the principles of nonintervention and self-determination. In each case, I try to show that the idea of state autonomy as conventionally understood provides an inadequate foundation for the principles involved, and that conceptions of domestic social justice are required to make good the inadequacies. However, I do not, in the present discussion, consider the content of the appropriate conceptions of justice.

It is important to stress, in advance, that my interest here is in the idea of state autonomy and the extent to which the associated moral concerns furnish a basis, *in principle*, for opposing intervention and supporting self-determination. I do not wish to foreclose the very likely possibility that particular cases of potential intervention or self-determination might involve other moral or prudential considerations that could prove in those cases to be overriding.

One further point of clarification is in order. Although nonintervention and self-determination have been discussed extensively as principles of international law, I shall consider them from a different point of view. My concern is to examine these principles as principles of international political theory, much as many theorists have viewed the principle of equal liberty as a principle of the political theory of the state rather than as an element of positive law. Accordingly, I shall ask how these principles may be justified morally, and how their justifications influence the contents of the principles. The relation of normative political theory to the international law of self-determination and nonintervention is a distinct issue, since a theory of international legal interpretation is required to explain how normative principles come into the determination of international law. I shall not pursue that problem here.

1. State Autonomy and Individual Liberty

IN THIS and the following sections, I propose a criticism and reconstruction of the idea of state autonomy by exploring the moral foundations of the principle of nonintervention. Historically, this principle is the most important embodiment of the modern idea that states should be treated as autonomous entities; it is also the main structural principle of a conception of the world, dominant since the mid-seventeenth century, as an order of largely self-sufficient states. Previously, a different conception of international order had been ascendant; in that conception, exemplified by Grotius, states were regarded as elements of a larger moral order, and their boundaries were not viewed as barriers to external moral assessment or political interference.[2] Grotius is often called the father of modern international law, but in this respect the label is incorrect. He argues, not for the nonintervention principle, but for the distinct principle that intervention is sometimes justifiable (for example, when necessary to stop oppression in another state).[3] The prohibition of intervention was formulated by later writers—largely Wolff and Vattel—who argued that the rights of sovereign states, or considerations of international stability, or both, required virtually unlimited toleration in international affairs.

From a philosophical point of view, the nonintervention principle, and various arguments usually given in its support, can be seen to embody the considerations that make the ideal of state autonomy intuitively most attractive. These considerations flow from two analogies with the political theory of the state, namely, the analogy of states and persons, and the resulting analogy of nonintervention and equal liberty. By considering arguments for the nonintervention principle based on these analogies, we can make more explicit the meaning and import of the ideal of state autonomy and assess its continuing relevance.

[2] See P. H. Winfield, "The History of Intervention in International Law," pp. 132-34; Hedley Bull, "The Grotian Conception of International Society."

[3] Hugo Grotius, *De jure belli ac pacis libri tres* [1625], II, xxv, sec. vi, p. 582.

It is worth pausing to consider the scope of the nonintervention principle. It prohibits intervention, but what, exactly,
is intervention? At the most general level, intervention refers
to actions or policies designed to influence the affairs of a
sovereign state and carried out by an agent external to that
state. But there is considerable dispute in the recent literature
about how to interpret the concept more precisely.

At one end of the range of available definitions are narrow
conceptions that identify intervention with "coercive interference" by a state in the political affairs of another state involving "the use or threat of force."[4] There is considerable inde-
terminacy even in such a narrow definition. This results from
the vagueness of the concepts of coercion, of force, of a state's
political affairs, and of interference. The most restrictive interpretation would be that intervention is a policy carried out
by a government, aimed at changing the structure of political
authority in another state against its will, using military force.

In addition to the moral objections that can be brought
against other forms of interference, military intervention is
subject to a variety of challenges that apply to all uses of
armed force in international affairs. Such challenges complicate the case against interference by obscuring those moral
objections that apply independently of the presence or absence of military violence. In order to concentrate on these
concerns, I shall bracket the case of military intervention and
limit what I shall call the narrow definition of intervention to
policies of interference that involve threats of military force
but fall short of the actual use of violence.

This definition could be broadened by enlarging any or all
of its conditions. For example, forms of coercion not involving threats of military force (like threats of economic sanctions or subversion) could be allowed into the definition.[5] On
this view, intervention is marked by compulsion rather than

---

[4] R. J. Vincent, *Nonintervention and International Order*, p. 8. This definition
derives from Oppenheim. See L. Oppenheim, *International Law: A Treatise*,
vol. 1, *Peace*, p. 305.

[5] "Economic pressures on other states; diplomatic demands backed up with
political threats to force a state to curb freedom of speech, press, and radio;
fifth column activities; the inciting of another state's peoples to rise against its

merely by armed force.[6] At least one writer has argued that intervention should simply be identified with influence.[7] Thus, bilateral economic aid has been claimed to constitute an instrument of intervention because political conditions are often attached.[8] Alternatively, or in addition, one might broaden the definition by allowing that other actors than state governments can practice intervention, especially such "non-national" actors as multinational corporations and terrorist groups, or such international actors as the United Nations and regional organizations.[9] Finally, the definition could be broadened further by allowing that intervention can have other goals than a change in the formal structure of authority in another state.[10] For example, perhaps intervention could aim at inducing a government to change a particular policy against its will, at altering the balance of power between competing groups or classes, or at producing a change in the structure of economic activity within a state. Although none of these necessarily involves a change in constitutional structures, all of them have in common the fact that they involve producing internal changes regardless of the wishes of the government of the state intervened in. In this sense they might be said to constitute coercive interference.

One might think that the breadth and vagueness of a definition of intervention enlarged along these lines is a reason either to restrict the definition as narrowly as possible or to

government; and a multitude of other refined techniques of interference must in many instances come under the heading of intervention." A.V.W. Thomas and A. J. Thomas, Jr., *Non-Intervention*, p. 69.

[6] Ibid., p. 71. Compare Hersch Lauterpacht, *International Law and Human Rights*, p. 167; Manfred Halpern, *The Morality and Politics of Intervention*, p. 9.

[7] James N. Rosenau, "Intervention as a Scientific Concept," p. 159.

[8] David A. Baldwin, "Foreign Aid, Intervention, and Influence," p. 426. There is a somewhat different view in Michael N. Cardozo, "Intervention: Benefaction as Justification," pp. 79-82.

[9] For these suggestions, see, respectively, Peter B. Evans, "National Autonomy and Economic Development"; and Richard A. Falk, "On Legislative Intervention by the United Nations in the International Affairs of Sovereign States," *Legal Order in a Violent World*, esp. pp. 341-42.

[10] For the view that "straightforward efforts to induce changes in particular policies of another government" are *not* instances of intervention, see Oran Young, "Intervention and International Systems," p. 178.

abandon the concept of intervention as an anachronism.[11]
Or, one might conclude that intervention conventionally
applies to several types of situations that have few features in
common, with the result that each type needs to be examined
separately.[12] But there is reason to hesitate about drawing any
of these conclusions. The controversy about the definition of
intervention masks a question of substantive political ethics—
what forms of interference in a state's internal affairs are impermissible, and why? In the recent literature, arguments
about this question have been formulated as arguments about
how to interpret the definition of intervention. On the premise that all intervention is impermissible, this approach attempts to define intervention so that any and all actions and
policies that constitute impermissible interference in a state's
internal affairs count as intervention. The most obvious flaw
in this approach is its premise that all intervention is impermissible. This is a substantive claim that needs a justification.
A deeper flaw is the tacit assumption that the three main elements of the *definition* of intervention—its form, its agent, and
its goal—capture all of the considerations that might enter
into arguments about the *permissibility* of intervention. As we
shall see, this is not obviously true. It would be better to separate questions of definition from questions of political ethics.
We might provisionally accept the broadest reasonable definition of intervention and then consider the normative issue of
when intervention is impermissible, and why. If it turns out
that there are cases in which some forms of intervention are
morally permissible, one should acknowledge that fact rather
than conceal it behind a cumbersome and mystifying definition.

   We can begin our consideration of the normative issue by

----

[11] For the restrictionist view, see Vincent, *Nonintervention*, pp. 6-13. An-
drew M. Scott urges that the principle of nonintervention is obsolete in *The
Revolution in Statecraft*, p. 107. He puts his view in a more moderate form in
"Nonintervention and Conditional Intervention," p. 209.

[12] "Intervention," John Norton Moore claims, is "a monochromatic term
for a polychromatic reality." "Intervention," *Law and the Indo-China War*, p.
83. See also "The Control of Foreign Intervention in Internal Conflict," *Law
and the Indo-China War*, pp. 126-27.

examining Christian Wolff's argument for the nonintervention principle, because his argument clearly captures the analogy of states and persons, and because it has been influential in the subsequent development of international thought. He writes, "[N]ations are regarded as individual free persons living in a state of nature."[13] Following out the analogy, he holds that nations, like persons, are moral equals: "Since by nature all nations are equal, since moreover all men are equal in a moral sense whose rights and obligations are the same; the rights and obligations of all nations are also by nature the same."[14] The "rights and obligations" of a nation are defined by its "sovereignty" which is "originally . . . absolute" but can be limited by laws of nations which impose restrictions equally on every state.[15] The nonintervention rule follows directly: "Since by nature no nation has a right to any act which pertains to the exercise of the sovereignty of another nation . . . ; no ruler of a state has the right to interfere in the government of another, consequently cannot establish anything in its state or do anything, and the government of the ruler of one state is not subject to the decision of the ruler of any other state."[16] Wolff has been interpreted as proposing an "absolute" prohibition of intervention.[17] However, he allows that the community of states "as a whole" has a right to "coerce" any state to comply with the law of nations.[18] The prohibition is absolute only with regard to states, which may not interfere in the affairs of other equally sovereign states.[19]

The intuitive appeal of this sort of argument results from the analogy with personal liberty. We are likely to think that a person's liberty to pursue his own ends without interference

[13] Christian Wolff, *Jus gentium methodo scientifica pertractatum* [1749], sec. 2, p. 9.

[14] Ibid., sec. 17, p. 16.   [15] Ibid., sec. 255, p. 130; secs. 3-6, pp. 9-10.

[16] Ibid., sec. 257, p. 131.

[17] Thomas and Thomas, *Non-Intervention*, p. 5.

[18] Wolff, *Jus gentium*, sec. 13, p. 14; Vincent, *Nonintervention*, p. 28.

[19] Vattel follows Wolff in this formulation. See Emerich de Vattel, *The Law of Nations or the Principles of Natural Law* [*Le droit des gens*] [1758], II, sec. 54, p. 131. The principle of state equality is hardly arcane. John Rawls also sees it as the basic principle of international relations. See *A Theory of Justice*, p. 378.

is an important good, that it is better to have more of it than less, and that there is no moral warrant for interfering with a person's liberty to pursue his ends as long as this pursuit does not offend the equal liberty of others to do the same. The argument for this view holds that a person's choice and pursuit of ends has intrinsic value which cannot be overridden simply by considerations of the social good; instead, we are to respect persons as autonomous agents who are not to be made subject to the will of another unless an appropriate justification, itself related to the preservation of a maximal system of equal liberties, can be supplied.

Reading "states" for "persons" in the last paragraph gives a reasonably close reconstruction of Wolff's argument for nonintervention. Indeed, several contemporary writers put the argument for nonintervention in similar terms.[20] However, the argument can be no more than suggestive until we probe further into the analogy of persons and states. In particular, we must ask under what conditions it makes sense to think that states have a right to be respected as sources of ends in the same way as do persons. What is the moral content of the right of state autonomy?

One view is that states have such a right under all conditions. Like persons, states might be conceived as moral beings which are organic wholes with the capacity to realize their nature in the choice and pursuit of ends.[21] Here Wolff's analogy is at its strongest, but it is difficult to know what to make of the idea of the state as a moral being analogous to the person. After all, states qua states do not think or will or act in pursuit of ends; only people (or perhaps sentient beings), alone or in groups, do these things. Unless some independent sense can be given to the idea of the state as a moral agent, this view cannot be very persuasive.

The state might be given a moral character by constructing

[20] See, for example, S. I. Benn and R. S. Peters, *The Principles of Political Thought*, pp. 429-31; Vincent, *Nonintervention*, p. 345.

[21] This view derives from Hegel. See *Hegel's Philosophy of Right* [1821], secs. 257-59, pp. 155-60; secs. 321-29, pp. 208-12; sec. 351, p. 219. See also Bernard Bosanquet, *The Philosophical Theory of the State* [1899], chs. 10-11; see esp. pp. 298-99.

its rights and liberties on a foundation of individual rights and liberties. As Michael Walzer writes, "the rights of states rest on the consent of their members." The social contract to which citizens consent is to be understood as a metaphor "for a process of association and mutuality, the ongoing character of which the state claims to protect against external encroachment."[22] Thus, the state safeguards more than individual lives and liberties; it also protects its citizens' "shared life and liberty, the independent community they have made."[23] But it is the consent of the individual citizens that provides the underpinnings of the state's autonomy and secures the analogy with individual liberty: "[G]iven a genuine 'contract,' it makes sense to say that the territorial integrity and political sovereignty can be defended in exactly the same way as individual life and liberty."[24]

Exactly why does the consent of the citizens justify a right of autonomy for their government? One might have something like the following in mind. The principle of state autonomy gives rise to claims by those who speak for a state that the state should not be interfered with in its internal or self-regarding actions. Such interference is a form of coercion, because it involves imposing institutions and policies on people against their will. Thus, it is natural to think that a state's autonomy might be defended in terms of the liberties of persons which would be offended by the exercise of coercion by external agents against domestic political institutions. One might say, following Benn and Peters, that states are "associations of individuals with their own common interests and aspirations, expressed within a common tradition."[25] Then the autonomy of states would rest on one aspect of the autonomy of persons, namely, their liberty to associate in pursuit of common ends. State governments should not be interfered with because they are, in fact, representatives of persons exercising their freedom of association. The liberty of states is a consequence of the liberty of persons to associate.

It is important to distinguish between two kinds of appeals

---

[22] Walzer, *Just and Unjust Wars*, p. 54.   [23] Ibid.
[24] Ibid.   [25] Benn and Peters, *Principles*, p. 429.

to freedom of association in assessing arguments of this type. One holds that a condition of the state's moral legitimacy is that it protect the freedom of its citizens to associate.[26] The other holds that the state should not be interfered with because it is itself a free association, that is, a group of persons freely associated in the pursuit of common ends. The present argument involves the second kind of appeal to freedom of association,[27] and once this is recognized, the difficulty with the argument becomes clear.

The difficulty is familiar and applies to virtually all attempts to justify civil government as a special case of freedom of association. The objection is simply that there are few, if any, governments to which all (or even some) of the governed have actually consented, and therefore that there are few, if any, governments that are in fact free associations. Governments are not like voluntary associations in the sense that people freely organize them, join them, depart from them, and dissolve them, according to the dictates of their desires and interests. Governments are more like a fixed part of the social landscape, into which people are born and within which all but the most fortunate are confined regardless of whether or not they expressly agree to their terms of association.[28]

But if the institutions of the state are not like free associations in the sense that people can freely join them and depart from them, it still might be said that these institutions derive their legitimacy from periodic reaffirmation of the support of their citizens. Perhaps voting, for example, can be interpreted as an act that implies the voter's consent to his or her political institutions; or, as Locke maintains, perhaps the failure to depart signifies "tacit consent" to the obligation to comply

[26] The term "legitimacy" is ambiguous. It might refer to a government's actual standing among its citizens (the "de facto" sense). Or it might refer to the moral standing of a government: roughly, its right to be obeyed (the "de jure" sense). Throughout, I employ the term in the second, de jure, sense.

[27] As Walzer makes clear in his sympathetic discussion of Mill's view about nonintervention, "We are to treat states as self-determining communities, [Mill] argues, whether or not their internal political arrangements are free." Walzer, *Just and Unjust Wars*, p. 87.

[28] See David Hume, "Of the Original Contract" [1748], esp. pp. 456-62; and, more recently, Hanna Pitkin, "Obligation and Consent—I," pp. 990-96.

with one's government.[29] It might even be thought that the failure to participate actively in political dissent is a sign of consent.[30] Now, in fact, it does not seem that any of these acts (or nonacts) would be sufficient to establish the legitimacy of institutions of government. Political institutions have a deep and pervasive effect on the prospects of people living under them, on their preferences, and on their abilities to act (or not act) on their preferences. In particular, institutions define the processes through which consent can or cannot be expressed and influence the availability of the means necessary to participate in these processes. These institutions themselves stand in need of justification, but such a justification cannot be provided in terms of consent.[31]

These points, taken together, suggest that few, if any, governments can be shown to be morally legitimate by appeal to considerations of actual or tacit consent. Nevertheless, we are prepared to recognize the possibility that some governments might be morally legitimate even though they lack a truly consensual or voluntary foundation. Standards of legitimacy are to be sought elsewhere than in the actual prior agreement of the governed.

These observations are familiar enough in recent discussions of consent theory, and so I shall not pursue them further. What is important is that the weakness of the argument from consent to legitimacy also undermines the argument from consent to autonomy. If domestic governments are nonvoluntary in the sense that they exercise coercive power without the prior and active consent of their members, then violation of a state's autonomy by an external agent cannot be criticized *simply* because it involves the exercise of coercion against persons without their consent. In that case, domestic governments would be subject to a similar criticism, and there would be few, if any, governments that could be regarded as

[29] John Locke, *Two Treatises of Government* [1689], II, secs. 119, 121, pp. 365-67.

[30] Such a view seems to be implied in Walzer, *Just and Unjust Wars*, pp. 54 and 98.

[31] For a further discussion of these points, see A. John Simmons, "Tacit Consent and Political Obligation," esp. pp. 278-88.

legitimate. But this is a position that few would be inclined to accept, since we are likely to believe that some governments that are not genuine voluntary associations (and the legitimacy of which therefore is not based on the expressed consent of their members) might be legitimate nonetheless. This reasoning produces a dilemma for the view of state autonomy outlined above: if legitimate domestic governments exercise coercive power over their own citizens without their consent, and if illegitimate violations of autonomy by external agents might be described in precisely the same way, how can one form of coercion be distinguished from the other?

Once the view that civil government is a special case of freedom of association is abandoned, one must recognize that government inevitably involves the use of coercion without the consent of those against whom it is used. Thus, to distinguish the coercion resulting from external interference from that resulting from the ordinary operations of government, one needs an account of the conditions that make it possible for us to regard the latter as legitimate. This is the truth that remains from the attempt to link autonomy and legitimacy after the philosophical difficulties of theories of legitimacy based on actual or tacit consent are cleared away. But if actual and tacit consent are not, in most cases, appropriate conditions of legitimacy, it remains to ask, what is? A plausible approach to this question is through the idea of a hypothetical contract: a government is legitimate if it *would be* consented to by rational persons subject to its rule. This is merely an alternative way of understanding the idea of an original contract as the mechanism for justifying principles of justice.[32] Then the argument against interference is that it violates principles that would be consented to by rational citizens as expressing the terms of their association. One might say that the analogue of the moral autonomy of persons, at the level of states, is a state's conformity with appropriate principles of

[32] Obviously, much more needs to be said to work out the details of a hypothetical-contract approach to the derivation of principles of social justice, but since nothing in what follows depends on our adopting any particular version of the contract doctrine, I shall not pursue this matter here.

domestic justice.[33] The autonomy of states is the outer face of their legitimacy.

This may seem implausible for reasons related to the analogy of states and persons. I have claimed that only states whose institutions satisfy appropriate principles of justice can legitimately demand to be respected as autonomous sources of ends. But surely I would not restrict the set of persons who can demand respect as sources of ends in an analogous manner. For example, one would not want to argue that only the righteous, the virtuous, or the psychologically well integrated should be respected as autonomous beings. That such considerations can seem to undermine the view of state autonomy sketched above illustrates how deeply the analogy of states and persons has penetrated our perceptions of the state, and at what cost. In fact, my argument has been that it is *because* all persons should be respected as sources of ends that we should not allow all states to claim a right of autonomy. Assuming that it is part of the justice of institutions that they treat their members in some sense as autonomous persons, then the claim that unjust states should not be accorded the respect demanded by the principle of state autonomy follows from the claim that it is only considerations of personal autonomy, appropriately interpreted, that constitute the moral personality of the state. This is not so implausible after all, if one keeps in mind that states, unlike persons, lack the unity of consciousness and the rational will that constitute the identity of persons. If states are not simply voluntary associations, neither are they organic wholes with the unity and integrity that attaches to persons qua persons. It should come as no surprise that this lack of analogy leads to a lack of analogy on the matter of autonomy.

My account of state autonomy might provide some warrant for interference in another state's affairs when the state's institutions are unjust according to appropriate principles of justice and the interference would promote the development

---

[33] I say "appropriate principles of justice" to suggest that it is possible that different principles of justice may apply to different types of societies in view of variations, e.g., in levels of socioeconomic development.

of a just domestic constitution within the state. This position
may be like that taken by Kant and, to a lesser extent, by Mill.
In *Perpetual Peace*, Kant lists the nonintervention principle as
a "preliminary article" and gives arguments based on respect
for a state's internal decision-making process and considerations of international stability. But he states as a "definitive
[and presumably more basic] article" the principle that "the
civil constitution of every state shall be republican."[34] Several
commentators interpret him as holding that the nonintervention rule does not apply to forms of intervention that might
promote or defend the development or survival of republican
forms of government.[35] Similarly, Mill claims in "A Few
Words on Non-intervention" and in "Vindication of the
French Revolution of February, 1848" that intervention is
legitimate when it is for the benefit of "nations which are still
barbarous" or in support of a free people "struggling against
a foreign yoke."[36]

This position might seem so implausible as to cast doubt on
the account of autonomy of which it is a consequence. The
recent history of international relations appears to teach
nothing so eloquently as the folly of intervention in the cause
of justice.[37] I shall argue in the following section that there
are considerations that weigh against interference even with
governments that are unjust. For the present, however, one
should note that "the perils of reform intervention" need not
undermine the view of autonomy sketched above. It does not

[34] Immanuel Kant, *Perpetual Peace* [1795], pp. 96 and 99.

[35] See, for example, Karl Loewenstein, *Political Reconstruction*, pp. 18-20;
Carl J. Friedrich, *Inevitable Peace*, p. 178. As an exegetical matter, this interpretation seems to me tenuous, although perhaps the claim is philosophically correct nonetheless. One must understand Kant's views on political
change in light of his view of history, and from this perspective it seems more
likely that he would have thought republican government would emerge
through domestic conflict—"an independent state . . . struggling with its
internal ills" (*Perpetual Peace*, p. 96)—than through external intervention.
What is incontestable is that he nowhere makes any explicit claim regarding
the priority of republicanism over nonintervention.

[36] John Stuart Mill, "A Few Words on Non-intervention" [1859], pp. 167
and 176; "Vindication of the French Revolution of February, 1848" [1849],
pp. 382-83.

[37] As Ernest W. Lefever argues in "The Perils of Reform Intervention."

necessarily follow from the morally objectionable results of recent examples of interventionary diplomacy that all interference in unjust states is morally wrong. An alternative interpretation would be that interference has been guided by inappropriate principles, or that appropriate principles have been incorrectly applied, or both. It seems likely that the main objections to a general permission to intervene in the cause of justice are practical rather than theoretical in the sense that they hold such intervention, in practice, to be difficult to calculate and control. I explore these possibilities in the following section.

2. Nonintervention, Paternalism, and Neutrality

THERE are three main arguments for a general prohibition of intervention in international relations. The first, considered above, draws on the idea that states, like persons, have a right to be respected as autonomous sources of ends. However, as I have suggested, a state's claim to autonomy in this sense rests on the conformity of its institutions with appropriate principles of justice. If this were the only basis for the principle of nonintervention, its scope would be reduced considerably since it would only apply to just states. The argument from autonomy suggests that interference in an unjust state's affairs might be justified when it would promote the development of a just domestic constitution in the state.

Two further arguments for the nonintervention principle apply—though, as I shall claim, not always decisively—to circumstances in which neither personal liberties nor just institutions would be protected by observance of the nonintervention standard. These arguments carry further the analogy of nonintervention and respect for individual liberty. To the extent that these arguments are successful, the scope of the nonintervention rule is broader than that of the principle of state autonomy as reinterpreted above.

One of these is analogous to Mill's argument against paternalism in *On Liberty*. There Mill claims that government is not justified in interfering with a person's self-regarding behavior even when it appears that the person, if left alone, is likely to act in ways that would not be good for him. The reason is that the individual is in a better position than anyone else, and certainly than any government, to determine his own interests. Although he might be wrong in particular cases, the adverse consequences of a general permission to interfere on paternalistic grounds would far outweigh the potential benefits.[38] A similar argument has been made for the nonintervention principle by Benn and Peters and by Vincent. They have claimed that intervention in a state's internal affairs cannot be justified on paternalistic grounds because the intervening state is unlikely to be impartial and because, in any event, a state is more likely to know its own best interests than any other state.[39] Thus, "[t]he duty of non-interference rests on the assumption that the claims of a state's members will generally be better served if they are left to work out their own salvation."[40]

The crucial element here is that the assumption involved is empirical. Like the analogous claim in Mill's argument against paternalism, it is a contingent matter whether a state is in a better position than any other state to assess its members' interests and resolve their claims. Mill's claim against paternalism seems highly plausible once the exceptions he mentions (children, the "uncultivated") are taken into account. Indeed, it is plausible even in some of the exceptional cases. But it is less clear that the assumption about governments is empirically plausible, or rather, that it is plausible in enough cases to warrant a general prohibition of interference.[41] On

[38] John Stuart Mill, *On Liberty* [1859], ch. 4, p. 277.

[39] Benn and Peters, *Principles*, pp. 429-30; Vincent, *Nonintervention*, p. 345. The argument generalizes a claim made by Mill with regard to intervention in internal wars in "civilized" states. See "Non-intervention," pp. 173-74.

[40] Benn and Peters, *Principles*, p. 431.

[41] A similar reply might be made to Vincent's claim (*Nonintervention*, p. 330) that respect for sovereignty is required to protect the security of life, sanctity of contracts, and stability of property presumably provided to individuals by states. It is not at all obvious that states always or usually succeed in fulfilling these goals, much less that they do so fairly for all of their citizens. It is not

the other hand, experience would seem to support the assumption that governments are seldom impartial and hence would be unlikely to make correct judgments about the interests of people on whose behalf they claim to be intervening. But this leaves open the possibility that intervention could be justified when there are good reasons for thinking that a correct judgment has been reached.[42] Another possibility is that of intervention under the auspices of an international organization (like the U.N.), which might not (I do not say, *will* not) be subject to the partiality that characterizes the decisions of particular governments.[43] For these reasons, antipaternalist arguments are less decisive in the nonintervention case than in the analogous case of individual liberty.

A sophisticated variation of the antipaternalist argument is found in Mill's essay on nonintervention and has recently been elaborated by Walzer. Mill argues against intervention even in states that lack free institutions on the ground that peoples must achieve freedom for themselves; only thus can they develop "the virtues needful for maintaining freedom."[44] Invoking the analogy of states and persons, Walzer claims that "the members of a political community must seek their own freedom, just as the individual must cultivate his own virtue."[45] Intervention would only be justified to offset other external interference with the process of political development through which free institutions either are or are not successfully established.

This version of the antipaternalist argument brings in a theory of political development to explain why, as Benn and Peters put it, "the claims of a state's members will generally be better served if they are left to work out their own salvation." But it does not thereby defeat the objection noted above; the

even obvious that they should fulfill these goals, e.g., when their internal arrangements are in other respects unjust.

[42] As Manfred Halpern, for example, suggests in pointing out the importance of "knowledge" in making decisions about intervention. See *The Morality and Politics of Intervention*, pp. 14-20.

[43] See further, Falk, "On Legislative Intervention by the United Nations . . . ," *Legal Order in a Violent World*, pp. 349-52.

[44] Mill, "Non-intervention," p. 175.

[45] Walzer, *Just and Unjust Wars*, p. 87.

explanation still involves an empirical assumption that requires substantiation. Mill thought that substantiation might be drawn from the experience of European states, and, as I have noted, he exempts from the scope of his nonintervention principle "nations which are still barbarous." The limitations of his evidence and the exemption of many non-European states reduce considerably the plausibility of his claim as part of a general argument against intervention. Walzer does not offer any evidence to support his generalization and in fact falls back on a quite different argument from state autonomy.[46]

Even if its empirical assumptions could be substantiated, the Mill-Walzer view would fail to support a generalized prohibition of intervention for another reason. The view concentrates on the establishment of free institutions and holds that intervention to promote this end is likely to be either ineffectual or superfluous. It leaves open other paternalistic justifications for intervention, of which many can be imagined, ranging from satisfaction of a population's basic material needs to establishment of a government committed to supporting one or another type of economic system. Either of these reasons for intervention might be comprehended by principles of social justice appropriate to the state involved and so might be permitted by the conception of state autonomy that I have proposed. Of course, this objection might be met by reformulating the Mill-Walzer view in terms of social justice rather than political freedom; then the view would be that people must be left free to seek justice for themselves because just institutions are likely to endure only when they have been struggled for by those who will live under their sway. But this reformulation would require an even more demanding empirical theory of political development, and such a theory would probably be even more difficult to substantiate than the theory on which Mill and Walzer actually rely.

Finally, it should be noted that the view allows an exception in case the development of a state is already being interfered with. (This exception is the basis of Walzer's argument for the

[46] Ibid., pp. 87-88.

permissibility of counterintervention and of intervention in support of secessionist movements "once they have demonstrated their representative character.")[47] The argument for the exception depends upon a distinction between internal and external (or domestic and foreign) agents of political change; internal agents, as compatriots, are not to be interfered with, but external agents, as foreigners, may become subject to counterintervention since they are themselves interfering with a domestic process of change. However, this distinction loses its moral significance if my argument against the consensual basis of autonomy is accepted, for then there would be no difference in principle between coercion by internal agents and by external ones. This point aside, in a world characterized by high levels of political and economic interdependence, one wonders whether there can be any pure cases of domestic political change, untouched by significant external influences. The exceptions are likely to overwhelm any generalized prohibition of intervention based on the importance of allowing peoples to work out their own salvation. For these reasons, Mill's and Walzer's more sophisticated versions of the antipaternalist argument against intervention do not appear to lend much additional strength to it.

A third argument is suggested by Hall's proposal for a neutral nonintervention standard governing intervention in internal war.[48] The virtue of such a standard is that it is impartial between competing conceptions of the political good in internal wars. Following Hall's argument, we might say that the virtue of a generalized nonintervention principle is its impartiality between competing conceptions of the good in international relations. As Vincent puts it, in a legal context, "if the principle of nonintervention is taken as a part of law which is law, however weak, its impartiality between contending political doctrines might be said to recommend it as a legal norm."[49] The nonintervention standard is similar in this re-

[47] Ibid., p. 108; see also pp. 91-101.
[48] William E. Hall, *International Law* [1880], p. 347. For a more recent discussion, see Wolfgang Friedmann, "Intervention, Civil War and the Role of International Law," p. 158.
[49] Vincent, *Nonintervention*, p. 386; compare p. 344.

spect to "neutral" principles of constitutional interpretation, which can be endorsed in a wide variety of cases without regard for the outcome of any particular one.[50] It might be noted, to continue the analogy with individual liberty, that the equal-liberty principle has also been said to be neutral in the sense that it allows persons to pursue their own conceptions of the good without requiring them to subordinate their aims to considerations of social utility or of any particular social ideal.[51]

My interest is in whether this sort of impartiality recommends the nonintervention principle as a basic moral principle of international relations, independently of various other arguments that might be given for it. Is it really a neutral principle at all? The test of a principle's neutrality is whether reasonable persons would endorse it as the basis for resolving the relevant conflicts without regard for the outcomes that the principle would produce in any particular dispute. The legal principle that the accused is assumed innocent until proven guilty, for example, is neutral because it is reasonable to endorse it for all criminal cases, regardless of the consequences of observing it in any particular trial. Now it is not obvious that nonintervention is neutral in this way. If one seriously believed that God ordained a universal church to rule the world in His name, or that persons possess certain rights that no government may permissibly infringe, or that a universal conception of justice requires governments to conduct their internal affairs according to a specific set of rules, then one would not endorse nonintervention as the most basic principle of international relations. My point is not that these hypothetical beliefs embarrass the nonintervention principle, but rather that nonintervention is not, as Vincent puts it, an "amoral" principle.[52] It is rooted in a substantive

[margin handwritten note: Definition of: what is a neutral principle]

---

[50] The canonical formulation of this view of constitutional principles is Herbert Wechsler, "Toward Neutral Principles of Constitutional Law," pp. 1-35.

[51] This reasoning is the source of one of Rawls's arguments for his first principle of justice. See *A Theory of Justice*, pp. 205-11.

[52] Vincent, *Nonintervention*, p. 344. "Impartial" would have been a more appropriate term.

conception of how the world should be arranged of which a
necessary element is the belief that there is no "coherent and
pervasive morality which transcends international frontiers
and which might then inform and justify particular acts of intervention."[53] To one who holds a conflicting belief, the
nonintervention principle would not be a neutral principle at
all. Its apparent impartiality does not provide a reason for
endorsing it independently of whatever can be said for the
substantive conception on which it rests.[54]

An analogous objection is often advanced with regard to a
similar argument for equal liberty. It is claimed that the
equal-liberty principle would seem nonneutral to a person
whose most deeply held beliefs entailed that certain actions
protected by the liberty principle should not be permitted to
take place. The true believer, for example, would not accept
as neutral a principle protecting religious liberty.[55] However,
the objection to equal liberty as an impartial principle differs
from the analogous objection to nonintervention in the following way. Despite its nonneutrality from the point of view
of, for example, a true believer, the equal-liberty principle
might be defended by showing that it is required to protect
the pursuit of self-determined ends by autonomous agents,
which is itself a central feature of an ideal of social life that is
based on the criterion of respect for persons. This criterion,
we may suppose, has strong independent support. But such a
defense would be of little help in the analogous case of nonintervention. As we have already seen, arguments for nonintervention by analogy with respect for persons fall far short of
what would be required to support a general prohibition of
intervention, because there are many states in which it is simply false that the state's institutions conform to appropriate
principles of justice.

This discussion suggests that an exceptionless noninterven-

[53] Ibid., pp. 345-46.
[54] As I argue below, I believe that there are principles of international justice that require us to regard the nonintervention rule as nonneutral in the
sense given above.
[55] See Gerald Dworkin's criticism of Rawls's view in "Non-neutral Principles," pp. 501-6.

tion principle cannot be supported by arguments analogous to those usually given for the principle of equal liberty in domestic society, despite the striking, though superficial, similarity between the functions of these principles in their respective realms. The most that can be said is that considerations analogous to those that support the equal-liberty principle protect against intervention those states whose institutions conform to appropriate principles of justice and those whose institutions are more likely to become just in the absence of outside interference than with outside assistance.

There remains a potentially large class of states that are not directly protected against intervention by the view sketched above. These are states that are unjust according to the appropriate principles of justice and that are unlikely to become just if, in Benn and Peters's words, their members are "left to work out their own salvation." The view advanced above imposes limits on the range and types of intervention that can be considered permissible even in these cases. First, and most important, a certain type of justification must be available for intervention in the affairs of such a state. Specifically, the justification must appeal to the likelihood that intervention will (on balance) promote the development of conditions in which appropriate principles of justice can be satisfied. Second, there must be some assurance that the decision to intervene is taken with adequate information and safeguards against self-serving activities by the intervening party. This is especially important in view of the difficulties of formulating principles of justice appropriate to societies whose socioeconomic and cultural characteristics differ significantly from those of the societies to which western theories of justice are typically addressed. In contemporary international politics, adequate assurance may be available only when intervention has the approval of fairly constituted international bodies, although one ought not to assume that existing international organizations are so constituted. These limits to intervention are consequences of the view of nonintervention sketched above.

There are, of course, a variety of other considerations that place limits on the forms and purposes of permissible intervention just as they would on many other types of political action. Thus, depending upon one's view of the moral legitimacy of violence as an instrument of political change, some or all uses of military force for interventionary purposes would be ruled out. Also, even if some contemplated act of intervention were permissible under the nonintervention principle—perhaps, for example, the use of nonviolent techniques by a U.N. force against a racist regime—it might be that the costs of such an action, either to the intervenor or to the international community, would outweigh its probable benefits. Within the limits set by the nonintervention principle, there is likely to be considerable latitude for this type of balancing. Thus, even if intervention would be permissible according to autonomy criteria, it might be inappropriate for other reasons. My critique of the idea of state autonomy implies that there are circumstances in which intervention might be morally permissible, but it does not imply that such intervention is always morally required.

This discussion helps to explain the disagreement about definitions of intervention noted at the outset. The disagreement is the result of attempting to define intervention coextensively with the range of actions prohibited by the nonintervention principle. However, if my account of the moral basis of nonintervention is correct, this range varies according to the justice of the institutions of the state that is the target of external action. When the target state is just, or is likely to become just if left free from external interference, the prohibition of intervention is based on respect for the rights of persons to associate in the pursuit of common ends, or to live in just regimes (provided that they do not infringe on the rights of others to do the same). In this class of cases, the relevant sense of intervention is very broad. It extends to any activity that interferes with the legitimate exercise of these rights and is not limited, as is the narrow definition, to coercive interference by one government in the affairs of another with the intention of altering its constitutional structure. Thus, the nonintervention principle prohibits any use of power that interferes with the normal decision-making procedures of a state that is a member of this class. Presumably this includes subversion, payoffs to government officials, conditional bilateral aid, and similar techniques of influence.[56]

On the other hand, if the target state is neither just nor likely to become just if left to its own devices, the situation is more complicated. Interference would be permissible on three conditions. First, it must meet the standards noted above (i.e., promote justice and be carried out with adequate information and assurances against self-serving actions by the intervening agent). Second, it must not run afoul of other relevant moral restraints on political action. Third, it must not be too costly in terms of the other goals of international politics. Since these conditions might be met or not met in a great variety of ways, it does not seem possible simply to enumerate the kinds of actions forbidden by the nonintervention principle with respect to unjust states. The definitional issue will persist as long as it is maintained that whatever counts as intervention must be *impermissible* interference.

3. Self-determination

CONCEPTS of liberty are sometimes divided into "negative" and "positive" varieties. While the distinction is open to criticism, it suggests an analogous distinction with respect to the ideal of state autonomy. The negative aspect of state autonomy is expressed by the principle of nonintervention, which protects the right of a state already recognized as independent "to choose its political, economic, social and cultural systems, without interference in any form by another State."[57] The positive aspect of state autonomy is expressed by the principle of self-determination, which holds that colonies or

[56] The specific features of the appropriate definition may vary somewhat from case to case. There is a further discussion in Thomas and Thomas, *Non-Intervention*, pp. 68-69.

[57] General Assembly Resolution 2,131 (XX), 21 December 1965. United Nations General Assembly, *Official Records: Twentieth Session*, Supp. no. 14 (A/6,014) (New York, 1966), p. 12.

other entities under foreign control have a right to independent statehood.

The difference between these two aspects of state autonomy is that nonintervention imposes a negative requirement that other states not interfere, while self-determination imposes a positive requirement that other states (here, specifically, the colonial or dominant power) stop exercising control over entities claiming the right to be allowed independent statehood.[58] Nonintervention is a conservative principle in the sense that its observance tends to preserve the structure of the international order against all nonconsensual changes. Self-determination, however, requires that the structure of the international order be changed and might support intervention by third parties in a group's struggle for independence from foreign rule. While nonintervention takes the political order as it is, self-determination looks behind the political order to the order of social (cultural, ethnic, linguistic) groups and supports efforts to bring political boundaries into alignment with boundaries between groups. Thus, rather than reinforcing each other, the principles of self-determination and of nonintervention may conflict.

Self-determination is one of the most important and most obscure principles of contemporary international law and practice. The principle is important as the justification of the most far-reaching political realignments in recent international history, those associated with the collapse of imperialism and the post-World War II movement toward colonial independence. As a result, the principle has rapidly been accepted as a main principle of international law. The concept is twice mentioned in the United Nations Charter (articles 2[4] and 55) and is cited as authority for the General Assembly's call for "the granting of independence to colonial countries and peoples" in Resolution 1,514 (XX) of 14 December 1960.[59] In the last fifteen years, the General Assembly has

[58] This difference is sometimes put in terms of a distinction between "internal" and "external" self-determination, where internal self-determination refers to nonintervention. See Rupert Emerson, "Self-Determination," pp. 465-66.
[59] "All peoples have the right to self-determination; by virtue of that right

reaffirmed this call almost annually, each time citing the principle of self-determination as if it were a self-evident first principle.[60]

While self-determination derives its importance from its role in the justification of colonial independence, it derives its obscurity from attempts to use it to justify other international realignments. In the mid-nineteenth century, the principle was formulated (e.g., by Mazzini) to justify the unification of such fragmented nations as Italy and Germany. Early in the twentieth century, it was appealed to by Woodrow Wilson, among others, in negotiations over the post-World War I boundaries in Europe and the settlement of colonial claims.[61] Lenin relied on the principle to promote opposition to colonial regimes, and in his polemic with Bukharin, Luxemburg, and others to characterize nationalism as a revolutionary force in the age of imperialism.[62] More recently, the principle has been invoked in support of the struggles of oppressed racial majorities (in Rhodesia and South Africa) for self-rule. It has been appealed to in criticism of the effects on poor countries of private foreign investment and multinational corpo-

they freely determine their political status and freely pursue their economic, social and cultural development." United Nations General Assembly, *Official Records: Fifteenth Session*, Supp. no. 16 (A/4,684) (New York, 1961), p. 67.

[60] The most important recent statement of "the principle of equal rights and self-determination of peoples" is in the "Declaration . . . concerning Friendly Relations and Co-operation among States." Annex to Resolution 2,625(XXV), 24 October 1970. United Nations General Assembly, *Official Records: Twenty-fifth Session*, Supp. no. 28 (A/8,028) (New York, 1971), pp. 123-24. For more detailed discussions of the recent career of the principle in United Nations practice, see Rosalyn Higgins, *The Development of International Law through the Political Organs of the United Nations*, pp. 90-106; and Emerson, "Self-Determination," pp. 459-75. There is a skeptical view of the principle's status in international law in Leo Gross, "The Right of Self-Determination in International Law."

[61] See, for example, Alfred Cobban, *The Nation State and National Self-determination*, pp. 52-53. Unfortunately, Wilson never managed to formulate the principle very clearly or to explore the possible difficulties in its application.

[62] V. I. Lenin, "The Socialist Revolution and the Right of Nations to Self-Determination," pp. 153-54. See also Stephen F. Cohen, *Bukharin and the Bolshevik Revolution*, pp. 34-38.

rate activity. What may become another period of international realignment has been signaled by the demands of racial and cultural minorities within established states for recognition as independent peoples under this principle.

As the diversity of appeals to self-determination suggests, the principle can be interpreted in a variety of ways. Indeed, it has become so flexible a rhetorical device that some might think it to have lost its moral content. Although, as I shall argue, such a conclusion would be extreme, the principle as stated above is ambiguous in at least three important ways, all illustrated by the various appeals to it mentioned. First, it is not clear whether the "self" in "self-determination" refers to the government or to the population of a group. Does the principle simply require the creation of an independent government among a previously dependent group, or does it require, in addition, that the new government be "self-government," i.e., institutionally responsible to its people? A second ambiguity concerns the identities of groups eligible to claim a right of self-determination. Standard applications of the principle involve colonial populations with memberships that are, in some sense, already established; but why should the scope of the principle be so restricted? Finally, one might wonder what kind of "independence" would satisfy the principle. Is the severing of legal bonds sufficient, or does the principle also require dissolution of the economic and social relationships that may permit foreigners to continue to exert influence inside the colonized area even after formal independence has been achieved?

These are the philosophical perplexities that any account of the moral basis of self-determination should address. I shall attempt to do so by beginning with standard cases of colonial self-determination, and asking whether and to what extent the moral arguments in those cases shed light on the ambiguities distinguished above. My overall concern is to see how our common-sense understanding of self-determination is affected by my earlier criticisms of the idea of state autonomy.

Perhaps the most obvious justification of self-determination follows from the prima facie impermissibility of governing people without their consent.[63] Arguments of this variety hold that the state legitimately exercises coercive power over its members only if they have previously consented to their terms of association. Thus, colonial rule, which is seldom consensual, is illegitimate and must give way to a form of government to which the governed have agreed. On this view, self-determination is merely a special case of freedom of association; to deny a group this right is to infringe what is widely thought to be a fundamental personal liberty.

I have considered the inadequacies of freedom of association as the basis of governmental legitimacy in my discussion of nonintervention. I argued that there are few, if any, governments that can be described accurately as free associations in the sense of actually having been consented to by all of their citizens. Nevertheless, we are prepared to regard non-voluntary political institutions as legitimate provided they conform to appropriate principles of justice. These considerations undermine the argument for self-determination in the following way. If government in general need not be based on consent, then colonial rule cannot be opposed simply because it is not based on consent. The successor governments to colonial ones—that is, the indigenous governments that take over after colonies gain their independence—will be as arbitrary as the colonial governments themselves in the sense that neither can be justified by considerations of consent. Mill pictured self-determination as liberation from repressive foreign "yokes" imposed on people without their consent.[64] But if successor governments are similarly nonconsensual, one might wonder what makes a domestic yoke more acceptable than a foreign one.

A possible response would be that colonial independence is usually marked by plebiscites, free elections of government officials, and the like. One might say that such measures of consent provide a justification of claims for self-determina-

Colonial rule

---

[63] Mill justified his principle of national self-determination on similar grounds, among others: "[T]he question of government ought to be decided by the governed." *Considerations on Representative Government* [1861], ch. 16, p. 547. See also John Plamenatz, *On Alien Rule and Self-Government*, p. 1.

[64] Mill, "Non-intervention," p. 176.

tion in two ways. First, they express a desire for independence that deserves respect regardless of the justice of colonial arrangements. Persons have a right to withdraw from the political institutions of which they are members even when the institutions are perfectly just, provided, at least, that their particular outstanding obligations have been satisfied. Second, consent to new institutions expressed through these devices provides the institutions with some measure of legitimacy even if they do not conform to appropriate principles of justice. Unjust institutions may carry out policies that are actually favored by the vast bulk of a population, and it may well be the case that postcolonial governments, even when they are no more just than colonial ones, are preferable for this reason.

This response is unsatisfactory. First, its premise is problematic. While such measures of consent as plebiscites and free elections of government officials may be typical of the achievement of colonial independence, they are not present in all such cases. Consider, for example, cases in which it is institutionally impossible to conduct free and fair elections but claims of a right to self-determination are pressed by revolutionary leaders on behalf of the population of a colony. Even in the absence of a majority's expressed desire for independence, such claims sometimes seem to be justifiable. If this is correct, majority consent to colonial independence is not *necessary* to justify claims of a right to self-determination pressed on behalf of a colony's population. Furthermore, majority consent does not seem *sufficient* to justify such claims. As I pointed out above, the institutions through which consent is expressed are themselves in need of justification. Furthermore, in most cases of colonial self-determination, there will probably be minorities who do not give their consent to the new arrangements, either because they oppose independence altogether or because they favor a different postcolonial government than that supported by the majority. The independent government requires a justification against the competing preferences of such minorities, but such a justification cannot be provided in terms of consent. The independent government also requires a justification from the point of view of others who are nonvoluntarily subject to its control, like succeeding generations of citizens, children, the illiterate, and those who are simply too apolitical to care. In all of these cases, the majority's expressed desire for independence is not sufficient to justify its claim for self-determination. Something more needs to be said.

Although the argument from consent to self-determination is inadequate as given above, it suggests the direction in which to look for a more satisfactory account. As in the case of non-intervention, we might formulate the argument in terms of hypothetical consent. Then the argument for self-determination is that colonial rule violates principles of justice that would be agreed to by rational citizens of the colony as expressing the terms of their association, and independence is required to remedy the injustices of colonial rule. Perhaps one principle that would be chosen is a principle of representative self-government: legitimate governments must include mechanisms that make government officials electorally responsible to their citizens. If such a principle would be chosen, then colonial rule almost always would be illegitimate since, almost always, it violates the principle of representative self-government. Thus majority consent might be taken into account as part of a broader doctrine of political legitimacy. But the principle of representative self-government is probably not the only principle that would be agreed to—another would be some sort of principle of just distribution—and perhaps it would not be agreed to at all. It is at least conceivable that representative institutions would be limited in their scope because of the demands of rapid and equitable economic development or the constraints of low levels of education and primitive systems of mass communication.[65] In any event, this reformulation of the argument for self-determination as a remedy for injustice helps to explain the fact that self-determination has been appealed to by those suffering a wide variety of perceived injustices. The claim may

[65] I do not mean to take a position here on the choice of principles for groups characterized by low levels of development or of well-being. I claim only that it is not obvious that all legitimate governments must include representative institutions in the sense familiar to liberal theory.

be as firmly justified on grounds of exploitation and distributive inequity as it is, on the more conventional interpretation, on grounds of an absence of representative institutions.

The idea that self-determination is a means for promoting conformity with principles that would be agreed to in a hypothetical social contract is supported by an analysis of the moral considerations underlying the foremost arguments of the apologists for imperialism and their critics. It has often been claimed that subject peoples must be prepared for political independence before being granted it. Perhaps Mill's formulation of this claim is the most famous: "[N]ations which are still barbarous have not got beyond the period during which it is likely to be for their benefit that they should be conquered and held in subjection by foreigners. Independence and nationality, so essential to the due growth and development of a people further advanced in improvement, are generally impediments to theirs."[66] Mill's view is an example of the more general position that colonialism is justified by its beneficial effects on subject peoples. Thus, for example, Disraeli defended military coercion of subject peoples on the ground that only British rule could provide "order and justice" and that these were good things for any political community,[67] and Marx thought that imperialism would lay the groundwork for economic and social modernization.[68] These justifications of colonialism implicitly hold that its effects are in the interests of the subject groups.

Today, such justifications are widely rejected. While one reason is that the effects of imperialism are more clearly understood, it is more interesting for present purposes to see what moral considerations are involved in the rejection of

[66] Mill, "Non-intervention," p. 167. It is worth noting that the General Assembly's "Declaration on the Granting of Independence to Colonial Countries and Peoples" specifically rules out such a justification for the continuance of colonial control. Resolution 1,514 (XV), 14 December 1960. *Official Records: Fifteenth Session*, Supp. no. 16 (A/4,684) (New York, 1961), p. 67.

[67] Speech to the House of Lords, 8 April 1878, quoted in Richard Koebner and Helmut Dan Schmidt, *Imperialism: The Story and Significance of a Political Word, 1840-1960*, pp. 136-37.

[68] Karl Marx, "The Future Results of British Rule in India" [1853].

these justifications of colonialism. In this regard, the main problem has to do with identifying the interests of subject groups in the absence of a fair social-decision procedure that would make them manifest. When a group is unable to make important choices for itself (because it lacks appropriate institutions), and when others are in a position to choose for it, how should the choices be made?

This is a typical problem of paternalism.[69] Some principle is needed for identifying those benefits or burdens that can permissibly be imposed on persons who are unable to give their consent to the imposition. A rough approximation of such a principle is that only benefits the recipients are unable to provide for themselves, but that they would rationally choose to have provided, if they were in a position to choose, should fall into this class.[70] Thus, two questions are relevant to the evaluation of the view that colonialism is justified by its beneficial effects on subject peoples. First, are the benefits a subject group might derive from alien rule such that they would be rationally agreed to by members of the subject group if they were in a position to choose for themselves? Second, would they agree to alien rule as the best way to secure these benefits (that is, would the cost involved be acceptable to them)?

If the potential benefits of colonial rule are described in a suitably general way as provision of social infrastrcture, agricultural development, education and technology, and so on, it seems relatively uncontroversial that rational members of subject groups would choose them (although there might be disagreement about the *form* in which these benefits should be provided) because these benefits are necessary for the improvement of living standards and the development of a capacity to sustain these improvements for subsequent generations. Some degree of socioeconomic development might also be necessary, as Mill claims, as a precondition of effective self-government. Perhaps this would not have been so two or

[69] The connection of imperialism with paternalism is discussed clearly by J. A. Hobson in his seminal, and still valuable, book, *Imperialism: A Study* [1902], pp. 228-32.

[70] Here I follow Gerald Dworkin, "Paternalism," pp. 119-25.

three centuries ago, but it seems inescapable today.[71] Certainly the demands of colonized areas after the last world war, and of poor countries today, lend support to this supposition. It is the second question—whether the cost of securing these benefits through colonial rule is acceptable—that is the heart of the case against colonialism. The argument usually given is that the colonial policies of the European powers imposed large costs on subject peoples by creating a variety of new social problems, increased distributive inequalities, structural economic distortions, and unbalanced economic growth which may have led, in some cases, to absolute as well as relative deprivation in the lower classes.[72] Furthermore, it is widely questioned whether colonial rule was more than marginally effective in providing the immediate benefits that have been advanced as its justification. In any event, it is unlikely that colonial policies generally helped prepare subject peoples for self-government; the instability of postcolonial democracies and the frequency of resort to authoritarian rule suggest that the opposite is more nearly the case.[73]

These claims seem plausible, but it is not necessary to settle the complex empirical issues raised by them here. The important points are that any moral defense or criticism of colonialism along these lines presupposes a principle distinguishing justified from unjustified paternalism, and that a plausible formulation of such a principle draws the distinction with reference to what the persons affected would consent to, if they were in a position to give their consent. If principles of social justice can be viewed as outcomes of a hypothetical social contract, it might be said that the moral argument about the supposed benefits of colonialism is an argument about

[71] See J. Roland Pennock, "Political Development, Political Systems, and Political Goods," pp. 420-26.

[72] A useful discussion of this broad issue, which is sensitive to the need to take account of the multiple causes of backwardness in ex-colonial areas, is Michael Barratt Brown, *After Imperialism*, esp. pp. 158-86.

[73] The question of the causal relevance of colonial conditions to postcolonial authoritarianism in new states has evoked a large empirical literature. As one might expect, findings vary widely with particular historical conditions and assumptions about historical explanation. See, for example, Aristide R. Zolberg, "Military Intervention in the New States of Tropical Africa."

whether, and to what extent, it promotes or impedes the development of just institutions among subject groups. This lends support to the proposal that claims of a right of colonial self-determination should be understood as remedies for social injustice.

In view of my earlier remarks about the arbitrariness of nonconsensual governments, someone might object that colonial regimes and postcolonial (independent) governments could be similar in the sense that neither conforms to the principles of justice that would be chosen by rational members of the group. While colonial rule is usually illegitimate according to these principles, there is no assurance that successor governments will be any more legitimate according to the same principles. Indeed, the historical record provides cases (e.g., that of the South Moluccans in Indonesia) in which the departure of imperialist powers was vocally regretted by members of colonial populations because of the harm they expected to suffer in consequence. Do such possibilities undermine the case for colonial self-determination?

Perhaps it is obvious enough that such an objection is overstated, but it is interesting to see why. The first thing to note is that the objection draws into question the empirical generalization that the granting of independence from colonial rule usually diminishes social injustice, but it does not touch the philosophical claim that self-determination, when it has a justification, should be justified as a remedy for injustice. Beyond this, while it seems unlikely that the generalization is entirely false, it may not be entirely true, either. What is certain is that members of colonized groups have the right to just institutions; whether they have a right of self-determination depends on the extent to which the granting of independence would, in their particular circumstances, help to minimize injustice.[74] While this seems frequently to have been true, it can only be settled definitely (if it can be settled at all) with reference to particular cases.

[74] The phrase "help to minimize injustice" is used advisedly. It may be that some cases—perhaps including that of the South Moluccans—require a complicated balancing of injustices avoided by, and those created by, decolonization. Obviously, the best political strategy is one that seeks to minimize overall

A potentially more serious objection to my view of the moral basis of colonial self-determination emerges from the possible conflict of justice and consent. Imagine the following kind of case. Country A is an imperial country, and area B, a territorially distinct area with generally accepted boundaries, is A's colony. Since A is the most benevolent of all possible imperial countries, there is no reason to think that granting independence to B will decrease the amount of social injustice in B; indeed, the opposite seems more likely because of various political and economic complications inside B which we don't need to explain. Nonetheless, the residents of B, in a fair and free election, overwhelmingly indicate their preference for national independence. On my view of self-determination, A should resist, but, intuitively, this seems implausible. Do such possibilities damage the view?

This objection is weaker than it may seem. It simply does not apply to many real world cases, for one or more of the following reasons: the imperial country involved is not as benevolent as the example requires; or, notwithstanding the benevolence of the imperial country, the long-term interests of justice would best be served by allowing the colony to develop an indigenous governing capacity, despite some short-term costs; or, the majority in favor of independence is not really overwhelming, and important problems of minority rights would be created by yielding to demands for the rapid granting of independence. Any of these conditions would diminish the force of the objection, either because the policy favored by the population would actually accord with justice, or because the supposed consent of the population should carry less weight than we assume at first glance.

The only case in which my view would not suffice is the case in which an overwhelming majority of the colonial population expresses a desire for national independence, great injustices would not be done to dissenting minorities, and the other injustices consequent to independence are known to and would be suffered by the majority itself. If all of these conditions

---

injustice, but it would be silly not to recognize that the elimination of some injustices might give rise to others.

hold, then it is difficult to imagine any reason why the expressed wishes of the population should not take precedence
over considerations of social justice. This is a matter about
which intuitions differ, but the view that expressed consent
takes priority over considerations of institutional justice finds
some support in the common-sense idea that apparent
wrongs can be legitimized by the actual, informed consent of
those who suffer them.[75]

In summary, claims of a right of self-determination, when
pressed by or on behalf of residents of a colony, are properly
understood as assertions that the granting of independence
would help reduce social injustice in the colony. This view
avoids the arbitrariness of flat assertions of a fundamental,
absolute right of independence (it can always be asked, why is
there such a right?) and the possible parochialism of views
linking independence to conceptions of representative self-
government prevalent in economically developed, western
societies. However, the view has the important consequence
that the validity of any particular claim of a right of self-
determination can only be assessed with the aid of complex
empirical considerations together with a theory of social justice appropriate to the group involved. These areas of complexity may help explain why applications of the principle are
so congenitally controversial.

At the beginning of this section, I noted three ambiguities
that any satisfactory account of the moral basis of self-determination should illuminate. For the first of these—whether
self-determination requires self-government inside a former
colony as well as the granting of political independence—the
solution should now be evident. Self-determination is a means
to the end of social justice. Part of the injustice of colonial rule
might be that it involves a denial of a right to representative
institutions, but whether this is, in fact, the case depends on
the contents of the principles of social justice appropriate to
particular groups. I have taken no position on the contents of
these principles, except to suppose that their contents may
vary from group to group (perhaps for reasons of cultural

[75] For a further discussion, see Michael A. Slote, "Desert, Consent and Justice," esp. pp. 332-36 and 343-47.

value or material circumstance) and that, as a result, we should not simply assume that social justice always requires representative institutions in the sense familiar to liberal political theory. If this supposition is correct, then no definite solution can be given to the first ambiguity that will apply to all cases. A resolution of the ambiguity for any particular case requires an exploration of the substantive requirements of social justice in that case.

There are two other ambiguities—whether self-determination properly applies to groups other than colonial populations, and whether it requires revision of informal (particularly economic) lines of influence as well as severance of formal political bonds. Some light is shed on both problems by my view of the basis of self-determination, but since both problems are complex, I shall discuss them separately in the following sections.

4. Eligibility, Boundaries, and Nationality

IN CONSIDERING only colonial cases, I have taken as given the identities of the groups eligible to assert claims under the principle of self-determination. Following U.N. practice, I have assumed that this question is to be settled independently of the justification of the principle itself.[76] Now I would like to examine this assumption.

The assumption is problematic because it is not clear why the groups eligible to claim a right of self-determination should be limited to those, like colonial populations, that are already recognized as territorially distinct.[77] Any plausible view of the justification of such claims will have implications for the question of eligibility, and there is no obvious reason to suppose that the answers will coincide with the often arbi-

[76] Higgins, *Development of International Law*, pp. 104-5; Vernon Van Dyke, *Human Rights, the United States, and World Community*, pp. 88-89.

[77] For an argument to this effect, see Stanley French and Andres Gutman, "The Principle of National Self-Determination," p. 140.

trary boundaries actually drawn by imperial powers for their colonies. For example, if self-determination is thought to be based on freedom of association, it seems reasonable to argue that any group that can agree on a constitution could claim a right to political independence under the principle. Or, if self-determination rests on the rights of people who share a common cultural heritage to form their own state, then the principle seems to support separatist movements by cultural minorities. One class of instances of this type—perhaps the most important historically—is made up of those involving claims of "national" groups for independent statehood. Because such claims have seemed especially strong, the fact that state and colonial boundaries often fail to coincide with those of national groups constitutes a major challenge to the assumption that the only entities eligible to claim the right of self-determination are those whose identities are already widely accepted.

One commentator has summarized our problem as follows: "On the surface [self-determination] seemed reasonable: let the people decide. It was in fact ridiculous because the people cannot decide until somebody decides who are the people."[78] One advantage of the view that the right of self-determination is derived from freedom of association is that it supplies a straightforward solution to this problem: the people should decide who the people are.[79] This is made plausible by the analogy with voluntary associations whose memberships are determined simply by including only those willing to accept the terms of membership. For convenience, we can say that, on this view, the groups to which self-determination applies are self-defining.

This solution to the eligibility question is the most radical one available. As Rupert Emerson writes: "In its most extreme version the right of self-determination could mean the right of any group of disaffected people to break away at their

[78] W. Ivor Jennings, *The Approach to Self-Government*, p. 56.

[79] Compare Mill's remark that "[o]ne hardly knows what any division of the human race should be free to do if not to determine with which of the various collective bodies of human beings they choose to associate themselves." *Considerations on Representative Government*, ch. 16, p. 547.

pleasure from the state to which they presently belong and establish a new state closer to their hearts' desire."[80] Apparently Emerson means to discredit "the most extreme version" of self-determination simply by exhibiting the possible consequences of its application. He invokes the prospect of sweeping changes in the world's political geography and implies that such changes would be undesirable. Leaving aside the empirical question of whether these changes would actually materialize, it is not clear that they would be undesirable if they did. Even if it is granted that such changes would involve adjustment costs, surely the costs might be justified as the unavoidable result of the exercise of individual rights of freedom of association.

If there is a decisive objection to the idea that groups eligible for self-determination are self-defining, it must lie deeper than this. Perhaps, as French and Gutman suggest, the problem is that application of this idea "is likely to result in conflicting claims. . . . Obviously it is impossible for all populations to determine which other populations they will be associated with."[81] They give the example of French separatism in Canada: some Québécois want an independent state while other Canadians want them to continue as part of a larger federated state.

Does the French and Gutman view count as an objection at all? Suppose that A, B, C, and D are all members of a state. A and B want to secede and establish an independent state, but C and D want to continue the existing arrangements. C and D's desires to the contrary do not seem to diminish A and B's rights to withdraw. At least this seems clear in the general case. Specific features of the parties' mutual relations would have to be brought in to explain why A and B's right to withdraw should be restricted. The general argument would be that A and B have obligations to C and D, and allowing A and B to secede would put them in a position to avoid satisfying their outstanding obligations. Whether this argument seriously restricts A and B's right to secede depends on the char-

[80] Rupert Emerson, *From Empire to Nation*, pp. 298-99.
[81] French and Gutman, "The Principle of National Self-Determination," pp. 143-44.

acter of the obligations involved. First, if the obligations flow from voluntary undertakings, such as promises, and if the obligations require the performance of specific actions, then A and B could put an end to the validity of C and D's opposing claims by satisfying their obligations. Second, the obligations might flow from A and B's voluntary acceptance of advantages provided by common institutions, such as an education. To the extent that A and B voluntarily acquired advantages from institutions supported by contributions from C and D, it seems plausible that C and D could appropriately demand some sort of reciprocal contribution from A and B as a condition of allowing them to withdraw, but here there are difficult problems about the form and amount of reciprocation that C and D could legitimately expect. In any event, A and B's right to secede would not be extinguished by such obligations, although the cost to them of compliance might make withdrawal seem less desirable. Third, it might seem that A and B could acquire obligations to C and D entirely nonvoluntarily; it might be thought that participation in common institutions that cannot practically be avoided gives rise to obligations to remain within the institutions. But why should this be so? If we grant that compensation is due for advantages voluntarily acquired at the relative expense of others, it is difficult to see how any further argument could be made out for the third category of obligations.[82] Two conclusions follow from these reflections. First, the right of withdrawal can be limited on the ground that outstanding obligations have not been satisfied only if the obligations have been voluntarily acquired. Second, the satisfaction of these obligations, either by performance or by compensation, puts an end to the validity of the competing claims of other members and leaves the way clear for withdrawal by the secessionist group. In general, if such obligations do not exist or have been satisfied, a self-defined group's right of self-determination is not undermined by the objection that others with whom they previously have been associated prefer to maintain the existing arrangements.

[82] For a brief, further discussion, see Thomas M. Scanlon, "Liberty, Contract and Contribution," p. 55.

As I noted above, the idea that groups eligible for self-determination are self-defining is made plausible by the analogy with voluntary associations and by the underlying thought that the right of self-determination is a special case of the right of freedom of association. The objections considered so far do not question these presuppositions, and that is why the objections seem unconvincing. Once we notice the crucial difference between voluntary associations and groups claiming a right of self-determination, however, it becomes clear why the self-definition solution to the eligibility problem is insufficient. The crucial difference, of course, is that voluntary associations are not *territorial* groups: they do not normally have to live together on a separate territory or to deprive others of the territory they inhabited previously. While the creation of a voluntary association involves a partitioning of some population, it does not involve a partitioning of territory.

Typical cases of self-determination, on the other hand, have an essential territorial component. A group's claim to be recognized as an independent political entity is accompanied by a claim that boundaries be redrawn to afford a separate territory to the independent group. The evaluation of such a claim raises questions that do not arise in cases of voluntary association and hence are invisible when self-determination is understood on that model. One of these questions concerns property rights. A group's successful exercise of self-determination results in a political realignment, which effectively redistributes access to natural resources and accumulated wealth. In some cases (probably most colonial cases, for example) this redistribution may have a moral warrant, but this is unlikely always to be true. Indeed, it seems impossible to say a priori whether the redistribution of access to wealth that results from the partitioning of a previously unified territorial unit will or will not be equitable to all concerned. Another question involves the personal and political rights of minorities within the territory claimed by or for the self-determining group. A minority in any given area may oppose the provisions for self-government, or, for that matter, may deny that any form of political independence would be desirable. Even when there is no expression of such minority views, it may be foreseeable that creation of an independent state on the territory will result in persecution or repression of, e.g., ethnic or racial subgroups. Such problems of minority rights do not arise on the voluntary-association model because voluntary associations include only those who actually consent to terms of membership. But those who find themselves in an area claimed for a self-determining group are more appropriately regarded as involuntary victims of circumstances for which they are not responsible; in most cases, they did not choose their geographical location, nor could they relocate without unreasonable cost.

In view of these considerations, self-definition must be rejected as a general solution to the eligibility question. There may be special cases in which it happens that a group's assertion of a right of self-determination is not embarrassed by problems of distributive justice or minority rights, but there is no reason to assume in advance that this will always be true. Whenever such problems arise and cannot be avoided, for example, by redrawing boundaries or resettling minorities, some further considerations must be advanced to settle the question of eligibility.

I observed earlier that few historical cases of self-determination resemble the free-association model. More often than not, rights of self-determination have been claimed on behalf of groups that have had no real opportunity to define themselves. In those cases, the identities of the groups have been held to consist in common and distinctive characteristics such as race, tribe, religion, or culture. Thus, it might be suggested that the groups eligible for self-determination are those united by some important common characteristic that distinguishes them from the larger population of which they are a part.[83] (I say "important" because, obviously, not *all* common and distinctive characteristics are relevant bases of claims of a right of self-determination. It is another matter to say what kinds of characteristics should count as important, and why. I consider this question below.)

[83] Van Dyke, *Human Rights*, pp. 85, 89-90; Emerson, "Self-Determination," pp. 464-65.

The common-characteristics approach to the eligibility problem may fit better with the history of self-determination, but it does not avoid the problems associated with territoriality. A priori, there is no reason to think that the distribution of racial, cultural, and other such groups over the earth's surface corresponds to the distribution of wealth in such a way that, even if it were possible for political boundaries to mirror group boundaries, the resulting distribution of access to wealth would be equitable to all. Further, it is not obvious that such a political realignment would preclude problems of minority rights: the fact that people have in common some important characteristic does not imply anything about their political preferences, nor does it imply that other causes of repression or persecution (e.g., distinctions based on *other*, perhaps cross-cutting, "important characteristics") are absent. For these reasons, the presence of common and distinctive characteristics does not seem to be sufficient to identify groups eligible for self-determination. In this respect, the common-characteristics approach is as inadequate as that based on self-definition. In another respect, the common-characteristics approach is even more inadequate. As suggested above, affirmative acts of self-definition, although historically rare, at least establish that those who identify themselves as members of a self-determining group actually do prefer a change in the political status quo. If it were possible to settle the problems associated with territoriality through political means, the expressed preferences of members of a separatist group might justify their claims to a right of self-determination. However, if the membership of the group is identified otherwise (e.g., by the presence of common and distinctive characteristics), even this presumption disappears, because it is not clear why *any* moral importance should attach to common characteristics. Even if problems of territoriality could be settled, why should cultural, racial, tribal, or religious groups be eligible for self-determination?

Our previous discussion of the justification of self-determination provides some help here. Since the exercise of self-determination by a group characteristically involves a change in the distribution of personal, political, and property rights, it requires a justification against the general presumption that existing arrangements should not be interfered with without good reasons. Such a justification might be provided by evidence that an overwhelming majority of those living in a common area have agreed to withdraw from the established government and create a new state on the territory they inhabit, provided that their voluntarily incurred outstanding obligations to others have somehow been satisfied, that personal rights would not be threatened, and that distributive injustice would not result. However, as I have observed, such cases are unlikely to arise. In more likely cases, a group's claim of self-determination must be justified by showing that its recognition is necessary to create or restore conditions consistent with appropriate principles of justice. Colonial cases arise as standard applications of self-determination because they typically involve great injustices, which cannot be rectified by any measures short of independent statehood. However, there is no reason to think that this condition applies *only* to colonial cases. It might be extended to other groups when it can be shown that independent statehood is a necessary political means for the satisfaction of appropriate principles of justice.

This perspective on the question of identifying units eligible to claim a right of self-determination illuminates an important and longstanding problem regarding the relationship of nationality to state boundaries. Theorists have disagreed over whether the principle of self-determination should apply to groups united by a common nationality.[84] The "nationalists" have argued for a rearrangement of state boundaries according to nationality, while the "multinationalists" have held that it is better to form states containing citizens of diverse nationalities.

J. S. Mill, an early proponent of the nationalist view, wrote: "Where the sentiment of nationality exists in any force, there is a *prima facie* case for uniting all the members of the nationality under the same government, and a government to

[84] For the purposes of the present discussion I assume that nationality can be given a reasonably coherent definition, although I shall question this assumption below.

themselves apart."[85] Mill made two arguments for this claim.
First, national unity under an independent government is
good in itself as a manifestation of freedom of association;
second, it is a necessary condition of fair representative institutions. The first of these is simply an application of the
general view that entities eligible to claim the right of self-
determination are self-defining. As given, Mill's argument for
the application of this principle to national groups is incomplete; the premise that national groups would, in fact, choose
to form their own independent government is suppressed.
But I have argued that this general view is insufficient in the
stronger sense that it does not provide enough criteria for distinguishing eligible from ineligible entities. It needs to be
shown that independent statehood is required to secure conditions supportive of institutions that satisfy appropriate
principles of justice. Mill's second argument constitutes such a
claim for the class of groups for which appropriate principles
prescribe fair representative institutions. (The argument
might be generalized by substituting considerations regarding social justice for those regarding fair representative institutions, but I shall not do so explicitly in this discussion.)

Mill's second argument is that "free institutions are next to
impossible in a country made up of different nationalities."[86]
The argument rests on three empirical claims. First, "a people
without fellow-feeling" cannot support "the united public
opinion, necessary to the working of representative government." Second, "the grand and only effectual security in the
last resort against the despotism of the government is in that
case wanting: the sympathy of the army and the people." Finally, diversity of nationality provides a natural division
which a government bent on establishing authoritarian rule
can exploit to maintain itself in power.[87] These claims have
formed the basis of the subsequent debate between those
favoring nationalist and those favoring multinationalist definitions of the state. Lord Acton, the first to criticize Mill's
empirical assumptions, argued that diversity of nationality
within a state "is a firm barrier against the intrusion of the

[85] Mill, *Considerations on Representative Government*, ch. 16, p. 547.
[86] Ibid.   [87] Ibid., pp. 547-48.

government beyond the political sphere," and that it encour-
ages the progress of civilization.[88] Ernest Barker later claimed
that Acton's view was contradicted by the facts and upheld
Mill's claim that multinationalism undermines democracy.[89]
More recently, Alfred Cobban has disputed the Mill-Barker
view on the basis of evidence drawn largely from twentieth-
century Europe, claiming that "the idea of the nation-state as
the sole basis of political organization must be abandoned."[90]

For our purposes, the issue raised by this debate is whether
diversity of nationality threatens the possibility of maintaining representative institutions sufficiently to warrant extending the principle of self-determination to national groups regardless of whether they occupy well-defined areas subject to
colonial rule. This question might be understood as straight-
forwardly empirical, as it has been by one recent researcher,
Walker Connor, whose comparative study of nationalism in
Europe, Africa, and South Asia confirmed "a broad-scale
trend toward political consciousness along lines of nationality" and suggested that "postwar developments indicate a link
between multinationalism and pressure for undemocratic
states."[91]

The problem here is to understand the meaning of the
family of terms including "nation," "nationality," "national
loyalty," and "nationalism." One might hesitate to accept the
normative implications of Connor's results without a clearer
account of these matters, since it is widely acknowledged that
some features associated with nationality are far more subject
to modification by political institutions than others. Analogously, some features that give rise to nationalism are less
deeply embedded in forms of social life than others.[92] Con-

[88] John E.E.D. Acton (Lord Acton), "Nationality" [1862], p. 290.

[89] Ernest Barker, *National Character and the Factors in its Formation*, pp. 16-17, 128-29.

[90] Cobban, *The Nation State and National Self-determination*, p. 130.

[91] Walker Connor, "Self-Determination: The New Phase," pp. 44, 50.

[92] See Acton, "Nationality," pp. 292-93; Barker, *National Character*, pp. 7-8; Karl W. Deutsch, *Nationalism and Social Communication*, esp. ch. 8. For a social-psychological view, see Herbert C. Kelman, "Patterns of Political In-volvement in the National System: A Social-Psychological Analysis of Political Legitimacy."

nor seems to understand nationality in terms of perceived membership in national groups. However, if perceptions of membership in national groups are largely the results of living under a common set of political institutions, then claims of self-determination would be considerably weakened, since it could be argued that groups claiming this right have not lived under existing institutions long enough for the requisite feelings of loyalty to develop, or, alternatively, that existing institutions should be modified to encourage more rapid assimilation of those who now perceive themselves as outsiders. Further empirical research is needed to see if it is possible to describe general conditions under which assimilation of this sort is unlikely.[93] These conditions, if they can be formulated, would identify those kinds of cases in which claims of self-determination could be justified.[94] In these cases, claims of self-determination would express grievances against injustices flowing from deep and relatively fixed features of the social and political life of a group. In view of the relative immutability of these divisive factors, self-determination could be justified as the only way for the oppressed group to secure conditions supportive of just institutions. (Of course, the *form* of self-determination—that is, the political and economic arrangements for independence—would also have to be consistent with appropriate principles of justice. See the following section.) While this solution to the eligibility problem has the disadvantage of relying heavily on empirical information that may be difficult to obtain, there seems to be no other way to define the range of permissible applications of the principle.

[93] Connor himself has suggested that "ethnic diversity" is one such condition, which leads to increasing rather than decreasing ethnic separatist demands as the level of economic development rises. However, since this is only sometimes true, it is clear that ethnic diversity does not always require separate statehood. Connor does not supply any way of identifying the circumstances under which the latter is more likely to be the case. Walker Connor, "Nation-Building or Nation-Destroying?"

[94] A preliminary formulation of such a condition holds that loyalties to existing political structures are unlikely to develop when the structures include groups differentiated by socioeconomic class accompanied by "cultural differences which cannot easily be blurred" like race, language, or religion. See Ernest Gellner, "Scale and Nation," p. 12.

5. Economic Dependence

ASSUMING that a group is eligible to claim a right of self-determination, is the right adequately satisfied by the granting of political independence if informal channels of foreign influence persist? More generally, can the exercise by foreigners of substantial political and economic influence over the internal affairs of an independent state properly be criticized as infringements of the state's right of self-determination?

This question has been raised by recent criticisms of the effects of foreign investment and multinational corporate activity on political and economic conditions in poor (and largely ex-colonial) countries. It has been argued widely that these forms of transnational economic relations interfere with "the ability of a nation-state as a collectivity to make decisions which shape its political and economic future."[95] States that are not autonomous in this respect are termed "dependent": such a state "is one which does not have control over the major decisions affecting its economy."[96]

"Economic dependence" can best be understood by comparing it with the political imperialism associated with the colonial period, of which economic dependence is alleged to be a lineal descendant. Imperialism, in its classical or nineteenth-century sense, refers to the systematic pursuit by a government of policies that meet two conditions: first, the policies involve the extension of political control to another country or territorially distinct group of people; second, this control is nonvoluntary from the point of view of the satellite country or group.[97] Dependence (or "economic imperialism") differs insofar as the control exercised over a satellite country

[95] Evans, "National Autonomy and Economic Development," p. 326. For a similar argument, see Osvaldo Sunkel, "Big Business and 'Dependencia,'" pp. 525-27.
[96] Barbara Stallings, *Economic Dependency in Africa and Latin America*, p. 6.
[97] For a slightly different analysis, see Sidney Morgenbesser, "Imperialism: Some Preliminary Distinctions," pp. 11-12.

or group utilizes economic rather than political means, and the agent exercising control is a foreign corporation or class rather than a government. Lenin notes the relationship in his tract on imperialism: "[I]t must be observed that finance capital and its foreign policy . . . give rise to a number of *transitional* forms of state dependence. Not only . . . the two main groups of countries, those owning colonies, and the colonies themselves, but also the diverse forms of dependent countries which, politically, are formally independent, but in fact, are enmeshed in the net of financial and diplomatic dependence, are typical of this epoch."[98] Similar views are held by many more recent writers, although there is controversy about the mechanism of economic imperialism—that is, about the nature of the phenomenon that now substitutes for political control. Theotonio Dos Santos, for example, urges that the colonial relationship is only one form of dependence brought about by the search by capitalist elites from rich countries for new markets for goods and capital; other forms combine political independence with indirect political and economic manipulation by the monopolies that control prices and supplies of manufactured goods and influence the distribution of aid and investment capital by foreign governments and international agencies.[99] Similarly, Paul Baran, identifying imperialism with its economic causes, finds that "contemporary imperialism" expresses itself in "comprador" (or subservient) governments in satellite states, which enforce policies favorable to metropolitan sources of investment and aid, making possible "the continued exploitation of underdeveloped countries."[100] In discussing the same theme, Suzanne Bodenheimer concludes that "the infrastructure of dependency [i.e., subservient governments and supporting social

[98] V. I. Lenin, *Imperialism, the Highest Stage of Capitalism*, p. 263 (emphasis in original). See also Karl Marx, *A Contribution to the Critique of Political Economy* [1859], pp. 202-3; and Hobson, *Imperialism*, pp. 5, 64-70, and 75-79.

[99] Theotonio Dos Santos, "The Structure of Dependence," pp. 231-32.

[100] Paul A. Baran, *The Political Economy of Growth*, pp. 196 and 205ff. The idea of a "comprador" elite derives from Mao Tse-tung, "The Chinese Revolution and the Chinese Communist Party," pp. 88-89.

structures] may be seen as the functional equivalent of a formal colonial apparatus."[101] Although there is disagreement about more precise definitions of dependence, it may be useful to note that a satellite country's economic dependence is often measured by the extent to which sources of imported capital, personnel, and technologies, and markets for major exports, are concentrated in a few metropolitan countries.[102]

Most contemporary theorists of dependence argue that the economic dependence of satellite on metropolitan countries retards economic growth, creates outward-looking elites who must service foreign interests to maintain their positions, and results in skewed patterns of growth and distribution within satellite economies and societies.[103] Some carry the argument a step further by claiming that the system of foreign aid, trade, and investment is not only relatively but absolutely harmful to satellite countries.[104] The results of economic dependence, furthermore, are held to be similar to the economic results of political imperialism during the colonial period, even though economic dependence does not necessarily involve direct intervention by a metropolitan government in the official political life of a satellite group. In both cases, undesirable economic and social conditions are imposed on satellite groups without their consent.

Many of these claims are the subjects of considerable empirical dispute.[105] However, it is neither possible nor necessary to resolve these issues here. The question I wish to raise

[101] Suzanne Bodenheimer, "Dependency and Imperialism: The Roots of Latin American Underdevelopment," p. 339.

[102] See, for example, Stallings, *Economic Dependency*, p. 7.

[103] The most influential, and the clearest, formulation of these hypotheses is by André Gunder Frank, "The Development of Underdevelopment," pp. 9-14.

[104] André Gunder Frank, "Capitalist Development of Underdevelopment in Chile," p. 3.

[105] See, for example, Robert R. Kaufman, Daniel S. Geller, and Harry I. Chernotsky, "A Preliminary Test of the Theory of Dependency," which argues that available measures of dependence do not consistently predict adverse effects on economic development. For the opposite view, see Christopher Chase-Dunn, "The Effects of International Economic Dependence on Development and Inequality: A Cross-national Study."

is, supposing for the sake of discussion that the claims noted above are largely correct, does the principle of self-determination support moral criticisms of economic dependence? I shall argue that it is especially unfortunate that criticisms of dependence have been framed in terms of deprivations of national autonomy. Such criticisms are inadequate, for reasons canvassed earlier, and more appropriate criticisms, based on substantive principles of justice, are more far-reaching.

As I remarked above, both political imperialism and economic dependence involve the imposition of political and economic institutions and practices on people without their consent. The moral objection to such policies is that they infringe the right of self-determination. However, as I have argued, it is not obvious what such a right requires, who is eligible to claim it, or why we should object to offenses against it. The clearest cases are those in which the satellite group is organized as a state with a fair social-decision procedure. When a foreign agent imposes political or economic conditions on such a group without its consent, the foreign agent violates the political rights of the members of the satellite group. But it seems unlikely that very many real world situations resemble this clear case. The more likely case is that in which the satellite group, if it has a developed state apparatus at all, lacks fair participatory institutions. From the point of view of persons nonvoluntarily subject to a regime, and unable effectively to express or withhold their consent to it, it appears to make little moral difference whether the regime is imposed by other members of their own community or by foreign agents. In either case the exercise of coercive power requires a justification. It is necessary to judge regimes of either kind by more substantive criteria than the simple criterion of political autonomy. As I have suggested previously, these criteria are supplied by the principles of justice appropriate to the society involved.

This reasoning has special importance in application to the circumstances of dependence. If the main moral objection to dependence is thought to rest on infringements of a state's right to self-determination, and thus of its political autonomy, it would be natural to conclude that the moral defects could be remedied by the development of an indigenous state apparatus capable of reclaiming political and economic control from foreign agents like multinational corporations and foreign investors. This, at least, seems to be the presumption of some recent discussions of dependence.[106] However, if my claim is correct that the ideal of state autonomy provides insufficient moral grounds for criticizing economic dependence, then it is a mistake to think that its moral flaws can be eliminated simply by returning political and economic control to indigenous agents. The objectionable features of dependence—like excessive exercises of state coercive power or large internal distributive inequalities—might be reproduced by an apparently autonomous state. What is required is an account of the more substantive criteria by which nonvoluntary regimes should be evaluated. Of course, it might be argued on empirical grounds that political autonomy is a necessary condition of a regime's satisfying those substantive criteria by which nonvoluntary political and economic arrangements gain their moral legitimacy. But, if I am right, political autonomy is not a sufficient condition of a regime's legitimacy; it remains to ask whether autonomous regimes satisfy appropriate principles of justice.

These remarks show that the third ambiguity of self-determination—whether it requires the severing of informal channels of influence as well as the granting of formal independence—also has no clear solution. Like the other ambiguities considered, this one arises because the principle of self-determination should be understood as a means to the end of social justice, and the argument for its application to particular cases is contingent on the truth of empirical hypotheses linking application of the principle to the promotion of justice or the prevention of injustice. Where it is true that the international economic relations characteristic of dependence contribute to the maintenance of domestic injustice in dependent countries, or where they impede efforts to promote the growth of just institutions, there is clearly room

[106] See, for example, Sunkel, "Big Business and 'Dependencia,' " p. 531; Theodore H. Moran, *The Multinational Corporation and the Politics of Dependence*, pp. 258-60; and Alfred Stepan, *The State and Society*, esp. ch. 7.

for moral criticism. But it is misleading to formulate such criticisms in terms of offenses against the principle of self-determination or denials of a right to national autonomy.

6. State Autonomy
and Domestic Social Justice

I HAVE argued that the principle of state autonomy—the central element of the morality of states—lacks a coherent moral foundation. There are no compelling reasons of principle for abstaining from judgments regarding the justice of the domestic political and economic institutions of other states.

This criticism of the received view has its most important application to the nonintervention principle. I have claimed that this principle does not apply equally to all states. Indeed, the same moral concerns that support the nonintervention principle in some circumstances might justify intervention in others. The relevant differences between the two sets of circumstances have to do with the justice of the domestic institutions of the potential target of intervention. Unjust institutions do not enjoy the same prima facie protection against external interference as do just institutions, and in fact, other things equal, interference with unjust institutions might be justified when it has a high probability of promoting domestic social justice. The nonintervention principle cannot be interpreted properly without considering the justice of the institutions of the states involved in particular instances of (potential) intervention.

Other concepts related to the ideal of state autonomy—self-determination and economic dependence—also require reference to principles of justice appropriate to the societies involved in order to be understood and interpreted properly. The strongest moral argument for self-determination is that political independence is necessary for the elimination of social injustice and for the development of just institutions; the strongest moral argument against economic dependence is that the associated forms of international economic relations produce or support unjust domestic institutions.

These points illustrate my more general claims about the autonomy of states. The idea that states should be respected as autonomous sources of ends, and hence should not be interfered with, arises as an analogue of the idea that individual persons should be respected as autonomous beings. But the analogy is faulty. The analogue of individual autonomy, at the level of states, is conformity of their basic institutions with appropriate principles of justice.

If these conclusions are correct, then there is one point at which the theoretical division between international relations and domestic society breaks down. On the view I have proposed, the principle of state autonomy—a principle of international political theory—cannot be interpreted correctly without bringing in considerations of social justice usually thought to belong to the political theory of the state.

It follows that a complete normative theory of international relations would require an account of domestic social justice, but I cannot provide such an account in this book. The most obvious reason is that the subject of social justice raises complex and persistent philosophical problems, which deserve far more extensive exploration than space and time allow.[107]

An additional complication involves the controversial nature of the supposition that principles of social justice appropriate to many existing societies may diverge in important ways from the principles usually thought appropriate to developed, western, industrial societies. This is denied by those who assume that the less-developed countries should conform to the conception of justice that applies to developed ones.[108] The supposition is apparently endorsed by those who argue that the requirements of economic development justify some relaxation of the standards that constrain the structure

---

[107] There is, of course, a vast recent literature on the subject. An especially helpful introductory discussion, which is sensitive to the different possible conceptions of justice, is David Miller, *Social Justice*, ch. 1.

[108] See, for example, Daniel P. Moynihan, "The United States in Opposition," esp. pp. 42-44.

and operation of institutions in developed countries.[109] Clearly, a great deal depends on which philosophical path is followed, including the interpretation of the international doctrine of human rights and the evolution of normative standards to justify and structure the empirical study of economic and political development.[110]

While the complexity and controversial nature of these matters provide two reasons for avoiding them here, a third is that detailed attention to the subject of domestic social justice would deflect us from other pressing international issues. It may be true, as representatives of developing countries have argued, that the rapid development of their societies requires a new international economic order as well as changes in social and political institutions internal to their own societies. Analogously, the development of just domestic institutions in many societies may depend on the elimination of international distributive injustice. Since this issue is less familiar to us than problems of domestic social justice—partly because it is ignored by the morality of states—I turn to it in the following part.

[109] Such views are maintained in Rawls, *A Theory of Justice*, pp. 302 and 542.

[110] On human rights, see my "Human Rights and Social Justice." On the relationship of normative theory and the study of political development, see Pennock, "Political Development, Political Systems, and Political Goods," pp. 420-26.

PART THREE

International Distributive Justice

Current events have brought into sharp focus the realiza-
tion that . . . there is a close inter-relationship between the
prosperity of the developed countries and the growth and
development of the developing countries. . . . Interna-
tional cooperation for development is the shared goal and
common duty of all countries.[1]

[1] "Declaration on the Establishment of a New International Eco-
nomic Order," Resolution 3,201 (S-VI), 1 May 1974. United Nations
General Assembly, *Official Records: Sixth Special Session*, Supp. no. 1
(A/9,559) (New York, 1974), p. 3.

I T IS no part of the morality of states that residents of relatively affluent societies have obligations founded on justice to promote economic development elsewhere. Indeed, the tradition of international political theory is virtually silent on the matter of international distributive justice. The most that might be said, consistently with the morality of states, is that the citizens of relatively affluent societies have obligations based on the duty of mutual aid to help those who, without help, would surely perish. The obligation to contribute to the welfare of persons elsewhere, on such a view, is an obligation *charity?* of charity.

or obligation

Obligations of justice might be thought to be more demanding than this, to require greater sacrifices on the part of the relatively well-off, and perhaps sacrifices of a different kind as well. Obligations of justice, unlike those of mutual aid, might also require efforts at large-scale institutional reform. The rhetoric of the General Assembly's "Declaration on the Establishment of a New International Economic Order" suggests that it is this sort of obligation that requires wealthy countries to increase substantially their contributions to less-developed countries, and radically to restructure the world economic system. Do such obligations exist?

This question does not pose special theoretical problems for the utilitarian, for whom the distinction between obligations of humanitarian aid and obligations of social justice is a second-order distinction. Since utility-maximizing calculations need not respect national boundaries, there is a method of decision available when different kinds of obligations conflict. Contractarian political theories, on the other hand, might be expected to encounter problems when they are applied to questions of global distributive justice. Contractarian principles usually rest on the relations in which people stand in a national community united by common acceptance of a conception of justice. It is not obvious that contractarian principles with such a justification support any redistributive obligations between persons situated in different national societies.

[margin handwritten note: Countries have an Obligation to aid each other]

Nevertheless, I shall argue that a strong case can be made on contractarian grounds that persons of diverse citizenship have distributive obligations to one another analogous to those of citizens of the same state. International distributive obligations are founded on justice and not merely on mutual aid. As a critique and reinterpretation of Rawls's theory of justice,[2] the argument explores in more detail the observation (offered in part one) that international relations is coming more and more to resemble domestic society in several respects relevant to the justification of principles of (domestic) social justice. The intuitive idea is that it is wrong to limit the application of contractarian principles of social justice to the nation-state; instead, these principles ought to apply globally.[3] The argument raises interesting problems for Rawls's theory, and, more important, it illuminates several central features of the question of global distributive justice. In view of increasingly visible global distributive inequalities, famine, and environmental deterioration, it can hardly be denied that this question poses one of the main political challenges of the foreseeable future.

My discussion has six parts. I begin by reviewing Rawls's brief remarks on international justice and show that these make sense only on the empirical assumption that nation-states are self-sufficient. Even if this assumption is correct, I then claim, Rawls's discussion of international justice is incomplete in important respects, for it neglects certain problems about natural resources. In section 3, I go on to question the empirical foundation of the self-sufficiency assumption and sketch the consequences for Rawlsian ideal theory of abandoning the assumption. Some objections to a global distributive principle are considered in sections 4 and 5. In con-

[2] John Rawls, *A Theory of Justice*.
[3] Such criticisms have been suggested by several writers. For example, Brian Barry, *The Liberal Theory of Justice*, pp. 128-33; Peter Danielson, "Theories, Intuitions and the Problem of World-Wide Distributive Justice"; Thomas M. Scanlon, "Rawls' Theory of Justice," pp. 1,066-67. For a discussion, see Robert Amdur, "Rawls' Theory of Justice: Domestic and International Perspectives."

clusion, I explore the relation of an ideal theory of international distributive justice to the nonideal world.

It should be emphasized that the main argument given here is hypothetical. I make no claim to provide independent support for a Rawlsian view of distributive justice; I only mean to explore the relevance of Rawls's view for international relations, and, *inter alia*, to point out some features of this view that require further development in the face of certain facts about the world. If one is inclined to reject Rawls's theory in the domestic case, then the case for a theory of global justice like the one suggested below is correspondingly weakened. My claim is that, if one finds Rawls's theory plausible, then the facts of contemporary international relations require that the theory be reinterpreted in the ways suggested here.

1. Social Cooperation, Boundaries, and the Basis of Justice

JUSTICE, Rawls says, is the first virtue of social institutions. Its "primary subject" is "the basic structure of society, or more exactly, the way in which the major social institutions distribute fundamental rights and duties and determine the division of advantages from social cooperation."[4]

The central problem for a theory of justice is to identify principles by which the basic structure of society can be appraised. The two principles proposed as a solution to this problem are:

1. Each person is to have an equal right to the most extensive total system of equal basic liberties compatible with a similar system of liberty for all.
2. Social and economic inequalities are to be arranged so that they are both: (a) to the greatest benefit of the least advantaged, consistent with the just savings principle

[4] Rawls, *A Theory of Justice*, p. 7.

[the "difference principle"], and (b) attached to offices
and positions open to all under conditions of fair
equality of opportunity.[5]

These principles are Rawls's preferred interpretation of the
"general conception" of justice, which applies in a wider
range of circumstances than those in which the two principles
are appropriate.[6]

Rawls's argument for the two principles makes use of the
idea of a hypothetical social contract. We are to imagine rational persons meeting in an "original position" to choose
among alternative principles of justice. The original position
is defined by a variety of conditions concerning the nature,
motivation, and knowledge of the parties, and by formal constraints on the type of principles they may consider, which are
supposed to represent features we normally associate with
moral choice. Chief among these conditions is a "veil of ignorance" that excludes from the original position knowledge
about the particular identities and interests of the parties,
their generation and place in society, and their society's history, level of development, and culture.[7] Rawls argues that rational persons meeting in these circumstances would choose
the two principles listed above as the most fundamental moral
standards for their social institutions.

Like Hume, Rawls regards society as a "cooperative venture
for mutual advantage."[8] Society is typically marked by both
an identity and a conflict of interests. Everyone (or almost
everyone) in society shares an interest in having access to the
various goods that social activity can provide. At the same

[5] Ibid., pp. 302-3.

[6] The general conception reads: "All social primary goods—liberty and
opportunity, income and wealth, and the bases of self-respect—are to be distributed equally unless an unequal distribution of any or all of these goods is
to the advantage of the least favored." (Ibid., p. 303.) For the purposes of this
discussion, I ignore the problem of when (and why) the two principles are to
be preferred to the general conception, and the problems that might result if
the general conception were applied globally.

[7] Ibid., pp. 130-42.

[8] Ibid., p. 4. Compare David Hume, *A Treatise of Human Nature* [1739-
1740], III, II, ii, pp. 484-89.

time, people's claims to these scarce goods may conflict. Principles are needed to identify institutions that will fairly distribute the benefits and burdens of social life.

The model of society as a cooperative scheme is very important for Rawls's theory, but it must not be taken too literally. It is important because it explains the social role of justice and specifies the characteristics of human activity by virtue of which the requirements of justice apply. Thus, principles of justice determine a fair distribution of the benefits and burdens produced by "social cooperation." If there were no such "cooperation," there would be no occasion for justice, since there would be no joint product with respect to which conflicting claims might be pressed, nor would there be any common institutions (e.g., enforceable property rights) to which principles could apply. But Rawls's model must not be taken too literally, since all of the parties to a particular social scheme may not actually *cooperate* in social activity, and each party may not actually be advantaged in comparison with what his or her position would be in the absence of that scheme. For *cooperation* example, there is no doubt that the *polis* of ancient Greece *may* constituted a scheme of social cooperation to which the requirements of justice should apply, yet its slaves were neither *benefit the rich* willing cooperators in social life, nor were they necessarily advantaged in comparison with what their situations would have *not the poor* been outside of their society. (For that matter, none of the parties may be advantaged. Perhaps there are societies in which everyone's position is depressed. Such a society would be strange, but there is no obvious reason why judgments about its justice, or lack of it, would be inappropriate.) To say that society is a "cooperative venture for mutual advantage" is to add certain elements of a social ideal to a description of the circumstances to which justice applies. These additional elements unnecessarily narrow the description of these circumstances. It would be better to say that the requirements of justice apply to institutions and practices (whether or not they are genuinely cooperative) in which social activity produces relative or absolute benefits or burdens that would not exist if the social activity did not take place. Henceforth, I shall take Rawls's characterization of society as a cooperative scheme as an elliptical description of social schemes meeting this condition.

Rawls's two principles characterize "a special case of the problem of justice." They do not characterize "the justice of the law of nations and of relations between states."[9] This is because the principles rest on morally significant features of an ongoing scheme of social cooperation. If national boundaries are thought to set off discrete and (more or less) self-sufficient schemes of social cooperation, as Rawls assumes, then the relations of persons situated in different nation-states cannot be regulated by principles of social justice.[10] As Rawls develops the theory, it is only after principles of social justice and principles for individuals (the "natural duties") are chosen, that principles for international relations are considered, and then only in the most perfunctory manner.

Rawls assumes that "the boundaries" of the cooperative schemes to which the two principles apply "are given by the notion of a self-contained national community." This assumption "is not relaxed until the derivation of the principles of justice for the law of nations."[11] In other words, the assumption that national communities are self-contained is relaxed when international justice is considered. What does this mean? If the societies of the world are now to be conceived as open, fully interdependent systems, the world as a whole would fit the description of a scheme of social cooperation, and the arguments for the two principles would apply, a fortiori, at the global level. The principles of justice for international politics would be the two principles for domestic society writ large, and this would be a very radical result, given the tendency to equality of the difference principle. On the other hand, if societies are thought to be *entirely* self-contained—that is, if they are to have no relations of any kind with persons, groups, or societies beyond their borders—then why consider international justice at all? Principles of justice are supposed to regulate conduct, but if, *ex hypothesi*, there is no possibility of international conduct, it is difficult to see why

[9] Rawls, *A Theory of Justice*, pp. 7-8.
[10] For the self-sufficiency assumption, see ibid., pp. 4, 8, and 457.
[11] Ibid., p. 457.

principles of justice for the law of nations should be of any interest whatsoever. Rawls's discussion of justice among nations suggests that neither of these alternatives describes his intention in the passage quoted. Some intermediate assumption is required. Apparently, nation-states are now to be conceived as "more or less"[12] self-sufficient, but not entirely self-contained. Probably he imagines a world of nation-states which interact only in marginal ways; perhaps they maintain diplomatic relations, participate in a postal union, maintain limited cultural exchanges, and so on. Certainly the self-sufficiency assumption requires that societies have no significant trade or other economic relations.

Why, in such a world, are principles of international justice of interest? Rawls says that the restriction to ideal theory has the consequence that each society's external behavior is controlled by its principles of justice and of individual right, preventing unjust wars and interference with human rights abroad.[13] So it cannot be the need to prohibit unjust wars that prompts his worries about the law of nations. The most plausible motivation for considering principles of justice for the law of nations is suggested by an aside regarding the difficulties of disarmament in which Rawls suggests that state relations are inherently unstable because it is particularly dangerous for any one to stick to the rules when there is no assurance that others will do the same.[14] Agreement on regulative principles would then provide each state with security about the others' external behavior and would represent the minimum conditions of peaceful coexistence.

For the purpose of justifying principles for nations, Rawls reinterprets the original position as a sort of international conference:

> [O]ne may extend the interpretation of the original position and think of the parties as representatives of different nations who must choose together the fundamental principles to adjudicate conflicting claims among states. Following out the conception of the initial situation, I assume that these representatives are deprived of various

[12] Ibid., p. 4.   [13] Ibid., p. 379.   [14] Ibid., p. 336.

kinds of information. While they know that they represent different nations each living under the normal circumstances of human life, they know nothing about the particular circumstances of their own society. . . . Once again the contracting parties, in this case representatives of states, are allowed only enough knowledge to make a rational choice to protect their interests but not so much that the more fortunate among them can take advantage of their special situation. This original position is fair between nations; it nullifies the contingencies and biases of historical fate.[15]

While he does not actually present arguments for any particular principles for nations, he claims that "there would be no surprises, since the principles chosen would, I think, be familiar ones."[16] The examples given are indeed familiar; they include principles of self-determination, nonintervention, the *pacta sunt servanda* rule, a principle of justifiable self-defense, and principles defining *jus in bello*.[17] These are supposed to be consequences of a basic principle of equality among nations, to which the parties in the reinterpreted original position would agree in order to protect and uphold their interests in successfully operating their respective societies and in securing compliance with the principles for individuals that protect human life.[18]

One might object to such reasoning that there is no guarantee that all of the world's states are internally just, or that if they are, they are just in the sense specified by the two principles. If some societies are unjust according to the two principles, some familiar and serious problems arise, In a world including South Africa or Cambodia, for example, one can easily imagine situations in which the principle of nonintervention would prevent other nations from intervening in support of an oppressed group fighting to establish a more

---

[15] Ibid., p. 378.   [16] Ibid.

[17] These principles form the basis of traditional international law. See the discussion, on which Rawls relies, in J. L. Brierly, *The Law of Nations*, esp. chs. 3-4.

[18] Rawls, *A Theory of Justice*, pp. 378 and 115.

just regime, and this might seem implausible. More generally, one might ask why a principle that defends a state's ability to pursue an immoral end is to count as a moral principle imposing a requirement of justice on other states.

Such an objection, while indicating a serious problem in the real world, would be inappropriate in this context because the law of nations, in Rawls, applies to a world of just states. Nothing in Rawls's theory specifically requires this assumption, but it seems consonant with the restriction to ideal theory and parallels the assumption of "strict compliance" in his arguments for the two principles in domestic societies. (The ideal-theory restriction means that Rawls's arguments are intended to establish principles for a just [or "well-ordered"] society. The principles of ideal theory do not apply directly to the nonideal world.)[19] It is important that the suggested justification of these traditional rules of international law rests on an ideal assumption not present in most discussions of this subject. It does not self-evidently follow that these rules ought to hold in the nonideal world; at a minimum, an additional condition would be required, limiting the scope of the traditional rules to cases in which their observance would promote the development of just institutions in presently unjust societies while observing the basic protection of human rights expressed by the natural duties and preserving a stable international order in which just societies can exist.[20]

Someone might think that other principles would be acknowledged, for example, regarding population control and regulation of the environment. Or perhaps, as Barry suggests, the parties would agree to form some sort of permanent international organization with consultative, diplomatic, and even collective security functions.[21] However, there is no obvious reason why such agreements would emerge from an

[19] On ideal theory, see ibid., pp. 8-9. I consider the relation between ideal principles and the nonideal world in section 6, below.

[20] It has been argued that such a condition should qualify the nonintervention rule in Rawlsian ideal theory as well. If so, the resulting principle would be extensionally equivalent to that proposed in part two, above. See Mark Wicclair, "Human Rights and Intervention: A Contractarian Analysis."

[21] Barry, *The Liberal Theory of Justice*, p. 132.

international original position, at least as long as the constituent societies are assumed to be largely self-sufficient. Probably the parties, if confronted with these possibilities, would reason that fundamental questions of justice are not raised by them, and such issues of policy as arise from time to time in the real world could be handled with traditional treaty mechanisms underwritten by the rule, already acknowledged, that treaties are to be observed. Other issues that are today subjects of international negotiation—those relating to international regulation of common areas like the sea and outer space—are of a different sort. They call for a kind of regulation that requires substantive cooperation among peoples in the use of areas not presently within the boundaries of any society. A cooperative scheme must be evolved, which would create new wealth to which no national society could have a legitimate prior claim. These issues would be excluded from consideration on the ground that the parties are assumed not to be concerned with devising such a scheme. As representatives of separate social schemes, their attention is turned inward, not outward. In coming together in an international original position, they are moved by considerations of equality between "independent peoples organized as states."[22] Their main interest is in providing conditions in which just domestic social orders might flourish.

2. Entitlements to Natural Resources

THUS far, the ideal theory of international justice bears a striking resemblance to that proposed in the Definitive Articles of Kant's *Perpetual Peace*.[23] Accepting for the time being the assumption of national self-sufficiency, Rawls's choice of principles seems unexceptionable. But would this list of principles exhaust those to which the parties would agree? Probably not. At least one kind of consideration, in-

[22] Rawls, *A Theory of Justice*, p. 378.
[23] Immanuel Kant, *Perpetual Peace* [1795], pp. 98-115.

volving natural resources, might give rise to moral conflict among states even in the absence of substantial social cooperation among them, and thus be a matter of concern in the international original position. The principles given so far do not take account of these considerations.

We can appreciate the moral importance of conflicting resource claims by distinguishing two elements that contribute to the material advancement of societies. One is human cooperative activity itself, which can be thought of as the human component of material advancement. The other is what Sidgwick called "the utilities derived from any portion of the earth's surface," the natural component.[24] While the first is the subject of the domestic principles of justice, the second is morally relevant even in the absence of a functioning scheme of international social cooperation. The parties to the international original position would know that natural resources are distributed unevenly over the earth's surface. Some areas are rich in resources, and societies established in such areas can be expected to exploit their natural riches and to prosper. Other societies do not fare so well, and despite the best efforts of their members, they may attain only a meager level of well-being because of resource scarcities.

The parties would view the distribution of resources much as Rawls says the parties to the domestic original-position deliberations view the distribution of natural talents. In that context, he says that natural endowments are "neither just nor unjust; nor is it unjust that men are born into society at any particular position. These are simply natural facts. What is just or unjust is the way that institutions deal with these facts."[25] A caste society, for example, is unjust because it distributes the benefits of social cooperation according to a rule that rests on morally arbitrary factors. Rawls's objection is that those who are less advantaged for reasons beyond their control cannot be asked to suffer the pains of inequality when

[24] Henry Sidgwick, *The Elements of Politics* [1891], p. 255; quoted in S. I. Benn and R. S. Peters, *The Principles of Political Thought*, p. 430. Sidgwick's entire discussion of putative national rights to land and resources is relevant here. See *Elements*, pp. 252-57.

[25] Rawls, *A Theory of Justice*, p. 102.

their sacrifices cannot be shown to advance their position in comparison with an initial position of equality.

Reasoning analogously, the parties to the international original position would view the natural distribution of resources as morally arbitrary.[26] The fact that someone happens to be located advantageously with respect to natural resources does not provide a reason why he or she should be entitled to exclude others from the benefits that might be derived from them. Therefore, the parties would think that resources (or the benefits derived from them) should be subject to redistribution under a resource redistribution principle. This view is subject to the immediate objection that Rawls's treatment of natural talents is troublesome. It seems vulnerable in at least two ways. First, it is not clear what it means to say that the distribution of talents is "arbitrary from a moral point of view."[27] While the distribution of natural talents is arbitrary in the sense that one cannot deserve to be born with the capacity, say, to play like Rubinstein, it does not obviously follow that the possession of such a talent needs any justification. On the contrary, simply having a talent seems to furnish prima facie warrant for making use of it in ways that are, for the possessor, possible and desirable. A person need not justify the possession of talents, despite the fact that one cannot be said to deserve them, because they are already one's own; the prima facie right to use and control talents is fixed by natural fact.

The other point of vulnerability is that natural capacities are parts of the self, in the development of which a person might take a special kind of pride. A person's decision to develop one talent, not to develop another, as well as his or her choice as to how the talent is to be formed, and the uses to which it is to be put, are likely to be important elements of the effort to shape an identity. The complex of developed talents might even be said to constitute the self; their exercise is a principal form of self-expression. Because the development of talents is so closely linked with the shaping of personal

[26] Compare Kant, *Perpetual Peace*, p. 106, where it is claimed that persons "have a right to communal possession of the earth's surface."
[27] Rawls, *A Theory of Justice*, p. 72.

identity, it might seem that one's claim to one's talents is protected by considerations of personal liberty. To interfere with
the development and use of talents is to interfere with a self.
Or so, at least, it might be argued.

Both of these are reasons to think that Rawls's discussion of
natural talents is problematic. Perhaps it can be defended
against objections like these, but that is not my concern here. I
want to argue only that objections of this sort do not apply to
the parallel claim that the distribution of natural resources is
similarly arbitrary. Like talents, resource endowments are arbitrary in the sense that they are not deserved. But unlike talents, resources are not naturally attached to persons. Resources are found "out there," available to the first taker.
Resources must be appropriated before they can be used,
whereas, in the talents case, the "appropriation" is a *fait accompli* of nature over which persons have no direct control.
Thus, while we might feel that the possession of talents con-
fers a right to control and benefit from their use, we feel
differently about resources. Appropriation may not always
need a justification; if the resources taken are of limited
value, or if, as Locke imagined, their appropriation leaves
"enough and as good" for everyone else, appropriation may
not present a problem. In a world of scarcity, however, the
situation is different. The appropriation of valuable resources
by some will leave others comparatively, and perhaps fatally,
disadvantaged. Those deprived without justification of scarce
resources needed to sustain and enhance their lives might
well press claims to equitable shares.

Furthermore, resources do not stand in the same relation
to personal identity as do talents. It would be inappropriate to
take the sort of pride in the diamond deposits in one's back
yard that one takes in the ability to play the *Appassionata*. This
is because natural resources come into the development of
personality (when they come in at all) in a more casual way
than do talents. As I have said, talents, in some sense, are
what the self is; they help constitute personality. The resources under one's feet, because they lack this natural connection with the self, seem more like contingent than necessary elements in the development of personality. Like talents,

resources are used in this process; they are worked on, shaped, and benefited from. But they are not there, as parts of the self, to begin with. They must first be appropriated, and prior to their appropriation, no one has any special natural claim on them. Considerations of personal liberty do not protect a right to appropriate and use resources in the same way that they protect the right to develop and use talents as one sees fit. There is no parallel, initial presumption against interference with the use of resources, since no one is initially placed in a naturally privileged relationship with them.

I conclude that the natural distribution of resources is a purer case of something being "arbitrary from a moral point of view" than the distribution of talents. Not only can one not be said to deserve the resources under one's feet; the other grounds on which one might assert an initial claim to talents are absent in the case of resources, as well.

The fact that national societies are assumed to be self-sufficient does not make the distribution of natural resources any less arbitrary. Citizens of a nation that finds itself on top of a gold mine do not gain a right to the wealth that might be derived from it *simply* because their nation is self-sufficient. But someone might argue that self-sufficiency, nevertheless, removes any possible grounds on which citizens of other nations might press claims to equitable shares. A possible view is that no justification for resource appropriation is necessary in the global state of nature. If, so to speak, social cooperation is the root of all social obligations, as it is in some versions of contract theory, then the view is correct. All rights would be "special rights" applying only when certain conditions of cooperation obtain.[28]

I believe that this is wrong. It seems plausible in most discussions of distributive justice because their subject is the distribution of the benefits of social cooperation. Where there is no social cooperation, there are no benefits or burdens of cooperation, and hence no problem of conflicting distributive claims concerning the fruits of cooperation. (This is why a

----

[28] William N. Nelson construes Rawlsian rights in this way in "Special Rights, General Rights, and Social Justice."

world of self-sufficient national societies is not subject to
something like a global difference principle.) But there is
nothing in this reasoning to suggest that we can *only* have
moral ties to those with whom we share membership in a
cooperative scheme. It is possible that other sorts of considerations might come into the justification of moral principles.
Rawls himself recognizes this in the case of the natural duties,
which are said to "apply to us without regard to our voluntary
acts," and, apparently, without regard to our institutional
memberships.[29]

In the case of natural resources, the parties to the international original position would know that resources are unevenly distributed with respect to population, that adequate
access to resources is a prerequisite for successful operation
of (domestic) cooperative schemes, and that resources are
scarce. They would view the natural distribution of resources
as arbitrary in the sense that no one has a natural prima facie
claim to the resources that happen to be under one's feet. The
appropriation of scarce resources by some requires a justification against the competing claims of others and the needs of
future generations. Not knowing the resource endowments
of their own societies, the parties would agree on a resource
redistribution principle that would give each society a fair
chance to develop just political institutions and an economy
capable of satisfying its members' basic needs.

There is no intuitively obvious standard of equity for such
matters; perhaps the standard would be population size, or
perhaps it would be more complicated, rewarding societies
for their members' efforts in extracting resources and taking
account of the different resource needs of societies with
different economies. The underlying principle is that each
person has an equal prima facie claim to a share of the total
available resources, but departures from this initial standard
could be justified (analogously to the operation of the difference principle) if the resulting inequalities were to the
greatest benefit of those least advantaged by the inequality.[30]
In any event, the resource redistribution principle would

---

[29] Rawls, *A Theory of Justice*, p. 114.   [30] Compare ibid., p. 151.

function in international society as the difference principle functions in domestic society. It provides assurance to persons in resource-poor societies that their adverse fate will not prevent them from realizing economic conditions sufficient to support just social institutions and to protect human rights guaranteed by the principles for individuals. In the absence of this assurance, these nations might resort to war as a means of securing the resources necessary to establish domestic justice, and it is not obvious that wars fought for this purpose would be unjust.[31]

Before turning to other issues, I must note a complication of which I cannot give a fully satisfactory account. The international original position parties are prevented by the veil of ignorance from knowing their generation; they would be concerned to minimize the risk that, when the veil is lifted, they might find themselves living in a world where resources have been largely depleted. Thus, part of the resource redistribution principle would set some standard for conservation against this possibility. The difficulties in formulating a standard of conservation are at least as formidable as those of defining the "just savings rate" in Rawls's discussion of justifiable rates of capital accumulation. I shall not pursue them here, except to point out that some provision for conservation as a matter of justice with respect to future generations would be necessary.[32]

[31] On this account, U. N. General Assembly Resolution 1,803 (XVII), which purports to establish "permanent sovereignty over natural resources," would be prima facie unjust. However, there are important mitigating factors. This resolution, as the text and the debates make clear, was adopted to defend developing nations against resource exploitation by foreign-owned businesses, and to support a national right of expropriation (with compensation) of foreign-owned mining and processing facilities in some circumstances. While the "permanent sovereignty" doctrine may be extreme, sovereignty-for-the-time-being might not be, if it can be shown (as I think it can) that resource-consuming nations have taken more than their fair share without returning adequate compensation from their own surpluses. United Nations General Assembly, *Official Records: Seventeenth Session*, Supp. no. 17 (A/5,217) (New York, 1963), pp. 15-16.

[32] Compare Rawls, *A Theory of Justice*, pp. 284-93. There is a discussion that takes account of problems of conservation in D. Clayton Hubin, "Justice and Future Generations."

In failing to recognize resource problems, Rawls follows other writers who have extended the social-contract idea to international relations.[33] Perhaps this is because they have attributed a greater symmetry to the domestic and international contracts than is in fact appropriate. Resource problems do not arise as distinct questions in the domestic case because their distribution and conservation are implicitly covered by the difference principle and the just-savings principle. When the scope of social cooperation is coextensive with the territorial boundaries of a society, it is unnecessary to distinguish natural and social contributions to the society's level of well-being. But when justice is considered internationally, we must face the likelihood of moral claims being pressed by members of the various social schemes which are arbitrarily placed with respect to the natural distribution of resources. My suggestion of a resource redistribution principle recognizes the fundamental character of these claims viewed from the perspective of the parties' interests in securing fair conditions for the development of their respective schemes.

3. Interdependence and Global Distributive Justice

THE case for an international resource redistribution principle is consistent with the assumption that states are self-sufficient cooperative schemes. Aside from humanitarian principles, like that of mutual aid, a global resource redistribution principle seems to be the strongest distributive principle applicable to a world of self-sufficient states.

Now, of course, the world is not made up of self-sufficient

---

[33] The closest thing to a fully worked-out international contract theory in the literature is Christian Wolff's doctrine of the *civitas maxima*, a hypothetical superlegislature made up of representatives of all states which was imagined to formulate rules for conduct based on the true interests of the states. The doctrine is developed in Wolff, *Jus gentium methodo scientifica pertractatum* [1749], esp. Prolegomena, sec. 9, p. 12. There is a helpful discussion in Walter Schiffer, *The Legal Community of Mankind*, pp. 69-78.

states. States participate in complex international economic, political, and cultural relationships that suggest the existence of a global scheme of social cooperation. As Kant notes, international economic cooperation creates a new basis for international morality.[34] If social cooperation is the foundation of distributive justice, then one might think that international economic interdependence lends support to a principle of global distributive justice similar to that which applies within domestic society. In this section I explore this idea.

International interdependence is reflected in the volume of transactions that flow across national boundaries—for example, communications, travel, trade, aid, and foreign investment. Although there has been some disagreement about the significance of the increase, the level of interdependence, measured by transaction flows and ratios of trade to gross national products, appears to have risen since 1945, reversing an interwar trend on the basis of which some have argued that rising interdependence is a myth. Furthermore, there is every reason to believe that the rising trend, if not the rate of increase, will continue in the years ahead.[35]

The main features of contemporary international interdependence relevant to questions of justice are the results of the growth of international investment and trade. Capital surpluses are not confined to reinvestment in the societies where they are produced, but instead are reinvested wherever conditions promise the highest yield without unacceptable risks. It is well known, for example, that large American corporations have systematically transferred significant portions of their capitalization to European, Latin American, and East Asian societies where labor costs are lower or markets are better. As a result of the long-term decline in tariffs and in nontariff barriers to trade, the rise of international advertising,

[34] Immanuel Kant, *The Metaphysical Elements of Justice* [1797], pp. 124-29. See also Kant, *Perpetual Peace*, pp. 106-8.

[35] Peter J. Katzenstein, "International Interdependence: Some Long-term Trends and Recent Changes." See also R. Rosecrance, et al., "Whither Interdependence?," esp. pp. 432-41. For a skeptical view, see Kenneth N. Waltz, "The Myth of National Interdependence." Waltz's view is challenged in Richard Rosecrance, "Interdependence: Myth or Reality," which also provides a review of some other relevant literature.

and the development of rapid international communications, a world market has grown in which demand for finished goods is relatively insensitive to their place of manufacture, and international trade has increased substantially. The main organizational form to evolve in response to these trends is, of course, the multinational corporation, which makes possible greater refinements in the global allocation of capital investment, the coordination of production, and the development of markets.[36]

It is clear that interdependence in trade and investment produces substantial aggregate economic benefits in the form of a higher global rate of economic growth as well as greater productive efficiency. These results would be predicted by neoclassical economic theory and seem to be confirmed by empirical studies, even those that recognize the presence of various political constraints on trade and of extensive oligopolistic practices among multinational corporations that might be thought to invalidate the predictions of economic theory.[37]

Interdependence helps economic growth

It is easier to demonstrate that a pattern of global interdependence exists, and that it yields substantial aggregate benefits, than to say with certainty how these benefits are distributed under existing institutions and practices or what burdens these institutions and practices impose on participants in the world economy. There is considerable controversy about these matters, and it is only possible here to offer some illustrative observations. There are several reasons for thinking that interdependence widens the income gap between rich and poor countries even though it produces absolute gains for almost all of them. Because states have differing factor

---

[36] The main texts on multinationals are Raymond Vernon, *Sovereignty at Bay* and C. Fred Bergsten, Thomas Horst, and Theodore H. Moran, *American Multinationals and American Interests.* There is a more critical discussion in Richard Barnet and Ronald Müller, *Global Reach*, esp. chs. 1-2.

[37] In this regard, a stronger empirical case can be made for the aggregate gains from foreign investment than for those from trade. On the gains from trade, see Richard N. Cooper, "Economic Assumptions of the Case for Liberal Trade." On the role of foreign investment in promoting global efficiency and growth, see Robert O. Keohane and Van Doorn Ooms, "The Multinational Firm and International Regulation," pp. 172-76.

endowments and varying access to technology, even "free" trade can lead to increasing international distributive inequalities (and, on some views, to absolute as well as relative declines in the well-being of the poorest classes) in the absence of continuing transfers to those least advantaged by international trade.[38] Direct foreign investment in the guise of multinational corporate expansion appears in some instances to exacerbate international inequality. With their monopolies on technology, access to large amounts of capital, and capacity to transfer factors of production from country to country, multinational corporations are often able to extract monopoly rents by fixing prices in excess of competitive levels.[39] The political power of the corporations, together with their ability to move profits from one country to another through transfer pricing, sometimes allows them to avoid the efforts of national governments to capture domestic profits through corporate taxes.[40] On the other hand, the international distribution of the gains from trade and investment depends significantly on the relative power of domestic governments to control the behavior of locally owned as well as multinational firms, and there is evidence that some developing countries are growing more powerful in this regard. Because this political factor can vary widely from one country to the next, it can be argued that it is not interdependence per se, but contingent features of particular domestic political arrangements, that account for the present, apparently uneven, distribution of the gains from trade and investment.[41]

In some cases, participation in the world economy produces political inequality as well. Let us say that a party to some relationship is vulnerable to the extent that the relationship would be costly for that party to break. When breaking a

[38] Ronald Findlay, *Trade and Specialization*, pp. 118-22. For the view that trade absolutely impoverishes the global poor, see Michael Barratt Brown, *The Economics of Imperialism*, esp. ch. 5, pp. 96-126, and the references cited there.

[39] Constantine V. Vaitsos, *Intercountry Income Distribution and Transnational Enterprises*, pp. 19-30 and 42-65.

[40] Keohane and Ooms, "The Multinational Firm," pp. 177-78.

[41] Ibid., p. 178.

relationship would impose higher costs on one party than on another, the relatively less vulnerable party can use the threat to break the relationship as a form of power over the more vulnerable party. In international trade, the most vulnerable parties are usually those with a heavy concentration of exports in a few products and a heavy concentration of export markets in a few countries. The most striking political inequalities arising from asymmetrical vulnerability involve industrial countries and non-oil-exporting developing countries (although it is worth noting that such vulnerability is neither distributed equally among developing countries nor limited to them).[42] This sort of vulnerability explains, for example, why the oil-poor developing countries have been so unsuccessful in winning concessions on trade policy from the industrial countries. A similar kind of vulnerability explains why the industrial countries have been able virtually to dictate economic policies to some developing countries that rely heavily for credit on such sources as the World Bank.

Perhaps the most damaging burdens of interdependence have to do with its domestic consequences. These fall into two main classes. First, domestic governments are likely to experience difficulty in controlling their own economies, since domestic economic behavior is influenced by economic developments elsewhere. For example, the global monetary system allows disturbances (like price inflation) in some countries to be transmitted to others, complicating economic planning and possibly undercutting employment and incomes policies.[43] The other class of burdens involves the domestic distributive and structural effects of participation in the world economy. It is impossible to generalize in this area because the effect of trade and investment on domestic income distribution is a function of features peculiar to particular countries, such as relative factor endowments, domestic market

---

[42] Kal J. Holsti, "A New International Politics?" p. 516. For a more detailed discussion of the relative weakness of the poor countries, see Tony Smith, "Changing Configurations of Power in North-South Relations since 1945," esp. pp. 7-15.

[43] For a discussion, see Richard N. Cooper, "Economic Interdependence and Foreign Policy in the Seventies," esp. pp. 164-67.

imperfections, and government investment, tariff, and tax policies. However, with specific reference to the resource-poor developing countries, it is fair to say that participation in international trade and investment has often contributed to domestic income inequality in at least two separate ways: first, under prevailing political conditions, the gains from trade and the retained profits of foreign-owned firms have tended to be concentrated in the upper income classes; second, the political influence of foreign investors has (either directly or indirectly) supported governments committed to inegalitarian domestic distributive policies.[44] As above, it is important to add the caveat that the extent to which a country's international economic relations destabilize its domestic economy and contribute to internal inequality depends crucially on the policies pursued by its government.[45]

It is not only true that interdependence involves a pattern of transactions that produce substantial benefits and costs; their increased volume and significance have led to the development of a global regulative structure. The world economy has evolved its own financial and monetary institutions, which set exchange rates, regulate the money supply, influence capital flows, and enforce rules of international economic conduct. The system of trade is regulated by international agreements on tariff levels and other potential barriers to trade. To these global institutions should be added such informal practices of economic policy coordination among national governments as those of the Organization for Economic Cooperation and Development, which are aimed at achieving agreement on a variety of domestic policies of local and international relevance. Taken together, these institutions and practices can be considered as the constitutional

[44] Keohane and Ooms, "The Multinational Firm," pp. 179-80.

[45] From the point of view of social theory, the important question raised by this observation is, to what extent and under what conditions is a government's choice of policies relevant to domestic income distribution influenced by its international economic relations? Since my argument does not turn on any particular response to this question, I shall not pursue it here. There is an illuminating discussion in Richard R. Fagen, "Equity in the South in the Context of North-South Relations."

structure of the world economy; their activities have important distributive implications.[46]

I have been largely concerned with the economic institutions and processes characteristic of interdependence. But it should be noted that certain political and legal institutions also influence the global distribution of income and wealth. Thus, for example, international property rights assign exclusive ownership and control of a territory and its natural resources to the recognized government of the society established on it, or reserve partial or total control of common areas (the seas and outer space) to the international community.[47] Also, laws and conventions established or codified by treaty, and thus guaranteed by the *pacta sunt servanda* rule of customary international law, protect private foreign investment against expropriation without compensation.[48] Perhaps most important of all is the rule of nonintervention, which, when observed, has clear and sweeping effects on the welfare of people everywhere.[49]

These facts, by now part of the conventional (if controversial) wisdom of international relations, describe a world in which national boundaries cannot be regarded as the outer limits of social cooperation. International interdependence involves a complex and substantial pattern of social interaction, which produces benefits and burdens that would not exist if national economies were autarkic. In view of these considerations, Rawls's passing concern for the law of nations seems to miss the point of international justice altogether. In an interdependent world, confining principles of social justice to domestic societies has the effect of taxing poor nations so

[46] This is recognized by those who hold that alternative international economic regimes should be assessed according to their distributive effects. See, for example, Robert E. Baldwin and David A. Kay, "International Trade and International Relations," pp. 121-24; C. Fred Bergsten, Robert O. Keohane, and Joseph S. Nye, Jr., "International Economics and International Politics," pp. 31-32.

[47] Ian Brownlie, *Principles of Public International Law*, pp. 109-29.

[48] Ibid., pp. 516-28.

[49] For brief discussions, see James N. Rosenau, "Intervention as a Scientific Concept," pp. 161-63; and part two, above.

that others may benefit from living in "just" regimes. The two principles, so construed, might justify a wealthy society in denying aid to needy peoples elsewhere if the aid could be used domestically to promote a more nearly just regime. If the self-sufficiency assumption were empirically acceptable, such a result might be plausible, if controversial on other grounds.[50] But if participation in economic relations with the needy society has contributed to the wealth of the "nearly just" regime, its domestic "justice" seems to lose moral significance. In such situations, the principles of domestic "justice" will be genuine principles of justice only if they are consistent with principles of justice for the entire global scheme of social cooperation. Note that this conclusion does not require that national societies should have become entirely superfluous, or that the global economy should be completely integrated.[51] It is enough, for setting the limits of cooperative schemes, that some societies are able to increase their level of well-being via global trade and investment while others with whom they have economic relations do not fare so well.[52]

How should we formulate global principles? It has been

[50] For example, on consequentialist grounds. See Peter Singer, "Famine, Affluence, and Morality."

[51] This conclusion would hold even if it were true that wealthy nations like the United States continue to be economically self-sufficient, as Kenneth Waltz has (mistakenly, I think) argued. To refute the claim I make in the text, it would be necessary to show that all, or almost all, nations are self-sufficient in the sense given above, and that such foreign relations as they engage in produce no significant external effects. This, plainly, is not the case. Waltz, "The Myth of National Interdependence," pp. 205-23.

[52] In some cases the situation may be worse than this. It has been argued that some poor countries' relations with the rich have actually worsened economic conditions among the poor countries' worst-off groups. This raises the question of whether interdependence must actually benefit everyone involved to give rise to questions of justice. I think the answer is clearly negative; countries A and B are involved in social cooperation even if A (a rich country) could get along without B (a poor country), but instead exploits it, while B gets nothing out of its "cooperation" but exacerbated class divisions and Coca-Cola factories. This illustrates my remark (section 1, part three) that Rawls's characterization of a society as "a cooperative venture for mutual advantage" (A Theory of Justice, p. 4) may be misleading, since everyone need not be advantaged by the cooperative scheme in order for requirements of justice to apply.

suggested that Rawls's two principles, suitably reinterpreted, could themselves be applied globally.[53] The reasoning is as follows: if evidence of global economic and political interdependence shows the existence of a global scheme of social cooperation, we should not view national boundaries as having fundamental moral significance. Since boundaries are not coextensive with the scope of social cooperation, they do not mark the limits of social obligations. Thus the parties to the original position cannot be assumed to know that they are members of a particular national society, choosing principles of justice primarily for that society. The veil of ignorance must extend to all matters of national citizenship, and the principles chosen will therefore apply globally.[54] As Barry points out, a global interpretation of the original position is insensitive to the choice of principles.[55] Assuming that Rawls's arguments for the two principles are successful, there is no reason to think that the content of the principles would change as a result of enlarging the scope of the original position so that the principles would apply to the world as a whole. In particular, if the difference principle ("social and economic inequalities are to be arranged so that they are . . . to the greatest benefit of the least advantaged") would be chosen in the domestic original position, it would be chosen in the global original position as well.

I have noted that there is considerable controversy about the international and domestic distribution of the benefits and costs of interdependence. Clearly, we cannot settle this controversy here. Someone might object that an argument with potentially far-reaching conclusions should not be allowed to rest on such an insecure empirical foundation. But

[53] Barry, *The Liberal Theory of Justice*, pp. 128-32; and Scanlon, "Rawls' Theory of Justice," pp. 1,066-67.

[54] David Richards also argues that the principles apply globally. But he fails to notice the relationship between distributive justice and the morally relevant features of social cooperation on which its requirements rest. This relationship is needed to explain why the original position parties should be kept ignorant of their nationalities, and thus why Rawlsian principles of social justice should apply globally. See David A. J. Richards, *A Theory of Reasons for Action*, pp. 137-41.

[55] Barry, *The Liberal Theory of Justice*, p. 129.

this would misunderstand the argument, which does not depend on the accuracy of any particular claims regarding the distributional consequences of interdependence. What is important in demonstrating that interdependence constitutes social cooperation in the relevant sense is that international economic relations be shown to produce significant aggregate benefits and costs that would not exist if states were economically autarkic, and this, I believe, is beyond dispute. My claims about the distribution of these benefits and costs illustrate that aggregate benefits and costs do not exist simply as an aggregate, but rather fall under the control of one or another agent; *some* distribution is entailed by their very existence. But it is not necessary for my argument that the existing distribution conform to any particular pattern, nor, as it might be supposed, that the existing distribution is in any sense unjust. (Indeed, it is not clear that an argument terminating in a principle of distributive justice could coherently involve any such premise; we cannot say that any particular distribution is unjust until we know what justice is.) All that is required is that interdependence produce benefits and burdens; the role of a principle of distributive justice, then, would be to specify what a fair distribution of those benefits and burdens would be like.[56]

It is important to be clear who are the subjects of a global difference principle, especially because it has been questioned whether such a principle should apply to states rather than persons.[57] It seems obvious that an international difference principle applies to persons in the sense that it is the globally least advantaged representative person (or group of persons) whose position is to be maximized.[58] If one takes the position

[56] I previously suggested that the case for an international difference principle depends on the truth of hypotheses from "dependency theory" regarding the costs to poor countries of participation in international economic relations. The suggestion was excessive, since the argument needs only the more modest empirical claims made in the text above. The relevant passage is in "Justice and International Relations," pp. 373-75.

[57] For example, by Robert W. Tucker, *The Inequality of Nations*, pp. 62-64.

[58] This would be obscured if one supposed (as has Christopher Brewin) that the parties to the international original position "would be masterless or sovereign states." But the supposition is incorrect (and perhaps incoherent);

of the least-advantaged group as an index of distributive justice, there is no a priori reason to think that the membership of this group will be coextensive with that of any existing state. Thus, a global difference principle does not *necessarily* require transfers from rich countries as such to poor countries as such. While it is almost certainly the case that an international difference principle would require reductions in intercountry distributive inequalities, this would be because these inequalities are consequences of impermissible interpersonal inequalities. Furthermore, because the difference principle applies in the first instance to persons, it would also require intrastate inequalities to be minimized if necessary to maximize the position of the (globally) least advantaged group.

It is not inconsistent with this view to understand states as the primary "subjects" of international distributive responsibilities.[59] For it may be that states, as the primary actors in international politics, are more appropriately situated than individual persons to carry out whatever policies are required to implement global principles. Perhaps intercountry redistribution should be viewed as a second-best solution in the absence of a better strategy for satisfying a global difference principle. In any event, it should be understood that the international obligations of states are in some sense derivative of the more basic responsibilities that persons acquire as a result of the (global) relations in which they stand.[60]

---

the parties are *persons*, and the international original position is distinguished from the domestic one by stipulating the parties' ignorance of their citizenship. Brewin, "Justice in International Relations," p. 147.

[59] As Tucker suggests. *The Inequality of Nations*, pp. 62-64.

[60] The relation of individual and group responsibilities is a difficult issue, involving a variety of complications. I cannot pursue it here. See Joel Feinberg, "Collective Responsibility"; and Virginia Held, "Can A Random Collection of Individuals Be Morally Responsible?"

4. Contrasts between International and Domestic Society

THE conclusion that principles of distributive justice apply globally follows from the premise that international economic interdependence constitutes a scheme of social cooperation like those to which requirements of distributive justice have often been thought to apply. This is the most important normative consequence of my argument (in part one) that international relations is more like domestic society than it is often thought to be. One might accept this premise but reject the conclusion on either of two grounds. First, one might hold that interdependence is a necessary but not a sufficient condition for the global application of principles of justice, and that other necessary conditions (like the existence of political institutions or of a capacity for a sense of justice) do not obtain in international relations. Second, one might argue that special features of social cooperation within national societies organized as states override the requirements of global principles, so that these cannot be understood as ultimate. In this and the following sections, I explore these objections.

There is no doubt that the main difference between international relations and domestic society is the absence in the former case of effective decision-making and decision-enforcing institutions. There is no world constitution analogous to those explicit or implicit codes that define the structure of authority within states. And there is no world police force capable of enforcing compliance with world community policies. Instead, there is an array of processes and institutions through which states and other political actors attempt to influence one another and which, directly or indirectly, affect the prospects of the persons who live within their scope. These processes and institutions range from war and coercive diplomacy to ad hoc bargaining and transnational organizations. Even in the last case, which most resembles the political institutions of domestic society, there is a significantly diminished capacity to make decisions and enforce them

against offenders. Although one must grant (as I argued in
part one) that the international realm includes various
capacities for sanctions and enforcement of community decisions, one cannot plausibly argue that these are similar in
extent to those characteristic of most domestic societies. In
particular, there is at present no reliable way of enforcing
compliance with international redistributive policies. (The
United Nations, for example, has been unable to persuade
rich countries to contribute even three-quarters of one percent of their gross products to international development efforts.)

A related contrast between the international and domestic
realms is the absence of what might be called an international
sense of community. Within domestic society, the sense of
community is an important motivational basis for compliance
with laws and official decisions. Rawls recognizes this in arguing that compliance with the principles of justice rests on the
fact that persons have a capacity for a sense of justice, and
that this capacity would be developed by participation in the
life of a well-ordered society (i.e., one whose basic structure
conformed to the two principles).[61] In international relations,
there is no similar sense of community; nor are most people
moved to act by any commitment to ideals like global justice.
One might think that the world is simply too large, and its cultures too diverse, to support a global sense of justice. Unify-
ing symbols are scarce while sectional ones are all too available; and, in any event, it is a commonplace that the political
force of a symbol decreases in proportion to the degree of
abstraction of the symbol from the immediate needs and interests of individuals and small groups. Thus, it is unlikely
that a sense of global community comparable to the sense of
national community will develop.

How are these contrasts relevant to the argument for international distributive justice? Objections to global principles
might be constructed following the precept that morality
cannot demand the impossible. As Rawls points out, the parties to the original position would not choose principles they

[61] Rawls, *A Theory of Justice*, pp. 496-504.

know they cannot live by.[62] Nor, surely, would they choose principles that cannot be implemented. If the lack of effective, global political institutions, or of a sense of world community, makes impossible the implementation of global principles, then the parties would not agree to them.

Such objections are not persuasive because they misunderstand the relation between ideal theory and the real world. Ideal theory prescribes standards that serve as goals of political change in the nonideal world, assuming that a just society can, in due course, be achieved. The ideal cannot be undermined simply by pointing out that it cannot be achieved at present. One needs to distinguish two classes of reasons for which it may be impossible to implement an ideal. One class includes impediments to change that are themselves capable of modification over time; the other includes impediments that are unalterable and unavoidable. Only in the second case can one appeal to the claim of impossibility in arguing against an ideal, since, in the former case, such an argument can be defeated by pointing out the mutability of those social facts that are supposed to render the ideal unattainable in the present.

Both of the objections sketched seem to rely on impediments to implementation of a global difference principle that are capable of modification over time. There is no evidence that it is somehow given in the nature of things that people can neither develop sufficient motivation for compliance nor evolve institutions capable of enforcing global principles against offenders. I am not claiming that either of these would be easy or that we can foresee the dynamics by which they may come about. But this is not what ideal theory requires. It requires only that the necessary changes be possible, and it is at least not demonstrably false that this is the case.[63]

[62] Ibid., p. 145.

[63] "[T]he idea that something which has hitherto been unsuccessful will never be successful does not justify anyone in abandoning even a pragmatic or technical aim. . . . This applies even to moral aims, which, so long as it is not demonstrably impossible to fulfil them, amount to duties." Kant, "On the Common Saying: 'This May be True in Theory, but it does not Apply in Practice' " [1793], p. 89.

A different interpretation of these objections is that neither authoritative global institutions, nor a sense of global justice, would be desirable even if they were attainable. Perhaps authoritative institutions on such a scale would be radically inefficient, or unavoidably oppressive, politics being what it is.[64] Or, perhaps the sense of justice is important not only as a motive for compliance with principles of justice, but also as a source of a people's common, and distinctive, identity. This might be thought to be an important good because it speaks to people's need to belong to a group that is smaller than the whole population of the world.[65] If this is true, then a sense of global justice might seem to carry allegiance to political ideals farther than is desirable.

In response to these objections it might be pointed out that the institutions and sentiments on which compliance with global principles is based need not bear too close a resemblance to their domestic analogues. In each case, some function must be fulfilled to make possible the implementation of global principles, but these functions need not be fulfilled through mechanisms like those familiar in domestic society. It is a mistake to identify too closely the scope of the principles and the scope of the institutions necessary to implement them, for a variety of configurations of institutions can be imagined (for example, a coordinated set of regional institutions) that would implement the principles. Similarly, the supposed undesirability of a sense of global justice rests on a conflation of the regulative role of the sense of justice and many other functions fulfilled by loyalties to subgroups of the species. While a common allegiance to justice is necessary to promote compliance with its norms and to regulate institutions that implement them, there is no obvious reason why

[64] Such a view is suggested by Kenneth N. Waltz, *Man, The State, and War*, p. 228; and Inis L. Claude, *Power and International Relations*, pp. 206-28.

[65] See, e.g., Sigmund Freud, *Civilization and its Discontents* [1930], p. 61; and Emile Durkheim, *Moral Education* [1925], pp. 74-77. Durkheim does not draw the extreme conclusion that the need for state-centered loyalties entirely undermines international morality. In fact, he claims that domestic society "can enjoy moral primacy only on the condition that it is not conceived as an unscrupulous self-centered being." *Moral Education*, p. 79.

this would be inconsistent with the persistence of those loyalties to smaller groups necessary to feelings of belonging and identity.[66]

The contrasts between international and domestic society, then, do not damage the argument for a global application of the difference principle. But the effect of distinguishing ideal from nonideal theory for the purpose of defeating such objections does not make the objections disappear; it merely recognizes that their relevance is not to the ideal of global distributive justice, but rather to the problem of realizing this ideal. In general, this problem is likely to be more difficult in international relations than in domestic society because the institutional framework of international relations is less capable of bringing about the shifts in the distribution of wealth and power required by the global difference principle. Below, I shall consider this problem in more detail. For the present, I would like briefly to illustrate one way in which the relative weakness of international institutions complicates nonideal theory. The illustration is of general interest because it involves the relation of fair coercive institutions to the sacrifices that can be required of people by moral principles.

An important feature of fair coercive institutions (that is, coercive institutions that are just or nearly just) is that they give assurance to those whom they call upon to make sacrifices that others in similar circumstances will be compelled to make similar sacrifices. So far as it is possible, such institutions seek to remove the unfairness inherent in the possibility that some of their members can avoid contributing their fair share by becoming free riders.[67] It is not only fairness that

---

[66] As Herbert Kelman points out in "Education for the Concept of a Global Society," p. 661. Compare Rawls's discussion of this issue as it arises in domestic society: "[T]he institutional scheme in question may be so large that particular bonds never get widely built up. In any case, the citizen body as a whole is not generally bound together by fellow feeling between individuals, but by the acceptance of public principles of justice." (*A Theory of Justice*, p. 477.) There is nothing in the global interpretation that defeats this reasoning; if it is plausible at the national level, it is plausible at the global level as well.

[67] For a general discussion, see James M. Buchanan, *The Demand and Supply of Public Goods*, pp. 77-99, and the references cited there.

makes this a significant feature of coercive institutions; the perception that such institutions can assure a fair distribution of the burdens of social cooperation is likely to be an important source of the motivation for compliance. One reason that obligations of charity often seem weaker than obligations of justice is that charity is more often voluntary in the sense that its demands are not backed up by the coercive power of the state. One can beg off on the grounds that he or she would be unfairly disadvantaged by his or her contribution in comparison with others who do not contribute, or that his or her contribution, in the absence of cooperation by others, would be futile. But these alternatives are not available when there is assurance that each will be compelled to contribute his or her fair share.

Now in international relations this assurance is often absent. In this limited respect, the problem of bringing about international distributive justice is similar to that of escaping a Hobbesian state of nature. In both cases, the absence of fair coercive institutions—which makes more probable the absence of reliable expectations of reciprocal compliance—undermines the motivational basis for compliance with principles of justice. In both cases, the solution of the assurance problem is effective coordination of the actions of all of the actors involved. But there are important differences as well. First, the risks of voluntary compliance are different. Moral persons in Hobbes's state of nature risk death, while in international relations they risk relative deprivation. Hobbes's problem is survival, while the problem in the present case is international distributive justice. Second, as I argued in part one, there are greater possibilities for coordination in international relations than in the state of nature. The assurance problem is more easily solved. Third, international relations involves a variety of institutions, which can be adjusted to improve the justice of the distribution they produce, while the state of nature lacks analogous institutions bearing on personal security. In sum, one can imagine a variety of intermediate solutions to the problem of implementing international distributive principles—intermediate in the sense of bringing the actual distribution closer to the ideal than it is at present—but it is hard to see what an intermediate solution would mean in the state of nature.

Thus the relevance of the contrasts between international relations and domestic society is to be found in the area of nonideal theory. These contrasts do not undermine the argument for a global application of principles of justice, but rather complicate the moral reasoning as well as the political action involved in the effort to realize the ideal. Unlike the partially analogous problem of escaping from a Hobbesian state of nature, however, the complications in the nonideal theory of international relations render justified political action more difficult, but not impossible in principle. (See further section 6, below.)

Although conceding all that I have said so far, someone might object that there is still an important difference between domestic and international "social cooperation." While the terms of participation in domestic society apply to its members regardless of their consent and may therefore appropriately be assessed from the standpoint of justice, it might be thought that participation in the world economy is considerably more voluntary. After all, no state is required to participate in international trade or to accept foreign investment, and any state could withdraw at will (following the example, say, of Albania or Cambodia). By participating, states might be said to have accepted the terms of participation offered them, making further moral criticism of those terms otiose.

The objection seems plausible only because it locates the alleged voluntariness of international economic relations in the wrong place. Of course it is usually true that a party to some ongoing pattern of exchange can withdraw if the terms of exchange are too costly, but this is not the respect in which most international economic relationships are nonvoluntary from the point of view of their worse-off participants. Relationships might also be nonvoluntary if the relatively weaker partner lacks the resources to bargain effectively for different terms of exchange. In effect, the terms are set by the more powerful partner; they appear as a *fait accompli* to those who are unable to change them. Since withdrawal may be immensely costly (as, for example, it would be to a vulnerable poor country with only one export crop), there may be no practical alternative to accepting the terms of trade that are effectively dictated by those with greater power. This is not a situation to which one can be morally indifferent, because the reasons for the weak state's relative vulnerability are usually beyond its control, having to do, for example, with the uneven distribution of wealth-producing resources or the effects of past injustices.[68] It is a victim of natural and historical facts, from which others have no moral right to benefit. Thus, one needs to ask by what standards of fairness the international economic order can be assessed.

5. The Rights of States

I TURN now to another set of objections, according to which considerations of social cooperation at the national level justify distributive claims capable of overriding the requirements of a global difference principle. Typically, members of a wealthy nation might claim that they deserve a larger share than that provided by a global difference principle because of their superior technology, economic organization, and efficiency.[69]

Objections of this general sort might take several forms. First, it might be argued that even in an interdependent world, national society remains the primary locus of one's political identification. If one is moved to contribute to aggregate social welfare at any level, this level is most likely to be the national level. Therefore, differential rates of national

[68] Should a state be held responsible for its vulnerability or poverty to the extent that these are caused by the absence of effective population-control policies? I think not, but cannot argue it here. For a penetrating discussion, see Henry Shue, "Food, Population, and Wealth: Toward Global Principles of Justice."

[69] More crudely: "[N]ational wealth is something that is earned by the capacities of the country's people and the policies of its Government; it is not something that is just shifted around." Robert Moss, "Let's Look Out for No. 1!," p. 100.

contribution to the global welfare ought to be rewarded pro-
portionally. This is a plausible form of the objection; the
problem is that in this form it may not be an objection at all.
The difference principle itself recognizes the probability that
differential rates of reward may be needed as incentives for
contribution; it requires only that the distributive inequalities
that arise in such a system be to the greatest benefit of the
world's least advantaged group. To the extent that incentives
of the kind demanded by this version of the objection actually
do raise the economic expectations of the least advantaged
without harming them in other ways, they would not be inconsistent with the difference principle.

Such objections only count against a globalized difference
principle if they hold that a relatively wealthy nation could
claim more than its share under the difference principle.
That is, the objection must hold that some distributive inequalities are justified even though they are not to the
greatest benefit of the world's least advantaged group. How
could such claims be justified? One justification is on grounds
of personal entitlement, appealing to the intuition that value
created by someone's unaided labor or acquired through voluntary transfers is properly one's own, assuming that the initial distribution was just.[70] This second sort of argument
yields an extreme form of the objection. It holds that a nation
is entitled to its relative wealth because each of its citizens has
complied with the relevant rules of justice in acquiring raw
materials and transforming them into products of value.
These rules might require, respectively, that an equitable resource redistribution principle has been implemented, and
that no one's rights have been violated (for example, by imperial plunder) in the process of acquisition and production
leading to a nation's current economic position. (Note that my
arguments for a resource principle, in section 2, are not
touched by this sort of objection and would impose some
global distributive obligations even if the personal-entitlement view were correct in ruling out broader global principles.)

[70] This is Robert Nozick's view in *Anarchy, State, and Utopia*, ch. 7.

This interpretation of the objection is analogous to the conception of distributive justice that Rawls calls the "system of natural liberty." His objection to such views is that they allow people to compete for available positions on the basis of their talents, making no attempt to compensate for deprivations that some suffer because of natural chance and social contingencies. These things, as I have said, are held to be morally arbitrary, and hence unacceptable as standards for distribution.[71] I shall not rehearse this argument further here. But two things should be noted. The argument seems even more plausible from the global point of view since the disparity of possible starting points in world society is so much greater. The balance between "arbitrary" and "personal" contributions to my present well-being seems decisively tipped toward the arbitrary ones by the realization that, no matter what my talents, education, life goals, etc., I would have been virtually precluded from attaining my present level of well-being if I had been born in a much less developed society. Also, if Rawls's counterargument counts against natural-liberty views in the domestic case, then it defeats the present objection to a globalized difference principle as well. Citizens of a society cannot base their claims to a larger distributive share than that warranted by the difference principle on morally arbitrary factors.

A third, and probably the most plausible, form of this objection is that a wealthy nation may retain more than its share under a global difference principle, provided that some compensation for the benefits of global social cooperation is paid to less fortunate nations, and that the amount retained by the producing nation is used to promote domestic justice—for example, by increasing the prospects of the nation's own least favored group. The underlying intuition is that citizens owe some sort of special obligation to the less fortunate members of their own society that is capable of overriding their general obligation to improve the prospects of less advantaged groups elsewhere. This intuition is distinct from that in the personal-entitlement case, for it does not refer to any putative

[71] Rawls, *A Theory of Justice*, pp. 66-72.

individual right to the value created by one's labor or acquired through voluntary transfers. Instead, we are here concerned with supposedly conflicting rights and obligations that arise from membership in nested schemes of social cooperation, one embedded in the other.

An argument along these lines needs an account of how obligations to the sectional associations arise. It is tempting, though unhelpful, to bring in psychological considerations here: for example, one might point out that the sentiment of nationality is stronger than that of humanity and argue that the difference principle therefore applies in full force only inside national societies.[72] Now those who would pursue this line must recognize that any account of how institutional obligations arise that is sufficiently psychological to make plausible a general conflict of global and sectional obligations will probably be too psychological to apply to the large modern state.[73] If this is true, then proponents of this view face a dilemma: either they must endorse the strongly counterintuitive conclusion that obligations of justice may not even hold within large modern states and are appropriate primarily within smaller solidaristic communities or organic groups; or they must agree that obligations of justice may be justified by considerations other than those of strong common sentiment. The first alternative seems clearly unacceptable, but the second implies that domestic and international obligations cannot be distinguished with reference to the supposedly unique psychological features of membership in national societies.

Even if this last point is incorrect, there is a more fundamental problem with the suggestion that sentiments of nationality support especially strong intranational distributive obligations. The difficulty is that it is not obvious why we should attach objective moral weight to national sentiments even where they are widely felt. Why should sectional loyalties diminish global obligations based on participation in the world economy? (This question should be distinguished from that considered in section 4, concerning the realism of the as-

[72] For a suggestive account of a similar problem, see Michael Walzer, "The Obligation to Disobey."

[73] Compare Rawls, *A Theory of Justice*, p. 477.

sumption that persons are motivationally capable of acting on a global difference principle.)

To attempt to answer this question, it is necessary to look behind the sentiments that people experience to the forms of social interaction in which they take part. Accordingly, one might say that the greater degree or extent of social cooperation in national societies (compared with that in international society) justifies stronger intranational principles of justice. Imagine a world of two self-sufficient and internally just societies, A and B. Assume that this world satisfies the appropriate resource redistribution principle. Imagine also that the least-advantaged representative person in society A is considerably better off than his counterpart in society B. While the members of A may owe duties of mutual aid to the members of B, it is clear that they do not also have duties of justice, because the two societies, being individually self-sufficient, do not share membership in a cooperative scheme. Now suppose that the walls of self-sufficiency are breached very slightly; A trades its apples for B's pears. Does this mean that the difference principle suddenly applies to the world that comprises A and B, requiring A to share all of its wealth with B, even though almost all of its wealth is attributable to economic interaction within A? It seems not; one might say that an international difference principle can only command redistribution of the benefits derived from international social cooperation or economic interaction. It cannot touch the benefits of domestic cooperation.

It may be that some such objection will turn out to require modifications of a global difference principle. But there are reasons for doubting this. Roughly, it seems that there is a threshold of interdependence above which distributive requirements like a global difference principle are valid, but below which significantly weaker principles hold. To see why this formulation has intuitive appeal, consider another hypothetical case. Suppose that, *within* a society, there are closely knit local regions with higher levels of internal cooperation than the level of cooperation in society as a whole. Certainly there are many such regions within a society like the United States. The argument rehearsed above, applied to closely knit localities within national societies, would seem to give members of the localities special claims on portions of their wealth. This seems implausible, especially since such closely knit enclaves might well turn out to contain disproportionate numbers of the society's most advantaged classes. Why does this conclusion seem less plausible than that in the apples and pears case? It seems to me that the answer has to do with the fact that the apples and pears case looks like a case of voluntary, free market bargaining, which has only a marginal effect on the welfare of the members of each society, whereas we assume in the intranational case that there is a nonvoluntary society-wide system of economic institutions, which defines starting positions and assigns economic rights and duties. It is these institutions—what Rawls calls "the basic structure"[74]—that stand in need of justification, because, by defining the terms of cooperation, they have such deep and pervasive effects on the welfare of people to whom they apply regardless of consent.

The apples and pears case, of course, is hardly a faithful model of the contemporary world economy. Suppose that we add to the story to make it resemble the real world more closely. As my review of the current situation (section 3, part three) makes clear, we would have to add just those features of the contemporary world economy that find their domestic analogues in the basic structure to which principles of justice apply. As the web of transactions grows more complex, the resulting structure of economic and political institutions acquires great influence over the welfare of the participants, regardless of the extent to which any particular one makes use of the institutions. These features make the real world situation seem more like the case of subnational, closely knit regions, than like the apples and pears case.

These considerations suggest that the amount of social and economic interaction in a cooperative scheme does not provide a straightforward index of the strength of the distributive principle appropriate to it. The existence of a nonvoluntary institutional structure, and its pervasive effects on the

[74] Ibid., pp. 7-11.

welfare of the cooperators, seem to provide a better indication of the strength of the appropriate distributive requirements. This sort of consideration would not necessarily support a globalized difference principle in the apples and pears case; but it does explain why, above a threshold measure of social cooperation, the full force of the difference principle may come into play despite regional variations in the amount of cooperation.[75]

Someone might think that a fourth version of the objection could be formulated by taking into account considerations about capital accumulation on behalf of future generations within national societies. The argument would be that people have a right to assurance that the capital they save for the sake of their descendants will actually be used for that purpose, rather than be distributed globally as the global difference principle might require. The idea here is that national societies can be conceived as cooperative schemes extending over time, in which earlier generations make sacrifices to raise the level of well-being of succeeding generations.[76] On reflection, however, it should be clear that this view is not distinct from versions of the objection previously considered. In fact, it is parasitic on them; if the previous versions are found wanting, considerations about domestic capital accumulation do not strengthen them.

The key question is why these considerations are thought to undermine the argument for global redistribution. There seem to be two possible replies. First, on the model of inheritance, one might visualize capital accumulation as the result of saving within a family, with wealth passed from one generation to the next in a series of private transfers. On this

[75] I do not claim to have resolved entirely the problem that underlies this objection, although I believe that my remarks point in the right direction. It should be noticed, however, that what is at issue here is really a general problem for any theory that addresses itself to institutional structures rather than to particular transactions. One can always ask why institutional requirements should apply in full force to persons who make minimal use of the institutions they find themselves living under.

[76] Such an argument is made by W. H. Hutt, "Immigration under 'Economic Freedom,'" p. 36, quoted in Danielson, "Theories, Intuitions, and World-Wide Distributive Justice," p. 335.

view, considerations about capital accumulation count against global redistribution for the same reason that they count against all redistribution: redistribution involves a violation of rights of inheritance. But rights of inheritance, in this sense, are simply species of the more general right of voluntary transfer on which natural-liberty and personal-entitlement views are based. The rejection of such views takes with it the justification of unrestricted rights of inheritance and therefore dissolves the foundation of the related objections to global redistribution.

The other reply to the question about why considerations about capital accumulation undermine the argument for global redistribution involves the model of social savings. Capital accumulated by one generation is passed on within a society but is distributed according to the society's allocative decision procedure. The explanation of why social savings should be used for the benefit of the members of the society in which they were generated rather than be redistributed globally must be that members of a national society have special claims to (portions of) their wealth, perhaps based on a supposed obligation to give special attention to the needs of the less fortunate members of their own society. But, again, such a view needs an account of how special obligations to sectional associations arise, and the attempt to supply such an account will encounter the same problems discussed with respect to the third interpretation of the objection. It follows that considerations about capital accumulation on behalf of future generations do not lend any independent strength to the objection that members of domestic societies have special rights to portions of their own product that undermine a global difference principle.

I have considered several versions of the objection that relatively well-off states have special claims on portions of their domestic products that would offset their global redistributive obligations. None of these versions of the objection appears to damage the argument for a global difference principle. However, it is worth pointing out that global redistributive obligations would not be entirely extinguished even if one or another of these versions of the objection could be made convincing. Suppose, for example, that the second version, based on individual entitlement, could be defended. It would not follow that there are no international redistributive obligations founded on justice because that version of the objection involves two premises that are probably contrary to fact: first, that the distribution of natural resources conforms to the requirements of the global resource principle, and second, that the effects of past injustices (stemming either from resource exploitation or violation of the relevant principles of justice in acquisition and transfer) have been rectified. A showing that either premise is false would lend support to an argument for some global redistribution to compensate for the uneven distribution of natural resources or to rectify past injustices. Or suppose that the third version of the objection, based on the greater intensity of social cooperation inside as compared to across national boundaries, could be defended. At a minimum it would still follow from my previous arguments that a global resource principle applies and that that portion of the global product actually attributable to global (as opposed to domestic) social cooperation should be redistributed according to a suitably restricted difference principle. In any event, if this general line of objection could somehow be made good, the question would not be whether there are global distributive obligations founded on justice, but rather to what extent considerations relevant to the special features of cooperation within national societies modify the strongly egalitarian tendencies of the global standard. And, in view of the large distributive inequalities that currently exist, it seems likely that the existing distribution would still be unjust.

6. Applications to the Nonideal World

THUS far, we have reached two main conclusions. First, assuming national self-sufficiency, Rawls's derivation of the principles of justice for the law of nations is incomplete. He neglects resource redistribution, a subject that would surely be on the minds of the parties to the international original position. But second, the self-sufficiency assumption, upon which Rawls's entire consideration of the law of nations rests, is not justified by the facts of contemporary international relations. The state-centered image of the world has lost its normative relevance because of the rise of global economic interdependence. Hence, principles of distributive justice must apply in the first instance to the world as a whole, and derivatively to nation-states. The appropriate global principle is Rawls's difference principle, perhaps modified by some provision for intranational redistribution in relatively wealthy states once a threshold level of international redistributive obligations has been met. In conclusion, I would like to consider the implications of this ideal theory for international politics and global change in the nonideal world.

We might begin by asking, in general, what relevance social ideals have for politics in the real world. Their most obvious function is to describe a goal toward which efforts at political change should aim. A very important natural duty is the natural duty of justice, which "requires us to support and to comply with just institutions that exist and . . . constrains us to further just arrangements not yet established, at least if this can be done without too much cost to ourselves."[77] By supplying a description of the nature and aims of a just world order, ideal theory "provides . . . the only basis for the systematic grasp of these more pressing problems."[78] Ideal theory, then, supplies a set of criteria for the formulation and criticism of strategies of political action in the nonideal world, at least when the consequences of political action can be predicted with sufficient confidence to establish their relationship to the social ideal. Clearly, this task is not easy, given the complexities of social change and the uncertainties of prediction in political affairs. There is the additional complication that social change is often wrongly conceived as a progressive approximation of actual institutions to ideal prescriptions in which people's welfare steadily improves. An adequate social theory must avoid both the pitfalls of a false incrementalism

[77] Rawls, *A Theory of Justice*, p. 155.   [78] Ibid., p. 9.

and what economists call the problem of second best.[79] But a coherent social ideal is a necessary condition of any attempt to conquer these difficulties.

Ideal justice, in other words, comes into nonideal politics by way of the natural duty to secure just institutions where none presently exist. The moral problem posed by distinguishing ideal from nonideal theory is that in the nonideal world, the natural duty of justice is likely to conflict with other natural duties, while the theory provides no mechanism for resolving such conflicts. For example, it is possible that a political decision that is likely to make institutions more just may also involve violations of other natural duties, like the duty of mutual aid or the duty not to harm the innocent. Perhaps reforming some unjust institution will require disappointment of expectations formed under the old order. The principles of natural duty in the nonideal world are relatively unsystematic, and we have no way of knowing which should win out in case of conflict. Rawls recognizes the inevitability of irresolvable conflicts in some situations, but, as Feinberg has suggested, he underestimates the role that an intuitive balancing of conflicting duties must play in nonideal circumstances.[80] It may be that the solution to problems of political change in radically unjust situations must rely on a consequentialist calculation of costs and benefits.[81] If this is true, then political change in conditions of great injustice marks one kind of limit of the contract doctrine, for in these cases the principles of justice collapse into consequentialism. Nevertheless, these considerations shed light on the normative problems we encounter in coping with global injustice, as I shall try to show briefly with respect to the question of development aid and international economic reform.

The duty to further just institutions where none exist endows certain political claims made in the nonideal world with a moral seriousness that does not derive merely from the

[79] On the problem of second best, see Brian Barry, *Political Argument*, pp. 261-62.

[80] Rawls, *A Theory of Justice*, p. 303; Joel Feinberg, "Duty and Obligation in the Nonideal World."

[81] As Rawls implies. *A Theory of Justice*, pp. 352-53.

duties that bind people regardless of the existence of co-operative ties. When the contract doctrine is interpreted globally, claims made by, or on behalf of, the less advantaged in today's nonideal world appeal to principles of global justice as well as to the duty of mutual aid. Those who are in a position to respond to these claims must take account of the reasons provided by the principles of justice in weighing their response. Furthermore, by interpreting the principles globally, we remove a major source of justifying reasons for not responding more fully to such claims. These reasons derive from statist concerns—for example, from a supposed right to reinvest domestic surpluses in national societies that are already relatively favored from a global point of view. Obviously, political considerations may make unavoidable levels of domestic reinvestment in excess of those that would be ideally just. But it should not be argued that citizens of wealthy nations have general rights to retain their domestic products, which override their obligations to advance the welfare of less-advantaged persons elsewhere.

These theoretical points have several practical consequences. Most clearly, the existence of global redistributive obligations strengthens the moral case for foreign aid. In the past, aid has often been regarded as a kind of international charity. Like charitable contributions, contributions to the economic development of poor countries have been understood to be morally discretionary and properly subject to various kinds of political restrictions. Moreover, the duty to give aid could be acknowledged without compromising the moral basis of existing legal property rights. Once the existence of global redistributive obligations founded on justice is recognized, however, the view of aid as charity must be given up. It is inappropriate to regard foreign assistance as discretionary in the way charitable contributions are, nor can the attachment of political conditions be easily defended (except in one sort of case, noted below). Furthermore, one cannot acknowledge a duty of justice to contribute to economic development elsewhere without acknowledging that existing legal property rights lack a firm moral foundation. Aid should not be regarded as a voluntary contribution of a portion of a state's own wealth, but rather as a transfer of wealth required to redress distributive injustice.[82]

At the same time, the fact that the global difference principle ultimately applies to persons suggests that it might not be fully satisfied simply by intercountry transfers. I emphasized above that it is the least advantaged representative *person* whose position is to be maximized. In the context of nonideal theory, this has two important implications. First, in formulating aid programs, donor countries and agencies should take account of the special weight to be placed on improvements in the welfare of the world's worst-off groups, and with respect to particular recipient countries, attempt to direct aid primarily at the satisfaction of minimum human needs. (It does not follow, though, that the inability successfully to do so undercuts the case for aid.[83] Second-best policies may be available, and second-best policies are usually better than none.) Second, in countries where extreme poverty is partially a result of large domestic income inequalities, pressure should be brought if possible for changes in policy or structural reforms aimed at reducing internal inequalities. In both cases, it might be objected that the attempt to implement the global difference principle involves a violation of state autonomy; however, if the view taken in part two, above, is correct, in these cases such an objection would be invalid.

We should also consider the implications of a global difference principle for the reform of the international economic

[82] See Thomas Nagel, "Poverty and Food: Why Charity Is Not Enough," pp. 54-61. In this and the following several paragraphs, I assume for illustrative purposes that increased foreign assistance from rich countries, and reforms in the institutional structure of the world economy, can be designed and implemented in ways that actually would contribute to a long-term improvement in the absolute position of the world's worst-off groups. This assumption seems plausible, but it should not be mistaken for the different assumption that such an improvement will result from implementation of aid programs and institutional reforms alone. What is of overriding importance for most of the poor countries is that they should radically increase their agricultural productivity and develop modern industrial sectors. Foreign assistance and international economic reforms should be evaluated primarily in terms of the contributions they make to these largely indigenous processes. See further W. Arthur Lewis, *The Evolution of the International Economic Order.*

[83] As Richard Cooper suggests. "Panel Discussion," p. 355.

order. One reason is that the institutions and practices of international finance and trade influence the distribution of global income and wealth and can be adapted to help compensate for the unjust inequalities that arise under the institutional status quo. A more subtle, but perhaps a more important, reason for using these institutions for redistributive purposes is that doing so provides a way around the assurance problem noted above (section 4). As I observed, citizens of a wealthy nation might object to the relative sacrifices required for global redistribution on the ground that there is no assurance that wealthy persons elsewhere will do their share. In the absence of coercive global institutions capable of coordinating and enforcing redistributive policies, such sacrifices might give others unfair advantages. This objection does not defeat the force of redistributive obligations, but it does emphasize the importance of devising mechanisms for coordinating the redistributive policies of the various international actors so that the necessary assurance can be provided. For example, the rules governing international trade and finance, and the international institutions that implement them, might be adjusted to promote redistribution toward poor countries, and to encourage them to adjust their internal affairs so as to maximize the prospects of their (internally) least advantaged groups. These mechanisms minimize the assurance problem because they are embodied in institutions with the capacity to enforce compliance by excluding offenders from participation. While I cannot assess the relative desirability of these mechanisms of redistribution on economic grounds, one might argue on grounds of distributive justice for such policies as a generalized system of preferential tariffs for poor countries and the removal of nontariff barriers to trade, or for the use of Special Drawing Rights in the International Monetary Fund as a form of development assistance.[84] If this is true, then nondiscriminatory tariffs and

[84] On trade preferences for poor countries in developed-country markets, see Harry G. Johnson, *Economic Policies toward Less Developed Countries*, pp. 163-206; and, on the SDR "link," see James Howe, "SDRs and Development: Let's Spread Them Around."

distribution of additional international liquidity in proportion to present holdings of Special Drawing Rights are not "neutral," as it is sometimes alleged, since the effect of such policies is to perpetuate an unjust distribution. Perhaps some other mechanisms of redistribution would be preferable from the point of view of economic efficiency—for example, direct transfer payments to poor countries—but, since such mechanisms may well be politically impossible at present, and since they raise the assurance problem more sharply, they seem less preferable from the point of view of distributive justice than policies like those suggested above.[85]

Finally, I would like to note a more remote implication of the global interpretation of the contract doctrine. It is worth attention because it illustrates how global principles that apply primarily to institutions and their policies can influence thinking about individual action, and in particular, about participation in a nation's military forces. I indicated above that principles of justice, on a global view, apply primarily to the world as a whole and then derivatively to states. This suggests that global principles could supply reasons that are capable of overriding the rule that demands compliance with internally just domestic regimes. One important consequence is that conscientious refusal to participate in a nation's armed forces would have far broader possible justifications than on the account given in Rawls,[86] assuming for the moment that, given the great destructiveness of modern weapons and war strategies, participation in national armed forces can be justified at all. To take a somewhat unlikely example, a war of self-defense fought by an affluent nation against a poorer nation pressing legitimate claims under the global principles (for

[85] The generalized system of preferences and the SDR "link" are simply examples of mechanisms that might be used to promote global redistribution without raising the problem of assurance. There are many others, like "indexation" of commodity prices, transfer of technology on a concessional basis, and refinancing or forgiving of debts on an internationally coordinated schedule. See Reginald Herbold Green and Hans W. Singer, "Toward a Rational and Equitable New International Economic Order: A Case for Negotiated Structural Changes."

[86] Rawls, *A Theory of Justice*, pp. 377-82.

example, for increased food aid) might be unjustifiable, giving rise to a justified refusal to participate in the affluent nation's armed forces.

These points show that the contract doctrine, despite limitations noted here, sheds light on the distinctive normative problems of the shift from statist to global conceptions of world order. The extension of economic and cultural relationships beyond national borders has often been thought to undermine the moral legitimacy of the state; the extension of the contract doctrine gives a systematic account of why this is so, and of the consequences for problems of justice in the nonideal world, by emphasizing the role of social cooperation as the foundation of just social arrangements. When, as now, national boundaries do not set off discrete, self-sufficient societies, we may not regard them as morally decisive features of the earth's social geography. For purposes of moral choice, we must, instead, regard the world from the perspective of an original position from which matters of national citizenship are excluded by an extended veil of ignorance.

Conclusion

I HAVE argued that prevailing theoretical conceptions of international relations are inadequate and lead to incorrect normative principles of international practice. A more satisfactory normative theory of international politics should include a notion of state autonomy explicitly connected with considerations of domestic social justice, and principles of international distributive justice that establish a fair division of natural resources, income, and wealth among persons situated in diverse national societies. Such a theory not only helps to clarify and deepen our moral intuitions about particular issues in international politics, but also provides structure and purpose for the empirical study of international relations. I would like to conclude with some summary observations about these main points.

Most writers in the modern tradition of political theory, and many contemporary students of international politics, have conceived of international relations on the analogy of the state of nature. States are pictured as purposive and autonomous agents coexisting in an anarchic environment without significant social, political, or economic activity and devoid of stable expectations regarding the agents' behavior with respect to one another. According to the most extreme views, like Hobbes's, moral judgments are inappropriate in such an environment. But the conception of international relations as a state of nature is empirically inaccurate and theoretically misleading. It is inaccurate because it fails to capture either the increasingly complex pattern of social interaction characteristic of international relations or the variety of expectations, practices, and institutions that order these interactions. Indeed, international relations is coming more and more to resemble domestic society in these respects, which are analogous to those on which the justification of normative principles for domestic society depends. The more extreme conceptions are theoretically misleading as well, for they are versions of international moral skepticism, a position that one cannot consistently maintain without being pushed back into a more general skepticism about all morality.

Even some (like writers in the modern natural law tradition such as Pufendorf and Wolff) who have avoided international moral skepticism have been misled by the conception of international relations as a state of nature. This is because they infer from the analogy of states and persons that states have some sort of right of autonomy in international relations analogous to the right of autonomy possessed by persons in domestic society. In effect, the supposed autonomy of states insulates them from external moral criticism and political interference. This claim is the basis of traditional arguments for the nonintervention principle, and of more recent arguments for the principle of self-determination and against the effects of imperialism and economic dependence. Against this view, I argued that the idea that all states have a right of autonomy is incorrect because the analogy of states and persons is imperfect. States are not sources of ends in the same sense as are persons. Instead, states are systems of shared practices and institutions within which communities of persons establish and advance their ends. The appropriate analogue of individual autonomy in the international realm is not national autonomy but conformity of a society's basic institutions with appropriate principles of social justice.

The refutation of international moral skepticism and the critique of the idea of state autonomy clear the way for the formulation of a more satisfactory normative international political theory. One element that should be part of any such theory is an account of international distributive justice. International distributive principles establish the terms on which persons in distinct societies can fairly expect each other's cooperation in common institutions and practices. These terms involve the distribution of the benefits gained from natural resources as well as those gained from social cooperation proper. In criticizing the conception of international relations as a state of nature, I observed that international relations is coming more and more to resemble domestic society in several respects relevant to the justification of (domestic) principles of justice. In part three, I explored the implications of this observation by considering how Rawls's theory of domestic distributive justice might be extended to

international relations in recognition of the increasing extent
and significance of international economic interdependence.
The result is a global distributive principle that might require
radical changes in the structure of the world economic order
and in the distribution of natural resources, income, and
wealth. Moreover, because global distributive principles apply
ultimately to persons rather than states, they may require that
interstate transfers and international institutional reforms be
designed to achieve specific domestic distributional results.
Once again, I must stress that such principles—even radical
ones—furnish only a prima facie warrant for practical efforts
at structural and distributional reform, since hypotheses from
the empirical study of international political economy would
be required to specify in detail the character of desirable reforms and to assess the chances of success of attempts to implement them. This is one respect in which the program of
international studies should be shaped by normative concerns
(a respect in which international studies thus far has failed
conspicuously to provide much practical help).

The point of view suggested by my discussion might be distinguished from prevailing views as follows. The dominant
normative conception of international relations in Anglo-
American writing is the Hobbesian conception. It combines
the analogy of international relations and the state of nature
with a conception of ethics according to which moral judgment is inappropriate outside of sovereign political communities. This view I have called international moral skepticism. Against it, writers of the modern natural law tradition
have maintained that moral judgment is appropriate in the
global state of nature, but that the standards to which moral
judgment should appeal are relatively weak. In particular,
considerations of justice occupy an inferior position in this
conception, which values international order more highly.
This is the morality of states. If my main contentions are correct, however, a third conception of international morality is
increasingly plausible. Following Kant, we might call this a
cosmopolitan conception.[1] It is cosmopolitan in the sense that

[1] Kant uses this term to characterize the law of a possible universal community of nations. *The Metaphysical Elements of Justice* [1797], p. 125.

it is concerned with the moral relations of members of a universal community in which state boundaries have a merely derivative significance. There are no reasons of basic principle for exempting the internal affairs of states from external moral scrutiny, and it is possible that members of some states might have obligations of justice with respect to persons elsewhere.

It would be a mistake to assimilate the distinctions I have drawn among conceptions of normative international political theory to another tripartite distinction among approaches to the empirical study of international relations. As Robert Gilpin argues, international politics can be studied from "mercantilist," "liberal," or "Marxist" perspectives.[2] But it is not necessary (although it may often be true) that "mercantilists" also be skeptics, or "liberals" statists, or "Marxists" cosmopolitans.[3] These empirical approaches are not distinguished from one another by disagreement about principles of normative theory; rather, they divide according to the heuristic value they attribute to certain higher-order empirical generalizations about international political economy (e.g., for "Marxists," that outcomes in international politics are best predicted with reference to the relative positions of the actors in the structure of the world economy).[4] I certainly do not dispute the view, associated with Aristotle and Weber, that normative concerns justify and shape the empirical study of politics; I claim only that there is no necessary one-to-one correspondence between particular empirical approaches and the three conceptions of international political theory distinguished above.

As I have suggested at various points, a cosmopolitan conception of international morality is not equivalent to, nor does

[2] Robert Gilpin, *U.S. Power and the Multinational Corporation*, ch. 1.

[3] Was Marx himself a statist, or a cosmopolitan, or neither? Or, if his texts are ambiguous or noncommittal, does his international theory clearly presuppose either type of view? These questions are fascinating, and I regret that I am unable to provide satisfactory answers. For helpful comments, from different points of view, see R. N. Berki, "On Marxian Thought and the Problem of International Relations"; and Alan Gilbert, "Marx on Internationalism and War."

[4] Gilpin, *U.S. Power*, p. 30.

it necessarily imply, a political program like those often identified with political universalism, world federalism, or "world
order." It is important to distinguish moral structures from
political ones, and to recognize that global normative principles might be implemented otherwise than by global institutions conceived on the analogy of the state. This is true in the
context of ideal theory and even more so in the nonideal
world. Much of the misunderstanding of cosmopolitan normative theories, among their opponents, and of naiveté about
universalist political programs, among their advocates, stems
from failure to understand this fact. In the application of
principles to practice, normative and empirical considerations
interact in complex ways. I have tried to indicate some of
these in my discussion of nonintervention, self-determination, and international distributive justice. Basing decisions to
act on normative principles without paying attention to these
complexities is certain to yield bad decisions. (This is the ker-
nel of truth in the realist objections to "moralism" considered
in part one.)

Thus far, such systematic moral debate about international
relations as has taken place has been between adherents of
international skepticism and the morality of states. However,
as I hope to have made clear, the more pressing issues are
those that divide the morality of states from a cosmopolitan
morality. A normative political theory of international relations that takes account of my criticisms of prevailing views
would be cosmopolitan and would situate controversy about
morality in world affairs on more fruitful terrain.

Works Cited

Dates enclosed in brackets indicate the year of original publication. For articles in collections, this means the year the article was originally published. For works published in more than one edition, the date refers to the year of publication of the first edition.

1. WORKS FIRST PUBLISHED BEFORE 1900

Acton, John E.E.D. (Lord Acton). "Nationality" [1862]. *History of Freedom and Other Essays*. London: Macmillan and Co., 1922, pp. 270-300.

Austin, John. *The Province of Jurisprudence Determined* [1832]. London: Weidenfield and Nicolson, 1954.

Bodin, Jean. *Six Books of the Commonwealth* [1576]. Abridged and trans. M. J. Tooley. Oxford: Basil Blackwell, n.d. (1955).

Bosanquet, Bernard. *The Philosophical Theory of the State* [1899]. 3d ed. London: Macmillan and Co., 1920.

Grotius, Hugo. *De jure belli ac pacis libri tres* [1625]. Trans. Francis W. Kelsey. The Classics of International Law, no. 3, vol. 2. Oxford: Clarendon Press, 1925.

Hall, William E. *International Law* [1880]. 8th ed. Ed. A. Pearce Higgins. Oxford: Clarendon Press, 1924.

Hegel, G.W.F. *Hegel's Philosophy of Right* [1821]. Trans. T. M. Knox. Oxford: Clarendon Press, 1952.

Hobbes, Thomas. *De Corpore Politico* [1650]. *The English Works of Thomas Hobbes*. Ed. Sir William Molesworth. Vol. 4. London: John Bohn, 1845, pp. 77-228.

——. *Human Nature* [1650]. *The English Works of Thomas Hobbes*. Ed. Sir William Molesworth. Vol. 4. London: John Bohn, 1845, pp. 1-76.

——. *Leviathan* [1651]. *The English Works of Thomas Hobbes*. Ed. Sir William Molesworth. Vol. 3. London: John Bohn, 1841.

——. *Philosophical Rudiments concerning Government and Society* [De Cive] [1651]. *The English Works of Thomas Hobbes*. Ed. Sir William Molesworth. Vol. 2. London: John Bohn, 1841.

Hume, David. "Of the Original Contract" [1748]. *Essays: Moral, Political and Literary*. London: Oxford University Press, 1963, pp. 452-73.

Hume, David. *A Treatise of Human Nature* [1739-1740]. Ed. L. A. Selby-Bigge. Oxford: Clarendon Press, 1888.

Kant, Immanuel. *The Metaphysical Elements of Justice* [1797]. Part 1 of *The Metaphysics of Morals*. Trans. John Ladd. Indianapolis: Bobbs-Merrill, 1965.

———. "On the Common Saying: 'This May be True in Theory, but it does not Apply in Practice' " [1793]. *Kant's Political Writings*. Ed. Hans Reiss and trans. H. B. Nisbet. Cambridge: Cambridge University Press, 1971, pp. 61-92.

———. *Perpetual Peace* [1795]. *Kant's Political Writings*. Ed. Hans Reiss and trans. H. B. Nisbet. Cambridge: Cambridge University Press, 1971, pp. 93-130.

Locke, John. *Two Treatises of Government* [1689]. 2d ed. Ed. Peter Laslett. Cambridge: Cambridge University Press, 1967.

Machiavelli, Niccolò. *Discourses on the First Ten Books of Titus Livius* [1531]. Trans. Christian E. Detmold. *The Prince and the Discourses*. Ed. Max Lerner. New York: Random House, 1950, pp. 101-540.

———. *The Prince* [1532]. Trans. Luigi Ricci. *The Prince and the Discourses*. Ed. Max Lerner. New York: Random House, 1950, pp. 3-98.

Marx, Karl. *A Contribution to the Critique of Political Economy* [1859]. Trans. S. W. Ryazanskaya. New York: International Publishers, 1970.

———. "The Future Results of British Rule in India" [1853]. *Karl Marx on Colonialism and Modernization*. Ed. Shlomo Avineri. Garden City, N.Y.: Doubleday and Co., 1968, pp. 125-31.

Mill, John Stuart. *Considerations on Representative Government* [1861]. *Collected Works of John Stuart Mill*. Ed. J. M. Robson. Vol. 19. Toronto: University of Toronto Press, 1977, pp. 371-577.

———. "A Few Words on Non-intervention" [1859]. *Dissertations and Discussions: Political, Philosophical, and Historical*. Vol. 3. London: Longmans, Green, Reader, and Dyer, 1867, pp. 153-78.

———. *On Liberty* [1859]. *Collected Works of John Stuart Mill*. Ed. J. M. Robson. Vol. 18. Toronto: University of Toronto Press, 1977, pp. 217-310.

———. "Vindication of the French Revolution of February, 1848" [1849]. *Dissertations and Discussions: Political, Philosophical, and Historical*. Vol. 2. London: John W. Parker and Son, 1859, pp. 335-410.

Pufendorf, Samuel. *De jure naturae et gentium, libri octo* [1688]. Trans. C. H. and W. A. Oldfather. The Classics of International Law, no. 17, vol. 2. Oxford: Clarendon Press, 1934.

Rousseau, Jean-Jacques. *Discours sur l'inégalité* [1755]. *The Political Writings of Jean-Jacques Rousseau*. Ed. C. E. Vaughan. Vol. 1. New York: John Wiley and Sons, 1962, pp. 124-220.

——. *Du contrat social* [1762]. *The Political Writings of Jean-Jacques Rousseau*. Ed. C. E. Vaughan. Vol. 2. New York: John Wiley and Sons, 1962, pp. 21-134.

——. "L'état de guerre" [1896; written 1753-1755?]. *The Political Writings of Jean-Jacques Rousseau*. Ed. C. E. Vaughan. Vol. 1. New York: John Wiley and Sons, 1962, pp. 293-307.

Sidgwick, Henry. *The Elements of Politics* [1891]. 4th ed. London: Macmillan and Co., 1919.

Vattel, Emerich de. *The Law of Nations or the Principles of Natural Law* [*Le droit des gens*] [1758]. Trans. Charles G. Fenwick. The Classics of International Law, no. 4, vol. 3. Washington, D.C.: The Carnegie Institution, 1916.

Wolff, Christian. *Jus gentium methodo scientifica pertractatum* [1749]. Trans. Joseph H. Drake. The Classics of International Law, no. 13, vol. 2. Oxford: Clarendon Press, 1934.

2. WORKS FIRST PUBLISHED AFTER 1900

Acheson, Dean. "Ethics in International Relations Today." Address given at Amherst College, December 9, 1964. *The New York Times*, December 10, 1964, p. 16.

Amdur, Robert. "Rawls' Theory of Justice: Domestic and International Perspectives." *World Politics* 29, no. 3 (April 1977), pp. 438-61.

Aron, Raymond. *Peace and War: A Theory of International Relations*. Trans. Richard Howard and Annette Baker Fox. Garden City, N.Y.: Doubleday and Co., 1966.

Baier, Kurt. *The Moral Point of View: A Rational Basis for Ethics*. Ithaca, N.Y.: Cornell University Press, 1958.

Baldwin, David A. "Foreign Aid, Intervention, and Influence." *World Politics* 21, no. 3 (April 1969), pp. 425-47.

Baldwin, Robert E., and David A. Kay. "International Trade and International Relations." *International Organization* 29, no. 1 (Winter 1975), pp. 99-131.

Baran, Paul A. *The Political Economy of Growth* [1957]. New York: Monthly Review Press, 1968.

Barker, Ernest. *National Character and the Factors in Its Formation*. London: Methuen, 1927.

Barkun, Michael. *Law without Sanctions*. New Haven: Yale University Press, 1968.

Barnet, Richard, and Ronald Müller. *Global Reach*. New York: Simon and Schuster, 1974.

Barratt Brown, Michael. *After Imperialism*. Rev. ed. New York: Heineman, 1970.

———. *The Economics of Imperialism*. Harmondsworth, Middlesex: Penguin, 1974.

Barry, Brian. *The Liberal Theory of Justice*. Oxford: Clarendon Press, 1973.

———. *Political Argument*. London: Routledge and Kegan Paul, 1965.

———. "Warrender and His Critics." *Philosophy* 42, no. 164 (April 1968), pp. 117-37.

Beales, A.C.F. *The History of Peace: A Short Account of the Organized Movements for International Peace*. New York: Dial Press, 1931.

Beitz, Charles R. "Human Rights and Social Justice." *Human Rights and United States Foreign Policy: Principles and Applications*. Ed. Peter G. Brown and Douglas MacLean. Lexington, Mass.: Lexington Books, 1979.

———. "Justice and International Relations." *Philosophy and Public Affairs* 4, no. 4 (Summer 1975), pp. 360-89.

Benn, S. I., and R. S. Peters. *The Principles of Political Thought: Social Principles and the Democratic State* [1959]. New York: Free Press, 1965.

Bergsten, C. Fred, Thomas Horst, and Theodore H. Moran. *American Multinationals and American Interests*. Washington, D.C.: The Brookings Institution, 1978.

Bergsten, C. Fred, Robert O. Keohane, and Joseph S. Nye, Jr. "International Economics and International Politics: A Framework for Analysis." *International Organization* 29, no. 1 (Winter 1975), pp. 3-36.

Berki, R. N. "On Marxian Thought and the Problem of International Relations." *World Politics* 24, no. 1 (October 1971), pp. 80-105.

Bodenheimer, Suzanne. "Dependency and Imperialism: The Roots of Latin American Underdevelopment." *Politics and Society* 1, no. 3 (May 1971), pp. 327-57.

Bozeman, Adda B. *The Future of Law in a Multicultural World*. Princeton: Princeton University Press, 1971.

Brandt, Richard B. *Ethical Theory: The Problems of Normative and Critical Ethics*. Englewood Cliffs, N.J.: Prentice-Hall, 1959.

Brewin, Christopher. "Justice in International Relations." *The Reason of States*. Ed. Michael Donelan. London: George Allen and Unwin, 1978, pp. 142-52.

Brierly, J. L. *The Law of Nations*. 6th ed. Ed. Humphrey Waldock. Oxford: Clarendon Press, 1963.

Brown, Seyom. *New Forces in World Politics*. Washington, D.C.: The Brookings Institution, 1974.

Brownlie, Ian. *Principles of Public International Law*. 2d ed. Oxford: Clarendon Press, 1973.

Buchanan, James M. *The Demand and Supply of Public Goods*. Chicago: Rand McNally, 1968.

Bull, Hedley. "The Grotian Conception of International Society." *Diplomatic Investigations*. Ed. Herbert Butterfield and Martin Wight. London: George Allen and Unwin, 1966, pp. 51-73.

————. "Society and Anarchy in International Relations." *Diplomatic Investigations*. Ed. Herbert Butterfield and Martin Wight. London: George Allen and Unwin, 1966, pp. 35-50.

Cardozo, Michael N. "Intervention: Benefaction as Justification." *Essays on Intervention*. Ed. Roland J. Stanger. Columbus: Ohio State University Press, 1964, pp. 63-85.

Carr, Edward Hallett. *The Twenty Years' Crisis, 1919-1939*. 2d ed. New York: Harper and Row, 1964.

Chase-Dunn, Christopher. "The Effects of International Economic Dependence on Development and Inequality: A Cross-national Study." *American Sociological Review* 40, no. 6 (December 1975), pp. 720-38.

Claude, Inis L. *Power and International Relations*. New York: Random House, 1962.

Cobban, Alfred. *The Nation State and National Self-determination*. [Rev. ed.] London: Collins, 1969.

Cohen, Marshall, Thomas Nagel, and Thomas Scanlon, eds. *War and Moral Responsibility*. Princeton: Princeton University Press, 1974.

Cohen, Stephen F. *Bukharin and the Bolshevik Revolution: A Political Biography, 1888-1938*. New York: Alfred A. Knopf, 1973.

Connor, Walker. "Nation-Building or Nation-Destroying?" *World Politics* 24, no. 3 (April 1972), pp. 319-55.

————. "Self-Determination: The New Phase." *World Politics* 20, no. 1 (October 1967), pp. 30-53.

Cooper, Richard N. "Economic Assumptions of the Case for Liberal Trade." *Toward a New World Trade Policy: The Maidenhead Papers*. Ed. C. Fred Bergsten. Lexington, Mass.: Lexington Books, 1975, pp. 19-31.

Cooper, Richard N. "Economic Interdependence and Foreign Policy in the Seventies." *World Politics* 24, no. 2 (January 1972), pp. 159-81.

———. "Panel Discussion." *The New International Economic Order: The North-South Debate.* Ed. Jagdish N. Bhagwati. Cambridge, Mass.: MIT Press, 1977, pp. 354-58.

———. "Prolegomena to the Choice of an International Monetary System." *International Organization* 29, no. 1 (Winter 1975), pp. 63-97.

Cox, Richard. *Locke on War and Peace.* Oxford: Clarendon Press, 1960.

Danielson, Peter. "Theories, Intuitions and the Problem of World-Wide Distributive Justice." *Philosophy of the Social Sciences* 3, no. 4 (December 1973), pp. 331-40.

Denzer, Horst. *Moralphilosophie und Naturrecht bei Samuel Pufendorf.* Munich: C. H. Beck, 1972.

Deutsch, Karl W. *Nationalism and Social Communication: An Inquiry into the Foundations of Nationality.* 2d ed. Cambridge, Mass.: MIT Press, 1966.

Durkheim, Emile. *Moral Education* [1925]. Trans. Everett K. Wilson and Herman Schnurer. New York: Free Press, 1961.

Dworkin, Gerald. "Non-neutral Principles." *Journal of Philosophy* 71, no. 14 (August 15, 1974), pp. 491-506.

———. "Paternalism." *Morality and the Law.* Ed. Richard Wasserstrom. Belmont, Calif.: Wadsworth Publishing Co., 1971, pp. 107-26.

Emerson, Rupert. *From Empire to Nation.* Cambridge, Mass.: Harvard University Press, 1960.

———. "Self-Determination." *American Journal of International Law* 65, no. 3 (July 1971), pp. 459-75.

Evans, Peter B. "National Autonomy and Economic Development: Critical Perspectives on Multinational Corporations in Poor Countries." *Transnational Relations and World Politics.* Ed. Robert O. Keohane and Joseph S. Nye, Jr. Cambridge, Mass.: Harvard University Press, 1972, pp. 325-42.

Fagen, Richard R. "Equity in the South in the Context of North-South Relations." *Rich and Poor Nations in the Global Economy.* By Albert Fishlow et al. New York: McGraw-Hill, 1978.

Falk, Richard A. "International Jurisdiction: Horizontal and Vertical Conceptions of Legal Order." *Temple Law Quarterly* 32, no. 3 (Spring 1959), pp. 295-320.

————. *Legal Order in a Violent World*. Princeton: Princeton University Press, 1968, pp. 336-53.

Feinberg, Joel. "Collective Responsibility." *Journal of Philosophy* 65, no. 21 (November 7, 1968), pp. 674-88.

————. "Duty and Obligation in the Nonideal World." *Journal of Philosophy* 70, no. 9 (May 10, 1973), pp. 263-75.

Findlay, Ronald. *Trade and Specialization*. Harmondsworth, Middlesex: Penguin, 1970.

Fisher, Roger. "Bringing Law to Bear on Governments." *Harvard Law Review* 74, no. 6 (April 1961), pp. 1,130-40.

Foot, Philippa. "Moral Beliefs." *Proceedings of the Aristotelian Society*, n.s. 59 (1958-1959), pp. 83-104.

Frank, André Gunder. "Capitalist Development of Underdevelopment in Chile." *Capitalism and Underdevelopment in Latin America*. Rev. ed. New York: Monthly Review Press, 1969, pp. 1-120.

————. "The Development of Underdevelopment." *Latin America: Underdevelopment or Revolution*. New York: Monthly Review Press, 1969, pp. 3-20.

Frankel, Charles. *Morality and U.S. Foreign Policy*. Headline Series no. 224. New York: Foreign Policy Association, 1975.

Frankena, W. K. *Ethics*. 2d ed. Englewood Cliffs, N.J.: Prentice-Hall, 1973.

French, Stanley, and Andres Gutman. "The Principle of National Self-Determination." *Philosophy, Morality, and International Affairs*. Ed. Virginia Held, Sidney Morgenbesser, and Thomas Nagel. New York: Oxford University Press, 1974, pp. 138-53.

Freud, Sigmund. *Civilization and Its Discontents* [1930]. Trans. James Strachey. New York: Norton, 1961.

Friedmann, Wolfgang. *The Changing Structure of International Law*. New York: Columbia University Press, 1964.

————. "Intervention, Civil War and the Role of International Law." *The Vietnam War and International Law*. Ed. Richard A. Falk. [Vol. 1.] Princeton: Princeton University Press, 1968, pp. 151-59.

Friedrich, Carl J. *Inevitable Peace*. Cambridge, Mass.: Harvard University Press, 1948.

Fullinwider, Robert K. "War and Innocence." *Philosophy and Public Affairs* 5, no. 1 (Fall 1975), pp. 93-97.

Gallie, W. B. *Philosophers of Peace and War*. Cambridge: Cambridge University Press, 1978.

Gauthier, David P. *The Logic of Leviathan: The Moral and Political Theory of Thomas Hobbes*. Oxford: Clarendon Press, 1969.

Gauthier, David P. "Morality and Advantage." *Philosophical Review* 76, no. 4 (October 1967), pp. 460-75.

Gellner, Ernest. "Scale and Nation." *Philosophy of the Social Sciences* 3, no. 1 (March 1973), pp. 1-17.

Gierke, Otto von. *Natural Law and the Theory of Society.* Trans. and ed. Ernest Barker. 2 vols. Cambridge: Cambridge University Press, 1934.

Gilbert, Alan. "Marx on Internationalism and War." *Philosophy and Public Affairs* 7, no. 4 (Summer 1978), pp. 346-69.

Gilpin, Robert. *U.S. Power and the Multinational Corporation.* New York: Basic Books, 1975.

Gottlieb, Gidon. "The Nature of International Law: Toward a Second Concept of Law." *The Future of the International Legal Order.* Vol. 4: *The Structure of the International Environment.* Ed. Cyril E. Black and Richard A. Falk. Princeton: Princeton University Press, 1972, pp. 331-83.

Green, Reginald Herbold, and Hans W. Singer. "Toward a Rational and Equitable New International Economic Order: A Case for Negotiated Structural Changes." *World Development* 3, no. 6 (June 1975), pp. 427-44.

Gross, Leo. "The Right of Self-Determination in International Law." *New States in the Modern World.* Ed. Martin Kilson. Cambridge, Mass.: Harvard University Press, 1975, pp. 136-57.

Haas, Ernst B. *Beyond the Nation-State.* Stanford: Stanford University Press, 1964.

———. "The Study of Regional Integration." *Regional Integration.* Ed. Leon N. Lindberg and Stuart A. Scheingold. Cambridge, Mass.: Harvard University Press, 1971, pp. 3-42.

Haas, Ernst B., Robert L. Butterworth, and Joseph S. Nye. *Conflict Management by International Organizations.* Morristown, N.J.: General Learning Press, 1972.

Haas, Michael. "International Integration." *International Systems: A Behavioral Approach.* Ed. Michael Haas. New York: Chandler, 1974, pp. 203-28.

Halpern, Manfred. *The Morality and Politics of Intervention.* New York: Council on Religion and International Affairs, 1963.

Hart, H.L.A. "Are There Any Natural Rights?" *Philosophical Review* 64, no. 2 (April 1955), pp. 175-91.

———. *The Concept of Law.* Oxford: Clarendon Press, 1961.

Held, Virginia. "Can a Random Collection of Individuals Be Morally Responsible?" *Journal of Philosophy* 67, no. 14 (July 23, 1970), pp. 471-81.

Held, Virginia, Sidney Morgenbesser, and Thomas Nagel, eds. *Philosophy, Morality and International Affairs*. New York: Oxford University Press, 1974.

Higgins, Rosalyn. *The Development of International Law through the Political Organs of the United Nations*. London: Oxford University Press, 1963.

Hinsley, F. H. *Power and the Pursuit of Peace*. Cambridge: Cambridge University Press, 1963.

Hobson, J. A. *Imperialism: A Study* [1902]. 3d ed. London: George Allen and Unwin, 1954.

Hoffmann, Stanley. "Notes on the Elusiveness of Modern power." *International Journal* 30, no. 2 (Spring 1975), pp. 183-206.

———. *The State of War*. New York: Praeger, 1965.

Holsti, Kal J. "A New International Politics?" *International Organization* 32, no. 2 (Spring 1978), pp. 513-30.

Horsburgh, H.J.N. *Non-violence and Aggression: A Study of Gandhi's Moral Equivalent of War*. London: Oxford University Press, 1968.

Howe, James. "SDRs and Development: Let's Spread Them Around." *Foreign Policy*, no. 8 (Fall 1972), pp. 102-13.

Hubin, D. Clayton. "Justice and Future Generations." *Philosophy and Public Affairs* 6, no. 1 (Fall 1976), pp. 70-83.

Hutt, W. H. "Immigration under 'Economic Freedom.'" *Economic Issues in Immigration*. Ed. Charles Wilson. London: Institute of Economic Affairs, 1970, pp. 17-44.

Inkeles, Alex. "The Emerging Social Structure of the World." *World Politics* 27, no. 4 (July 1975), pp. 467-95.

Jennings, W. Ivor. *The Approach to Self-Government*. Cambridge: Cambridge University Press, 1956.

Johnson, Harry G. *Economic Policies toward Less Developed Countries*. Washington, D.C.: The Brookings Institution, 1967.

Katzenstein, Peter J. "International Interdependence: Some Long-term Trends and Recent Changes." *International Organization* 29, no. 4 (Autumn 1975), pp. 1,021-34.

Kaufman, Robert R., Daniel S. Geller, and Harry I. Chernotsky. "A Preliminary Test of the Theory of Dependency." *Comparative Politics* 7, no. 3 (April 1975), pp. 303-30.

Kelman, Herbert C. "Education for the Concept of a Global Society." *Social Education* 32, no. 7 (November 1968), pp. 661-68.

———. "Patterns of Political Involvement in the National System: A Social-Psychological Analysis of Political Legitimacy." *International Politics and Foreign Policy*. Rev. ed. Ed. James N. Rosenau. New York: Free Press, 1969, pp. 276-88.

Kennan, George F. *Realities of American Foreign Policy*. Princeton: Princeton University Press, 1954.

Keohane, Robert O., and Joseph S. Nye, Jr. *Power and Interdependence: World Politics in Transition*. Boston: Little, Brown, 1977.

————. "Transgovernmental Relations and International Organizations." *World Politics* 21, no. 1 (October 1974), pp. 39-62.

————, eds. *Transnational Relations and World Politics*. Cambridge, Mass.: Harvard University Press, 1972.

Keohane, Robert O., and Van Doorn Ooms. "The Multinational Firm and International Regulation." *International Organization* 29, no. 1 (Winter 1975), pp. 169-209.

Koebner, Richard, and Helmut Dan Schmitt. *Imperialism: The Story and Significance of A Political Word, 1840-1960*. Cambridge: Cambridge University Press, 1964.

Krieger, Leonard. *The Politics of Discretion: Pufendorf and the Acceptance of National Law*. Chicago: University of Chicago Press, 1965.

Lauterpacht, Hersch. *International Law and Human Rights*. London: Stevens, 1950.

Lefever, Ernest W. "The Perils of Reform Intervention." *Worldview* (February 1970), pp. 7-10.

Legault, Albert, and George Lindsey. *The Dynamics of the Nuclear Balance*. Ithaca, N.Y.: Cornell University Press, 1974.

Lenin, Vladimir Il'ich. *Imperialism, the Highest Stage of Capitalism* [1917]. *Collected Works*. Trans. Yuri Sdobnikov and ed. George Hanna. Vol. 22. Moscow: Progress Publishers, 1964, pp. 185-304.

————. "The Socialist Revolution and the Right of Nations to Self-Determination" [1916]. *Collected Works*. Trans. Yuri Sdobnikov and ed. George Hanna. Vol. 22. Moscow: Progress Publishers, 1964, pp. 143-56.

Lewis, W. Arthur. *The Evolution of the International Economic Order*. Princeton: Princeton University Press, 1978.

Loewenstein, Karl. *Political Reconstruction*. New York: Macmillan, 1946.

Mao Tse-tung. "The Chinese Revolution and the Chinese Communist Party" [1939]. *Selected Works of Mao Tse-tung*. Vol. 3. London: Lawrence and Wishart, 1954.

Midgley, E.B.F. *The Natural Law Tradition and the Theory of International Relations*. London: Paul Elek, 1975.

Miller, David. *Social Justice*. Oxford: Clarendon Press, 1976.

Miller, Lynn H. *Organizing Mankind: An Analysis of Contemporary International Organization*. Boston: Holbrook Press, 1972.

Mitrany, David. *A Working Peace System*. 4th ed. London: National Peace Council, 1946.

Moore, John Norton. *Law and the Indo-China War*. Princeton: Princeton University Press, 1972.

Moran, Theodore H. *The Multinational Corporation and the Politics of Dependence: Copper in Chile*. Princeton: Princeton University Press, 1974.

Morgenbesser, Sidney. "Imperialism: Some Preliminary Distinctions." *Philosophy and Public Affairs* 3, no. 1 (Fall 1973), pp. 3-44.

Morgenthau, Hans J. *In Defense of the National Interest*. New York: Alfred A. Knopf, 1952.

———. Letter to the editor. *International Affairs* 35, no. 4 (October 1959), p. 502.

———. *Politics Among Nations*. 5th ed. New York: Alfred A. Knopf, 1973.

———. "To Intervene or Not to Intervene." *Foreign Affairs* 45, no. 3 (April 1967), pp. 425-36.

———. "The Twilight of International Morality." *Ethics* 58, no. 2 (January 1948), pp. 79-99.

Morse, Edward L. "The Transformation of Foreign Policies: Modernization, Interdependence, and Externalization." *World Politics* 22, no. 3 (April 1970), pp. 371-92.

———. "Transnational Economic Processes." *Transnational Relations and World Politics*. Ed. Robert O. Keohane and Joseph S. Nye, Jr. Cambridge, Mass.: Harvard University Press, 1972, pp. 23-47.

Moss, Robert. "Let's Look Out for No. 1!" *The New York Times Magazine* (May 1, 1977), pp. 31, 99-106.

Moynihan, Daniel P. "The United States in Opposition." *Commentary* 59, no. 3 (March 1975), pp. 31-44.

Nagel, Thomas. "Hobbes's Concept of Obligation." *Philosophical Review* 68, no. 1 (January 1959), pp. 68-73.

———. *The Possibility of Altruism*. Oxford: Clarendon Press, 1970.

———. "Poverty and Food: Why Charity Is Not Enough." *Food Policy: The Responsibility of the United States in the Life and Death Choices*. Ed. Peter G. Brown and Henry Shue. New York: Free Press, 1977, pp. 54-62.

Nelson, William N. "Special Rights, General Rights, and Social Justice." *Philosophy and Public Affairs* 3, no. 4 (Summer 1974), pp. 410-30.

Northrup, F.S.C. *The Meeting of East and West*. New York: Macmillan, 1946.

Nozick, Robert. *Anarchy, State, and Utopia*. New York: Basic Books, 1974.

Nye, Joseph S., Jr. "Multinational Corporations in World Politics." *Foreign Affairs* 53, no. 1 (October 1974), pp. 153-75.

Nye, Joseph S., Jr. *Peace in Parts: Integration and Conflict in Regional Organization*. Boston: Little, Brown, 1971.

Oppenheim, Lassa F. L. *International Law: A Treatise*. 8th ed. Ed. Hersch Lauterpacht. 2 vols. London: Longmans, Green, 1955.

Parkinson, F. *The Philosophy of International Relations*. Sage Library of Social Research, vol. 52. Beverly Hills, Calif.: Sage Publications, 1977.

Pennock, J. Roland. "Political Development, Political Systems, and Political Goods." *World Politics* 18, no. 3 (April 1966), pp. 415-34.

Pitkin, Hanna Fenichel. "Obligation and Consent—I." *American Political Science Review* 59, no. 4 (December 1965), pp. 990-99.

Plamenatz, John. *On Alien Rule and Self-Government*. London: Longmans, 1960.

Rapoport, Anatol. *Strategy and Conscience*. New York: Schocken Books, 1964.

Raser, John R. "International Deterrence." *International Systems: A Behavioral Approach*. Ed. Michael Haas. New York: Chandler, 1974, pp. 301-24.

Rawls, John. *A Theory of Justice*. Cambridge, Mass.: Harvard University Press, 1971.

Richards, David A. J. *A Theory of Reasons for Action*. Oxford: Clarendon Press, 1971.

Rosecrance, Richard. "Interdependence: Myth or Reality." *World Politics* 26, no. 1 (October 1973), pp. 1-27.

———, et al. "Whither Interdependence?" *International Organization* 31, no. 3 (Summer 1977), pp. 425-71.

Rosenau, James N. "Intervention as a Scientific Concept." *Journal of Conflict Resolution* 13, no. 2 (June 1969), pp. 149-71.

Ruggie, John Gerard. "Collective Goods and Future International Collaboration." *American Political Science Review* 66, no. 3 (September 1972), pp. 874-93.

Santos, Theotonio Dos. "The Structure of Dependence." *American Economic Review* 60, no. 2 (May 1970), pp. 231-36.

Scanlon, Thomas M. "Liberty, Contract and Contribution." *Markets and Morals*. Ed. G. Dworkin, G. Bermant, and P. Brown. Washington, D.C.: Hemisphere, 1977, pp. 43-67.

———. "Nozick on Rights, Liberty, and Property." *Philosophy and Public Affairs* 6, no. 1 (Fall 1976), pp. 3-25.

———. "Rawls' Theory of Justice." *University of Pennsylvania Law Review* 121, no. 5 (May 1973), pp. 1,020-69.

Schiffer, Walter. *The Legal Community of Mankind*. New York: Columbia University Press, 1954.

Schlesinger, Arthur, Jr. "The Necessary Amorality of Foreign Affairs." *Harper's Magazine* 243, no. 1,455 (August 1971), pp. 72-73.

Scott, Andrew M. "Nonintervention and Conditional Intervention." *Journal of International Affairs* 22, no. 2 (1968), pp. 208-16.

————. *The Revolution in Statecraft.* New York: Random House, 1965.

Sewell, James Patrick. *Functionalism and World Politics.* Princeton: Princeton University Press, 1966.

Shue, Henry. "Food, Population, and Wealth: Toward Global Principles of Justice." Paper presented at the annual meeting of the American Political Science Association, Chicago, Illinois, September 2-5, 1976.

Simmons, A. John. "Tacit Consent and Political Obligation." *Philosophy and Public Affairs* 5, no. 3 (Spring 1976), pp. 274-91.

Singer, J. David, and Melvin Small. "Alliance Aggregation and the Onset of War, 1815-1914." *Quantitative International Politics.* Ed. J. David Singer. New York: Free Press, 1968, pp. 247-86.

Singer, Peter. "Famine, Affluence, and Morality." *Philosophy and Public Affairs* 1, no. 3 (Spring 1972), pp. 229-43.

Slote, Michael A. "Desert, Consent, and Justice." *Philosophy and Public Affairs* 2, no. 4 (Summer 1973), pp. 323-47.

Smith, Tony. "Changing Configurations of Power in North-South Relations since 1945." *International Organization* 31, no. 1 (Winter 1977), pp. 1-27.

Stallings, Barbara. *Economic Dependency in Africa and Latin America.* Sage Professional Papers in Comparative Politics, no. 01-031. Beverly Hills, Calif.: Sage Publications, 1972.

Stawell, F. Melian. *The Growth of International Thought.* The Home University Library. London: Thornton Butterworth, 1929.

Stepan, Alfred. *The State and Society: Peru in Comparative Perspective.* Princeton: Princeton University Press, 1978.

Sunkel, Osvaldo. "Big Business and 'Dependencia.'" *Foreign Affairs* 50, no. 3 (April 1972), pp. 517-31.

Thomas, Ann Van Wynen, and A. J. Thomas, Jr. *Non-Intervention: The Law and Its Impact in the Americas.* Dallas: Southern Methodist University Press, 1956.

Thompson, Kenneth W. *Political Realism and the Crisis of World Politics.* Princeton: Princeton University Press, 1960.

Tucker, Robert W. *The Inequality of Nations.* New York: Basic Books, 1977.

United Nations, General Assembly. *Official Records.* Fifteenth,

Seventeenth, Twentieth, and Twenty-fifth Sessions; Sixth Special Session. New York: United Nations, 1961, 1963, 1966, 1971; 1974.

Vaitsos, Constantine. *Intercountry Income Distribution and Transnational Enterprises.* Oxford: Clarendon Press, 1974.

Van Dyke, Vernon. *Human Rights, the United States, and World Community.* New York: Oxford University Press, 1970.

Vernon, Raymond. *Sovereignty at Bay.* New York: Basic Books, 1971.

Vincent, R. J. *Nonintervention and International Order.* Princeton: Princeton University Press, 1974.

Wallerstein, Immanuel. *The Modern World-System: Capitalist Agriculture and the Rise of the World Economy in the Sixteenth Century.* New York: Academic Press, 1974.

Waltz, Kenneth N. *Man, the State, and War.* New York: Columbia University Press, 1959.

———. "The Myth of National Interdependence." *The International Corporation.* Ed. Charles P. Kindleberger. Cambridge, Mass.: MIT Press, 1960, pp. 205-26.

Walzer, Michael. *Just and Unjust Wars.* New York: Basic Books, 1977.

———. "The Obligation to Disobey." *Obligations: Essays on Disobedience, War, and Citizenship.* Cambridge, Mass.: Harvard University Press, 1970, pp. 3-23.

Warrender, Howard. *The Political Philosophy of Hobbes: His Theory of Obligation.* Oxford: Clarendon Press, 1957.

Warwick, Donald P. "Transnational Participation and International Peace." *Transnational Relations and World Politics.* Ed. Robert O. Keohane and Joseph S. Nye, Jr. Cambridge, Mass.: Harvard University Press, 1972, pp. 305-24.

Wasserstrom, Richard, ed. *War and Morality.* Belmont, Calif.: Wadsworth Publishing Company, 1970.

Watkins, J.W.N. *Hobbes's System of Ideas.* 2d ed. London: Hutchinson University Library, 1973.

Wechsler, Herbert. "Toward Neutral Principles of Constitutional Law." *Harvard Law Review* 73, no. 1 (November 1959), pp. 1-35.

Wicclair, Mark. "Human Rights and Intervention: A Contractarian Analysis." *John Rawls' Theory of Social Justice: An Introduction.* Ed. Gene Blocker, Elizabeth Smith, and Robert Trevis. Athens: Ohio University Press, forthcoming.

Wight, Martin. "Why Is There No International Theory?" *Diplomatic Investigations.* Ed. Herbert Butterfield and Martin Wight. London: George Allen and Unwin, 1966, pp. 17-34.

Winfield, P. H. "The History of Intervention in International Law."

British Yearbook of International Law. Vol. 3, 1922-1923. London: Henry Frowde and Hodder and Stoughton, 1922, pp. 130-49.

Wolfers, Arnold. "Political Theory and International Relations." *The Anglo-American Tradition in Foreign Affairs*. Ed. Arnold Wolfers and Lawrence W. Martin. New Haven: Yale University Press, 1956, pp. ix-xxvii.

Wolin, Sheldon S. *Politics and Vision*. Boston: Little, Brown, 1960.

Young, Oran. "The Actors in World Politics." *The Analysis of International Politics*. Ed. James N. Rosenau et al. New York: Free Press, 1972, pp. 125-44.

———. "Intervention and International Systems." *Journal of International Affairs* 22, no. 2 (1968), pp. 177-86.

Zolberg, Aristide R. "Military Intervention in the New States of Tropical Africa: Elements of Comparative Analysis." *The Military Intervenes: Case Studies in Political Development*. Ed. Henry Bienen. New York: Russell Sage Foundation, 1968, pp. 71-102.

Index

Acheson, Dean, 20n
Acton, John E.E.D. (Lord Acton): on statehood and nationality, 113-14
Albania, 160
alliances, *see* coalitions of states
Amdur, Robert, 128n
anarchy, international, *see* international state of nature
Aquinas, St. Thomas, 7n
Aristotle, 182
Aron, Raymond: ambiguity of view of national interest, 20n; on primacy of national interest in international state of nature, 27-28
assurance problem: and fair coercive institutions, 158-59; in international relations, 46-50, 158-59; minimized in institutional reform, 174
Austin, John, 27n
autonomy of states: content of, 8, 76-81; critique of summarized, 121-22, 180; and economic dependence, 116; idea of, as application of analogy of states and persons, 8, 69; nonintervention as negative aspect of, 92; as outer face of moral legitimacy of states, 81; and possible justification of intervention, 81-83; self-determination as positive aspect of, 92-93; view of as based on consent of citizens, 76-79

Baier, Kurt, 46
Baldwin, David A., 73n
Baldwin, Robert C., 149n
Baran, Paul: economic structure of contemporary imperialism, 117
Barker, Ernest: defense of Mill on statehood and nationality, 114

Barkun, Michael, 47n
Barnet, Richard, 145n
Barratt, Michael Brown, 101n, 146n
Barry, Brian, 3n, 30n; on global application of Rawls's principles, 128n, 151n; on the problem of second best, 171n; on Rawls and international relations, 135
Beales, A.C.F., 7n
Beitz, Charles R., 123n, 152n
Benn, S. I., 76n, 90; anti-paternalist argument for nonintervention, 84, 85; states as free associations, 77
Bergsten, C. Fred, 145n, 149n
Berki, R. N., 182n
Bodenheimer, Suzanne: economic structure of dependency, 117-18
Bodin, Jean, 3; absence of common judge as reason for international skepticism, 26-27; on natural law, 26; on sovereignty, 25-26; "true kings" and "despots" distinguished, 26
Bosanquet, Bernard, 76n
boundaries: not morally decisive, 176; and nationality, 112-15; and problem of eligibility for self-determination, 105-106, 109; and property rights, 109; Rawls on, 132; significance in distributive justice, 161-69; and social cooperation, 151
Bozeman, Adda B., 17n
Brandt, Richard B., 19n
Brewin, Christopher, 152n
Brierly, J. L., 47n, 134n
Brown, Seyom, 44n
Brownlie, Ian, 149n
Buchanan, James M., 158n
Bukharin, N. I., 94
Bull, Hedley, 20n, 71n
bureaucrats, 39
Butterworth, Robert L., 38n

Cambodia, 134, 160
Canada, 107
Cardozo, Michael N., 73n
Carr, Edward Hallett, 32n
charity, 143; as basis of international distributive obligations, 127; contrasted with justice, as source of obligations, 127, 159; as inappropriate model for foreign aid, 172-73
Chase-Dunn, Christopher, 118n
Chernotsky, Harry I., 118n
Claude, Inis L., 157n
coalitions of states, 47; effects of on international conflict, 37-38
Cobban, Alfred, 94n; criticism of Mill-Barker view of nationality and statehood, 114
coercion: and assurance problem, 158-59; intervention as, 72-73; legitimacy of, by governments, 79-80. See also war
Cohen, Marshall, 9n
Cohen, Stephen F., 94n
collective goods: theory of, 49n
collective guilt and responsibility, 9, 153n
colonialism, see imperialism, self-determination
community: international sense of, 155-58
Connor, Walker, 114-15
conscientious refusal: and participation in armed forces, 175-76
consent: as basis of state autonomy, 76-79; and moral legitimacy of institutions, 78-79; possible conflict with justice, 103-104; and self-determination, 95-98; voting as a form of, 78-79; weakness of argument for political obligation, 78-80
consequentialism, 171
conservation of national resources, 142
Cooper, Richard N., 43n, 44n, 145n, 147n, 173n

cosmopolitan international theories, 9; characterized, 181-82; reasons for misunderstanding of, 183
counterintervention, 87
Cox, Richard, 60n
cultural relativism: problem not limited to international ethics, 19; as source of international skepticism, 13, 17-19

Danielson, Peter, 128n
Denzer, Horst, 60n
Deutsch, Karl W., 114n
difference principle: and equality, 132, 162; global, see international distributive justice; Rawls's formulation of, 129-30
Disraeli, Benjamin: justification of imperialism, 99
domestic society: contrasts with international relations, summarized, 49-50, 154-55, 159
Dos Santos, Theotonio: on economic dependence, 117n
Durkheim, Emile, 157n
Dworkin, Gerald, 89n, 100n

East Asia, 144
economic dependence, 69, 122; compared with imperialism, 116-17; as injustice, 119-20; as interference with state autonomy, 119-21; Lenin on, 117; nature and effects of, 118
economic development: relation of normative theory to study of, 123; and social justice, 81n, 98, 104-105, 122-23
economic imperialism, see economic dependence
economic inequality: and interdependence, 145-46
Emerson, Rupert, 93n, 94n, 110n; on self-determination, 106-107
environment, regulation of, 135
equality of states: Rawls on, 75n, 134; Christian Wolff on, 75

ethical egoism: compared to moral
    skepticism, 22
ethics, see morality
ethnic diversity, 115n
Europe, 144n
European Economic Community, 47
European Coal and Steel Commu-
    nity, 39
Evans, Peter B., 73n, 116n
expropriation, 149

Fagen, Richard R., 148n
Falk, Richard A., 48n, 73n, 85n
Feinberg, Joel, 153n; criticism of
    Rawls on nonideal theory, 171
Findlay, Ronald, 146n
Fisher, Roger, 47n
food: rights to, 175-76
Foot, Philippa, 57n
foreign aid, 172-73
foreign investment, 144-45; in de-
    pendency theory, 118; and eco-
    nomic dependence, 116; as inter-
    ference in internal affairs of states,
    69; and international inequality,
    145-48; and property rights, 149;
    voluntariness of acceptance of,
    160
Frank, André Gunder, 118n
Frankel, Charles, 20n
Frankena, W. K.: on morality and
    egoism, 23
freedom of association: and consent
    theory of political obligation,
    77-79; and eligibility for self-
    determination, 106-109; inappli-
    cable to self-determination, 109-
    110; and justification of self-
    determination principle, 96-98;
    two senses contrasted, 77-78
free rider problem, 57, 158
French Canada, 107
French, Stanley: on conflicting
    claims of self-determination, 107;
    eligibility for self-determination,
    105n
Freud, Sigmund, 157n

Friedmann, Wolfgang, 47n, 87n
Friedrich, Carl J., 82n
functional integration: theory of,
    38-40

Gallie, W. B., 9n
game theory, 42-43
Gauthier, David P., 31n; on morality
    and self-interest, 58n; on nuclear
    proliferation and equality of na-
    tional power, 41; on nuclear
    weapons in Hobbesian conception
    of international relations, 41-42
Geller, Daniel S., 118n
Gellner, Ernest, 115n
General Agreement on Tariffs and
    Trade, 43
Germany, 94
Gierke, Otto von, 28n, 60n
Gilbert, Alan, 182n
Gilpin, Robert, 182
global monetary system, 43, 47, 147,
    148, 173-75
Gottlieb, Gidon, 48n
Greece, ancient, 131
Green, Reginald Herbold, 175n
Gross, Leo, 94n
Grotius, Hugo, 7n; as father of
    modern international law, 71; on
    nonintervention, 71
Gutman, Andres: on conflicting
    claims of self-determination, 107;
    on eligibility for self-
    determination, 105n

Haas, Ernst B., 38n, 39n
Haas, Michael, 39n
Hall, William E.: neutral nininter-
    vention standard, 87-88
Halpern, Manfred, 73n, 85n
Hart, H.L.A.: on analogy between
    individuals and states, 48; on polit-
    ical obligation, 57n
Hegel, G.W.F., 76n
Held, Virginia, 9n, 153n
Higgins, Rosalyn, 94n, 105n
Hinsley, F. H., 7n

Hobbes, Thomas, 3, 10n, 62n; argument for international skepticism, 14; basis of moral obligation, 31-32; basis of stable expectations in state of nature, 46; *De Cive*, 29; dynamics of state of nature, 28-30, 32; equality in state of nature, 40; *Human Nature*, 29; importance of survival in state of nature, 159; inappropriateness of moral judgments in state of nature, 179; independence of parties in state of nature, 42; individualism of state of nature, 37; international Leviathan not necessary, 33n, 41n; international relations as a state of nature, 8, 14, 28-34, 64, 181; international state of nature as analytical device, 35-50; international state of nature as prescriptive device, 50-63; on laws of nature, 31, 50-51, 61n; *Leviathan*, 7n, 29; on morality and self-interest, 51, 55-58

Hobson, J. A., 100n, 117n

Hoffmann, Stanley, vii n, 44n, 45n

Holsti, Kal J., 147n

Horsburgh, H.J.N., 10n

Horst, Thomas, 145n

Howe, James, 174n

Hubin, D. Clayton, 142n

human rights: consequence of Rawls's assumptions for, 133; relation to social justice, 123

Hume, David, 78n; nature of society, 130

ideal theory: Kant on, 156n; Rawls on, 133, 135, 170-71; relation to nonideal world, 156-58

imperialism, 8, 69; Disraeli on, 99; economic, *see* economic dependence; Hobson on, 100n; as injustice, 101-102; main features of, compared with economic dependence, 116-17; Marx on, 99; J. S. Mill on, 99; as paternalism, 100-

102; and self-determination, 93, 94

incentives, 162

incrementalism, 170

inequality: domestic, 147-48; international, 145-48, 162

Inkeles, Alex, 44n

integration: functional, 38-40

interdependence, 3-4, 42-44; distributive effects of, 145-46; domestic effects, 147-48; evidence of, 144-45; history of in international relations, 4n; relevance of controversy about effects of, 151-52; as social cooperation, 143-50; and vulnerability, 146-47

international distributive justice, 125-76 *passim*; based on social cooperation, 150; as charity, 127; and debate about new economic order, 8; domestic obligations may limit, 165-66; and entitlements to natural resources, 136-43; and incentives, 162; in nonideal world, 169-75; objections based on contrast of international relations and domestic society, 154-61; objections based of right of states, 161-69; principle of, 150; subjects of, 152-53; utilitarian and contractarian approaches contrasted, 127

international institutions and practices: compared with domestic analogues, 154-55, 157; and international common interests, 43-46; lack of enforcement capability, 154-55; reasons for compliance with, 48; reform of guided by justice, 173-75; as results of interdependence, 148-49; significance of in argument for distributive principle, 166-67; undesirability of global authority, 157; voluntariness of participation in, 160-61

International law, 7n; and Austinian positivism, 26-27; customary, 47;

and interdependence, 149; Rawls on traditional rules of, 134-35; relation to political theory, 70; self-determination principle in, 93

International Monetary Fund, 43; Special Drawing Rights in, 174-75

international moral skepticism, 7-8, 15-27; argument from cultural relativism, 17-19; argument from international state of nature, 27-34, 49; argument from moralism, 20-21; argument from national interest, 21-25; argument from sovereignty, 25-27; critique of summarized, 64-65, 179; distinguished from general moral skepticism, 16-17; prevalence of, 5, 13, 15; sources of, 13. *See also* international state of nature, national interest

international political theory: and domestic justice, 122-23; and empirical political science, 181, 182; history of, 7; justification of principles of, 53-55, 59, 63, 149-51, 176; neglect of, 3, 10, 13; obstacles to, 5-6; possibility of, 13, 59; Rawls on, 132-36; relation of to international law, 70; relation to practice, 4-5, 170-72; relevance of recent changes to, 4; silence of tradition on distributive issues, 127; three modern approaches distinguished, 181-82. *See also* nonideal theory

international relations: analogy with domestic society, 8-9, 49-50, 128, 154-61; common interests in, 49-50; empirical study of, 6, 9, 181, 182; "idealist" approach to study of, 20; power in, 40-42, 44-46; states as actors in, 36-40. *See also* assurance problem, boundaries, interdependence, international institutions and practices, international law, war

international state of nature, 3-4;

analogy of states and persons in, 36, 52-54, 63, 69; analytical and prescriptive uses contrasted, 35, 53; analytical use of, 35-36, 63-64; assurance problem in, 158-59; basis of stable expectations in, 46-48; Hobbes on, 28-34; inaccuracy of traditional image of, 179; Kant on, 44-45; and moral justification, 14, 35, 50-63; omits important features of international relations, 49; prescriptive use of, 50-51, 64-65; Pufendorf on, 60-62; reasons for persistence of image, 47-48; Rousseau on, 33n, 45; as source of international skepticism, 13-14, 27-28, 31-34; as state of war, 14, 48-49

intervention: "broad definition" of, 74; controversy about definition of, 74, 91-92; economic aid as, 73; goals of, 73; and interdependence, 87; main objections practical rather than theoretical, 83; meaning of, 72-74; and military force, 72; moral limits on summarized, 91-92; "narrow definition" of, 72, non-national actors as agents of, 73; reform, perils of, 82. *See also* nonintervention principle

Italy, 94

Jennings, W. Ivor, 106n
Johnson, Harry G., 124n
jus ad bellum, 10
jus in bello, 47, 134
justice, Hobbes on, 29-30; Rawls on natural duty of, 171; sense of in international relations, 155, 157-58; of war, *see* just war. *See also* international distributive justice, social justice

just war, 9-10, 47, 133-34, 142, 175-76

Kant, Immanuel: on cosmopolitan international theory, 9, 181-82;

Kant, Immanuel (*cont.*)
   economic co-operation as basis of
   international morality, 144; effect
   of interdependence on conflict,
   45n; on nonintervention, 82; *Perpetual Peace*, 7n, 45n, 82; on possibility in ideal theory, 156n; on
   rights to earth's surface, 138n;
   theory of international justice, 136
Katzenstein, Peter J., 144n
Kaufman, Robert R., 118n
Kay, David A., 149n
Kelman, Herbert C., 114n, 158n
Kenna, George F., 12, 17n
Keohane, Robert O., 20n, 38n, 39n,
   43n, 46n, 145n, 146n, 148n, 149n
Koebner, Richard, 99n
Krieger, Leonard, 60n

Latin America, 144
Lauterpacht, Hersch, 73n
law of nations: Rawls on, 132, 133-
   34, 149, 170. *See also* international
   law, natural law
law of nature, *see* natural law
Lefever, Ernest W., 82n
Legault, Albert, 41n
legitimacy (moral) of institutions:
   contrasted with *de facto* legitimacy,
   78n; and hypothetical social contract, 80; not based on consent, 79;
   as subject of political theory, 13
Lenin, V. I.: on economic imperialism, 117; on self-
   determination, 94
liberal approach to international
   studies, 182
liberty: as analogy in argument
   against intervention, 71, 75-77,
   83-84, 88-90; in argument for
   self-determination, 92-93, 96-97,
   98, 100; considerations of relevant
   to natural talents, 139; and imperialism, 99-102; and nationality,
   112-14; as a neutral principle, 89;
   and paternalism, 100
Lindsey, George, 41n

Locke, John: importance of international relations in *Second Treatise*,
   60n; on state of nature, 59-60; on
   "tacit consent," 78-79
Loewenstein, Karl, 82n
loyalties: to nation-states, 157-58,
   164-65
Luxemburg, Rosa, 94

Machiavelli, Niccolò, 3; on the national interest as first principle,
   22-23; on public and private morality, 22; as skeptic, 23; on *virtù*
   and national interest, 22n
Mao Tse-tung, 117n
Marx, Karl, 182n; on economic imperialism, 117n; on imperialism,
   99
Marxist approach to international
   studies, 182
Mazzini, Giuseppe, 94
mercantilist approach to international studies, 182
Midgley, E.B.F., 7n
Mill, John Stuart, 106n; antipaternalist argument against intervention, 85-87; apology for imperialism, 99; argument against
   paternalism, 84; "A Few Words on
   Non-intervention," 82; on nationality, 112-14; on nonintervention, 78n, 82; *On Liberty*, 84; on
   self-determination, 96; "Vindication of the French Revolution of
   February, 1848," 82
Miller, David, 122n
Miller, Lynn H., 47n
Mitrany, David, 39n
Moore, John Norton, 74n
moral intuitions, 6, 17, 56
moralism: and argument for skepticism, 20-21; kernal of truth in, 183
morality: cannot demand the impossible, 155-56; Hobbes's view of,
   28-29; inadequacy of Hobbes's
   view, 56-58; intuitions about, 6,
   17, 56; nature of, 16, 23; and self-

interest, 56-58; skepticism about international, *see* international moral skepticism

morality of states, 8, 14; critique of summarized, 180; as main alternative to international skepticism, 14, 65; as natural law tradition, 8; and international distributive justice, 66, 127; and principle of state autonomy, 65-66, 69; main features analogous to liberalism, 66

moral skepticism: compared to ethical egoism, 22-23; distinguished from international moral skepticism, 16-17; generalized, 15-16

Moran, Theodore H., 120n, 145n

Morgenbesser, Sidney, 9n, 116n

Morgenthau, Hans, 19n; ambiguity of view of national interest, 20n; on intervention, 24n; on moral status of national interest, 54-55; national interest constrained by domestic morality, 25; on political realism and international morality, 19-21

Morse, Edward L., 43n, 44n

Moss, Robert, 161n

Moynihan, Daniel P., 122n

Müller, Ronald, 145n

multinational corporations, 39; and dependency theory, 117; and economic dependence, 116; and interdependence, 144-45; interference of, in internal affairs of states, 69; political power of, 146

mutual aid, *see* charity

Nagel, Thomas, 9n, 16n, 56n, 173n

national interest: ambiguity as evaluative standard, 20n; ambiguity of relation to individual interests, 52; as first principle of international morality, 23; and moral values of a state, 24-25; Machiavelli on, 21-23; relation to individual self-preservation, 52; relation to national survival,

52-55; skeptical argument from responsibilities of leaders to promote, 23-24; as source of international moral skepticism, 21-25

nationality: Acton on 113-14; Barker on, 114; Cobban on, 114; definition of, 114-15; J. S. Mill on, 112-14; moral significance of sentiments of, 164; and self-determination, 106, 112-15

nation-state, *see* state

natural law: Jean Bodin on, 26; Hobbes on, 31, 50-51, 61n; and international state of nature, 28; Locke on, 60; Pufendorf on, 60-61; relation of, to international skepticism, 59; tradition characterized as morality of states, 8

natural liberty: Rawls on system of, 163

natural moral requirements, 57, 58

natural resources: claims to as justification of war, 142; compared to natural talents, 137-40; conservation of, 142; entitlements to, 136-43; natural distribution of as morally arbitrary, 140; and property rights, 149

Nelson, William N., 140n

neutral principles, 88

New International Economic Order, 127, 173-75

nonideal theory: difficulties of, 183; and international distributive justice, 156-58, 169-76; problems likely to be more difficult in international than domestic politics, 158-60; Rawls on, 133, 135, 170-71

nonintervention principle, 8, 121; antipaternalist argument for, 84-87; application to just and unjust states contrasted, 90; argument by analogy with personal liberty, 21, 75-77, 83-84, 88, 89; argument from state autonomy, 71, 75-83; contrasted with self-

nonintervention principle (*cont.*)
determination principle, 93; derived from autonomy of states, 69; effects of, 149; history of, 71; Kant on, 82; J. S. Mill on, 82; main arguments for, 83; as neutral standard, 87-89; not exceptionless, 89-90; Rawls's justification of, 134; sources other than state autonomy, 90-91; Christian Wolff on, 75-76. *See also* intervention
nonviolence, 9, 10n, 44
North Atlantic Treaty Organization (NATO), 47
Northrup, F.S.C., 17n
Nozick, Robert, 162n
nuclear weapons and deterrence, 41-42
Nye, Joseph S., Jr., 20n, 38n, 39n, 43n, 46n, 149n

Ooms, Van Doorn, 145n, 146n, 148n
Oppenheim, L., 72n
Organization for Economic Cooperation and Development, 148
original contract, *see* social contract
original position: argument for resource redistribution principle, 141; constraint of possibility, 155-56; Rawls on, 130; Rawls's application of to international relations, 133-34; reinterpreted for international relations, 151
outer space: as common area, 149; exploitation of, 136

pacta sunt seranda rule, 149; Rawls's justification of, 134
Parkinson, F., 7n
paternalism: argument against applied to intervention, 84-87; and hypothetical social contracts, 101; and imperialism, 100-102; when justified, 100
Pennock, J. Roland, 101n, 123n
Peters, R. S., 76n, 90; antipaternalist

argument for nonintervention, 84, 85; states as free associations, 77
Pitkin, Hanna, 78n
Plamenatz, John, 96n
polis, 131
political development: hypotheses about, in antipaternalist argument against intervention, 85-86; relation of normative theory to study of, 123
political inequality, *see* vulnerability
political obligation: effects of international principles on, 175-76; impossibility of self-interest-based justification of, 57; and right of secession, 107-108
political realism: meaning of, 19-21; and national interest, 21-22; objection to moralism, 21; as research orientation, 20; as source of international skepticism, 13, 15. *See also* international moral skepticism
political theory: nature of, 4-5, 13. *See also* international political theory
population control policies, 135, 161n
positivism: legal, 27
power: in Hobbes, 36, 40-41; inequality of, in international relations, 40-42, 48; of multinational corporations, 146; nature of, in international relations, 41, 44-46; and vulnerability, 146-47
property rights: and international law, 149; lack of moral foundation of in international relations, 172; and self-determination, 109-110
Pufendorf, Samuel, 7n, 69; analogy of states and persons, 61-62; application of natural law to nations, 60-62; argument for state autonomy, 180; critique of Hobbes, 60, 65; *Of the Law of Nature and Nations (De jure naturae et gentium)*, 60

Québéçois, 107

Rapoport, Anatol, 43n
Raser, John R., 43n
Rawls, John, 136n, 164n; assumption of national self-sufficiency, 132, 170; *A Theory of Justice*, 8; conflicts among natural duties, 171; on conscientious refusal, 175; on distribution of natural talents, 137-40; on equality of states, 75n, 134; on equal liberty, 88n, 89n; failure to recognize resource problems, 143, 169-70; "general conception" of justice, 130; on "ideal theory," 133, 135, 170-71; importance of feasibility in choice of principles, 155-56; international original position, 133-34; on justice in developing societies, 123n; on just savings rate, 142; on law of nations, 132, 133-34, 149, 170; on natural duties, 132, 133, 141, 170; "original position," 130; principles of justice apply to "basic structure," 129, 166; sense of community as motivation for compliance with principles, 155; social unity achieved through common acceptance of principles, 158n; society as cooperative venture for mutual advantage, 130-32, 150n; on state boundaries, 132; on system of natural liberty, 137-38, 163; theory of distributive justice applied to international relations, 128-29, 151, 180-81; two principles of justice, 129-30; "veil of ignorance," 130
reform intervention, 82
regimes, 43. *See also* international institutions and practices
resource redistribution principle, 162; argument for in international original position, 138, 141; case for, not undermined by self-sufficiency assumption, 140-41; and intergenerational justice, 142; problems of formulating, 141-42;

strongest distributive principle applicable to self-sufficient states, 144. *See also* natural resources
Rhodesia (Zimbabwe), 94
Richards, David A. J., 151n
Rosecrance, Richard, 43n, 144n
Rosenau, James N., 73n, 149n
Rousseau, Jean-Jacques, 62n; on analogy of international relations and domestic society, 33n; effect of interdependence on conflict, 45n
Ruggie, John Gerard, 40n, 49n

Scanlon, Thomas, 9n, 128n, 151n; on secession and political obligation, 108n
Schiffer, Walter, 7n, 60n, 143n
Schlesinger, Arthur, Jr., 24n
Schmidt, Helmut Dan, 99n
Scott, Andrew M., 74n
seas: as common areas, 149; exploitation of, 136
secession: right of, 103-104, 107-108; as self-determination, 107-108
secessionist movements: intervention in support of, 87
second best: problem of, 171
sectional associations: rights of states as, 163-67
self-defense: ambiguity of national right of, 51-53; right of, in Hobbesian state of nature, 52; Rawls on, 134
self-determination principle, 8, 121; ambiguity of, 95, 104-105, 120; analogy with "positive" liberty, 92-93; argument from freedom of association, 95-96; and consent, 103-104; common characteristics approach to eligibility problem, 110-11; contrasted with nonintervention principle, 93; derived from autonomy of states, 69; and economic dependence, 116, 119-21; eligibility for, 105-115; eligibil-

self-determination principle (*cont.*)
ity problem and freedom of association, 106-109; eligibility problem and social justice, 111-12, 115;
history of, 93-95; importance of
empirical generalizations in justification of, 102, 104; inadequacy of
freedom of association view,
96-98; inapplicability of free association model to eligibility problem, 109-110; internal and external senses contrasted, 93n; justification of application to colonial
cases, 96-104; and nationality,
106, 112-15; problem of conflicting claims, 107-108; Rawls's justification of, 134; relation to social
justice summarized, 104; as remedy for social injustice, 98-99; territorial component, 109-110
self-government: and self-
determination, 98, 104
self-help, *see* self-defense
self-sufficiency of states: assumption
of does not undermine resource
redistribution principle, 140-41;
contrasted wtih interdependence,
143-44; implausibility of assumption of, 149-50; Rawls's assumption of, 128, 132, 136
sense of justice, 155-58
separatism, 106-12
Sewell, James Patrick, 39n
Shue, Henry, 161n
Sidgwick, Henry, 27n; on natural resources, 137
Simmons, A. John, 79n
Singer, Hans W., 175n
Singer, J. David, 37n
Singer, Peter, 150n
Slote, Michael A., 104n
Small, Melvin, 37n
Smith, Tony, 147n
Social contract: and international
distributive justice, 127-28, 175-
76; and justification of self-
determination principle, 98-102;

as mechanism for justifying principles of justice, 80; and paternalism, 101; Rawls's application to
international relations ignores resource problems, 143
social cooperation: distinction between natural and social components unnecessary in domestic
case, 143; international interdependence as, 42-44, 47-49, 143-
50; meaning of in Rawls's theory
of justice, 130-32, 150n; and national boundaries, 132; natural
and social components distinguished, 137; not only source of
moral ties, 141; problem of nested
schemes of, 163-67
social justice: basic problem of, 129;
consistency of domestic and international, 150; and critique of
imperialism, 101; and economic dependence, 119-20; and natural resources, 137; and nonintervention
principle, 80-83, 86, 89-92; possible conflict with consent, 103-104;
principles may vary with context,
81n, 98, 104-105, 122-23; Rawls's
principles of, 129-30; relation to
state autonomy summarized,
121-22; and self-determination
principle, 98-104; and state autonomy, 69, 80-81. *See also* international distributive justice
South Africa, 94, 134
South Moluccans (Indonesia), 102
sovereignty: Jean Bodin on, 26; over
natural resources, 142n; as source
of international moral skepticism,
25-27; Christian Wolff on, 75. *See
also* autonomy of states
Stallings, Barbara, 116n
state of nature: basis of stable expectations in, 46-48; Hobbes and
Locke contrasted, 59-60; Hobbes
on, 28-30, 37; Hobbes's view of, as
analytical device, 35; Hobbes's
view of, as moral construct, 50-51;

individualism of Hobbes's view of,
37; international relations as, *see*
international state of nature; as
state of war, 28-29

states: as actors in international relations, 36-40, 54; analogy with persons, 38, 52, 69, 75-76, 81; as associations, 78; autonomy of, *see*
autonomy of states; nature of, 38,
52, 76-77, 81; obligations to future
generations within, 167-169; role
of, in international political
theory, 54n; special rights to
domestic product of, 161-169; as
subjects of distributive obligations,
152-53. *See also* boundaries, social
cooperation

Stawell, F. Melian, 7n

Stepan, Alfred, 120n

strict compliance: Rawls's assumption of, 135

Sunkel, Osvaldo, 116n, 120n

tariffs, 144

Thomas, A. J., 73n, 75n, 92n

Thomas, A.V.W., 73n, 75n, 92n

Thompson, Kenneth W., 20n, 24n

trade, 144-45; argument for tariff
preferences for poor countries,
174; in dependency theory, 118;
gains from, 145-46; and international inequality, 145-48; international regulation of, 148; voluntariness of participation in, 160; and
vulnerability, 146-47

transfer pricing, 146

transnational actors: and Hobbesian
view of international relations,
38-39. *See also* multinational corporations

Tucker, Robert W., 152n, 153n

Ulyanov, V. I., *see* Lenin

United Nations, 73, 85, 155; defini-
tion of nonintervention, 92n;
General Assembly Declaration on
New Economic Order, 126n, 127;

rejection by General Assembly of
colonial paternalism, 99n; self-
determination principle in General Assembly, 93-94

United Nations Conference on
Trade and Development, 47

Universal Postal Union, 47

universalism, political, 182-83

utilitarianism: approach to international distributive justice, 127

Vaitsos, Constantine V., 146n

Van Dyke, Vernon, 105n, 110n

Vattel, Emerich de, 69, 75n; on
nonintervention, 71

"veil of ignorance": Rawls on, 130;
should exclude knowledge of citizenship, 151

Vernon, Raymond, 145n

Vincent, R. J., 75n, 76n; antipaternalist argument for nonintervention, 84; definition of intervention, 72n, 74n; neutrality of
nonintervention principle, 87-89;
on respect for sovereignty, 84n

violence, 9, 44-45, 72, 91. *See also* war

voting: as from of consent, 78-79;
and self-determination, 96-98

vulnerability: as political inequality,
146-47

Wallerstein, Immanuel, 4n

Waltz, Kenneth, 35n, 144n, 157n;
economic self-sufficiency of
United States, 150n

Walzer, Michael, 9n, 164n; antipaternalist argument against intervention, 85-86; consent theory
of state autonomy, 77, 79n; on
state sovereignty, 68

war: causes of, 7n, 35n, 37-38;
crimes of, 9-10, 134; its place in
international relations, 4, 48-49;
morality of, 9n, 10; moral problems set aside in this book, 10; as
result of international interdependence, 44-46; rules of, 47

Warrender, Howard, 41n
Warsaw Pact, 47
Warwick, Donald P., 40n
Wasserstrom, Richard, 9n
Watkins, J.W.N., 31n
Weber, Max, 182
Wechsler, Herbert, 88n
Wicclair, Mark, 135n
Wight, Martin, 3n, 7n
Wilson, Woodrow, 94
Winfield, P. H., 71n
Wolfers, Arnold, 7n
Wolff, Christian, 7n, 69, 71, 180; argument for nonintervention based on analogy of states and persons,

75-76; doctrine of *civitas maxima*, 143n
Wolin, Sheldon S., 22n
world economy, *see* interdependence
world federalism, 183
World Health Organization, 47
World Meteorological Organization, 39

Young, Oran, 37n, 73n

zero-sum game: international relations as, 42
Zimbabwe (Rhodesia), 94
Zolberg, Aristide R., 101n